# THE WAY OF THE HORSE

## A Sequel to The Forgotten Horses

## LYNN MANN

Coxstone Press

ISBN 978-1-7398314-8-6
Published by Coxstone Press 2022

*For Caroline*
*in memory of Miley*

# Chapter One

The heart-pounding, knee-shaking terror, which incapacitated me when the black-clad figures first appeared on the yard, begins to wane as I watch one of them hand a sheet of paper to Tania. They aren't here for me. Not this time, anyway. I stay in the shadow of the barn as five of the police unload quad bikes from their vans and rev them to life. Tania looks as relaxed as ever, despite two policemen standing closer to her than can be comfortable.

It's what they do. If she takes even one step backward, they'll know they have her. They'll move closer again, enjoying the effects of their intimidation and knowing that her fear will cause her to make a mistake and give them justification for the cruelty they intend to inflict upon her.

I take a step towards the edge of the shadow that has hidden me from them, but stop as Tania lifts a hand slightly at her hip and flicks her fingers in my direction. I look around and confirm that I am alone; the gesture was definitely meant for me. She wants me to stay where I am, but I won't just stand here and watch the police play with her as they did my parents. Tania may think she's invincible, having impressed Helen, the yard owner, into giving her the yard manager's role within weeks of her arrival, but she won't be able to impress her would-be tormentors.

I take another step forward and then another, my legs moving by themselves now as a cold rage rises within me, dispersing the remainder of my fear. I'll show those monsters that they can't just do whatever they want and get away with it. I step out into the sunshine but am forced to halt in my tracks as the quad bikes head straight for me at speed. They veer around me at the last moment, all five riders grinning nastily at me, and head towards the field. Why are they here? Who are they looking for?

I glance back at Tania, who is smiling as she now holds a hand to each of the policemen's faces while they continue to loom over her. The woman is insane. The men step back from her, both of them blinking rapidly. They look at one another and then back at her as if they've never seen her before. What did she do to them? Does she have some sort of chemical on her hands? Poison? No, that can't be it; she couldn't possibly be that stupid. She stands talking to them as if nothing untoward has happened, and they begin to nod and smile at whatever it is that she's telling them.

I jump at a scream coming from the field. I turn and squint into the sun. The horses have left the shade of the trees at the far end of the pasture and appear to be coming our way at a gallop, followed by the quad bikes. Why are the police herding the horses to the yard? Is this some kind of census? Not content with knowing and controlling everything we do, they're extending the policy to our animals?

The gate is open! The idiots, they didn't bother to close it when they took those wretched machines into the field. And the gate between the yard and the road is also open. The horses – our friends, our therapists who help those of us who attend the equine assisted therapy centre to cope with the madness that threatens to drown us every second of every day – will get out onto the road!

That can't happen; I can't risk harm coming to Honour or any of the other horses. Even if they don't get hurt, as the managers of this establishment, Tania and Helen will. They'll be charged with threatening the safety and comfort of the citizens of our "City Of Glory", as it's recently been renamed. They'll have the yard confiscated and put to use "serving the citizens" while they are put to work in one of the building crews responsible for the high rise apartment blocks and food factories going up everywhere, thrown in jail or shot, depending on their behaviour during and following arrest.

I can't reach the field gate in time, but I should be able to close the gate to the road. I start running and wonder why Tania is still standing with the policemen. Doesn't she see the danger? She's closer to the gate than I, why doesn't she react?

She shakes her head at me. She's smiling but her eyes bore into me, leaving me in no doubt that she doesn't want me to intervene. What the hell? One of the policemen moves in my direction but Tania puts a hand out and takes his, still smiling, still talking to him. He stops.

I falter. She's gone too far now, surely? Do I help her or carry on to the gate?

The pounding of hooves behind me gets my feet moving again and I hurtle onward. Tania moves quickly into my path. She shakes her head again and glances at the police, who are standing watching her as if for direction.

'Tania, what are you doing?' I whisper. 'You have to move, I have to shut the gate.'

'No, you need to stand aside and let what is about to happen, happen,' Tania says under her breath.

I sidestep around her and run on, but I'm too late. Three horses gallop around and past me, followed by more. I look about myself in horror as I hear the first hooves clatter onto the road.

'STOP!' I yell, as if it will make any difference to the panicking horses. The smell of their sweat floods my nostrils, accompanied by one I know very well; that of fear. I smelt it on my parents when they were tortured and then shot in front of me, and I've smelt it on myself ever since. I was fourteen when my parents were killed. I'm twenty-five now. I've only survived the past eleven years of smelling, tasting, seeing, hearing – even touching – fear wherever I go by finding refuge in the horses during my daily visits. Now that they are exuding that from which they have always protected me, I have nowhere to hide.

A miasma of terror envelops and then saturates me. I stop running and turn around on the spot, unsure where to run, what to do. Urine streams down the inside of my leg in a warm flow that glues my trousers to my skin.

Then Honour passes me. My Honour. She rescued me on the day I stumbled past her field with the police hot on my heels, taunting me about what had just befallen my parents and trying to provoke me into retaliating so that they could dispense the same "justice" to me. I was exhausted and terrified, but both were beginning to give way to anger. Another few minutes and I would have done exactly as the police wanted me to do, but as I staggered against a wooden fence and paused there to regain my breath, a soft, throaty noise made me look up. I recoiled from the large nostrils that blew warm, comforting breath over my face. Two large brown eyes gazed down at me. Kindness oozed out of them and into me, making me want to cry the tears I had so far refused to cry.

'He's breaking, we've got him now,' one of the police said and laughed. 'Go on, boy, show us what a baby you are. Don't bother crying for your parents though, they were thieving cowards who cared more about flouting the law than about you. If you're going to cry, at least do it about something worthwhile, like what we're planning to do to you.'

I knew that my parents were heroes for stockpiling food and quietly distributing it to those whose advancing years had resulted in ever decreasing food rations, not cowards, but the truth was, I was as angry with them for leaving me as I was with those chasing me. Anger sparked in me again and blazed into fury.

The throaty noise sounded close to my ear this time. A bristly lip nuzzled my face, accompanied by a long, slow outward breath of air. Kindness. Both the sound and touch were filled with it. I recognised it without any clue how that was possible, but there it was – there she was; a tall grey horse who... loved me.

I leant over the fence, wanting to be nearer to her. She lowered her head behind me and I felt a gentle pressure against my back as she held me close. I rested my forehead against her neck and breathed in her scent. Why was it familiar? Why was she familiar? And how did I know I could trust her – that she wouldn't bite me, that she would look after me – when I didn't know anything about any horse, let alone this one? She filled my senses with safety, and I closed my eyes tightly and clung to her, never wanting to let her go.

When I eventually did, when I opened my eyes and stood back from her, it was getting dark. I was alone – the police had gone! How long had they taunted me, tried to tempt me from the refuge I had found, before giving up?

'So, you've met Honour,' a kindly voice said. A woman with a tanned face and greying hair tied back in a tail stepped into sight from behind the grey mare.

'She... she helped me.'

'She's good at that. Would you like to come back and see her tomorrow?'

I had never been so sure of anything. 'Yes. Yes please.'

'Okay, well the yard entrance is just around that corner over there. I'm Helen, by the way. Come any time you like. You ought to be getting home now though, it'll be dark soon.'

I nodded. Home. I supposed that would be with my grandmother now. 'I'd better go and tell her what's happened,' I murmured to myself, then said to Helen, 'I'll see you tomorrow.'

I've come to the yard every day since that fateful one, and every single day, I've found Honour waiting for me. I'd have been dead a hundred times over if it weren't for her. I can't lose her.

The very thought strikes a whole new type of panic into me, one that gives me strength rather than sapping it from me. I can't lose her.

I run after her, my wet trouser leg flapping around my ankle. 'Honour, stop, it's me, calm down. Stop!'

A quad bike draws level with me as Honour gallops out onto the road. 'Just carry on as you are,' its rider growls, 'and you'll be shot for resisting authority.'

'You're herding them out onto the road on purpose? Why?'

His laugh sends chills down my spine. 'We're not just herding them onto the road, we're herding them out of the city. They're surplus to requirements, as very soon will you be if you don't get out of their – and by that, I mean our – way.'

His words reverberate in my head, getting louder each time they hit the sides and bounce back on themselves. As the last horse of Honour's herd passes me, the policeman stares at me, waiting to see what I'll do.

They're taking our horses away from us. They're taking Honour away from me. All of the hurt, the fear, the anger that Honour has soothed away over the years come flooding back and combine into a white hot rage. I'll stop them. I'll kill them. Him first. My eyes narrow. My intended victim's widen and brighten with anticipation.

A hand takes hold of mine. Tania whispers, 'Nathan, stop. Remember.'

My rage lessens. My face softens. My antagoniser looks between Tania and me and frowns, presumably fearing his intended sport may not be so after all, and as confused as I as to why that should be.

All of a sudden, some of the hoofbeats that were getting fainter become louder again. Some of the horses must have broken away from the herd and are coming back! Maybe Honour is among them! There is an eruption of hooting and jeering in the distance, and the hoofbeats gradually become fainter again.

I glare at the quad bike rider, who stands on his pedals waiting to jump off his bike and onto me if I give him even the tiniest reason. He grins and flicks his eyebrows up and down in invitation. Rage burns within me once more but just as I go to move towards him, Tania's hand tightens around mine.

It's as if lightning strikes out of nowhere. All I see, all I feel, is a bright, blinding white light.

Tania's voice is calm, soft, as she repeats, 'Nathan. Remember.'

And I do.

## Chapter Two

*I* remember my grandmother opening the front door with tear-streaked cheeks and red, puffy eyes. I jumped, not expecting anyone to admit me to my home, let alone Gran. As the strongest Weather-Singers in the area, she and my parents were supposed to have been helping to calm the storms that had been battering the villages along the coast. Before they had left, my parents sat me down and told me that, being as trustworthy as they knew me to be, and now fifteen, they deemed me ready and able to be left alone for the four days it would take them and Gran to travel to the coast, lend their strength to the Weather-Singers who had sent word asking for help, and travel home again. I had been thrilled and felt slightly annoyed that they were home a day early. But then I took in Gran's presence and appearance for the second time, and a shard of fear pierced my heart.

'Come in, Newson, there's something I have to tell you.'

Newson? My name is Nathan. But it wasn't. Not there. Not then. I was Newson.

'Gran? What are you doing here? What's happened?' I asked her.

She reached out and took one of my hands in both of hers. She gently pulled me to her, then put her arm around me and guided me inside. She lifted my back-sack off my shoulder and set it down by the door, then, her lips and hands trembling, beckoned me to go into the grey stone-walled front room ahead of her.

My heart began to pound in my chest as I tried to find an explanation for her behaviour other than the one I was terrified she was about to give.

'Sit down, Newson.'

I sat down gingerly on the edge of the sofa, afraid to be comfortable when the atmosphere was anything but.

Gran sat down beside me and took hold of my hand in hers again. 'There's no, um, no easy way to say this, so I'm just going to come straight out with it. My daughter and son-in-law, your mother and father... they aren't coming home, Newson. They... we... dealt with the weather quicker than we expected. It was beautiful on the coast. Long beaches with white sand, warm seawater lapping at our toes in the sunshine. Your parents loved it so much, I told them to enjoy it for a bit – to go for a walk, maybe give swimming a go, and then we'd head back here when they were ready. I left them on the beach, tearing around and laughing like a couple of children.'

She paused and swallowed before continuing. 'We're... we're hill people, aren't we? Your parents weren't stupid, they just didn't know the dangers. When they didn't return to where we were staying, the boats were sent out, but your parents couldn't be found. They... they must have drowned, Newson. Whether they went for a walk and were cut off from the beach by the tide, or whether they decided to try swimming and got caught in something called a rip tide, no one could say but apparently both are possibilities. I'm sorry, Newson, so very, very sorry.'

I leapt to my feet. 'They haven't been found? Well then, they must still be out there somewhere. Why did you come back here without them? You should have stayed to look for them until you found them. Come on, we need to get back there. I'll find them, I'll hear them calling for help wherever they are, they must be trapped, like in a cave or something. And I've got a loud voice, you know I have. They'll hear me calling and they'll hang on until we find them.' I ran to the door and then turned back to Gran. 'WHY ARE YOU STILL SITTING THERE? COME ON, WE HAVE TO GO.'

Gran remained where she was, staring at me through the tears that filled her eyes. 'The villagers there know that stretch of coast as well as they know their own families. They searched everywhere your parents could have been trapped, or... or taken by the tide. They went far out to sea and zigzagged back and forth across the bay as they made their way back to the beach, but found nothing. No sign whatsoever.'

I began to pace back and forth across the room. 'But if there's a possibility they were cut off by the tide coming in, then wouldn't it have brought them in with it? And if a rip... rip tide?' I stopped pacing for a moment and looked at Gran, who nodded. 'If a rip tide took them, then they'd have been found wherever that took them, wouldn't they? How can they just disappear? Maybe they never went near the water, maybe they walked somewhere else and fell down a hole? Or got trapped in quicksand? Do they have quicksand there? I learnt about it at school. Isn't that possible?'

'They left their shoes on the beach, love. It's far more likely that they either walked out to meet the sea and got trapped when it sneaked in around and behind them, or tried to swim in it once it had come in, but we checked everywhere else they could have gone just in case; I and the villagers who weren't out searching in boats did that. When we'd exhausted all of the possibilities, we had to accept that your parents had gone, Newson. I didn't want to believe it any more than you do, but we both have to.'

I threw myself onto the sofa beside Gran. 'But they must be somewhere, I mean people don't dissolve in seawater, do they? How can they have just disappeared?'

'No, people don't dissolve, any more than the animals who live in the sea do.'

I sat up straight, my throat dry and tight. 'Animals?' I whispered. 'You think they've been eaten?'

Gran held her arms out to me. 'Come here, love, I'm so very sorry.'

I just sat, staring at her unseeingly as I racked my brain for any other possible explanation for my parents' disappearance, however unlikely, however remote. Eventually, I crumpled in on myself. I pulled my knees up to my chin, wrapped my arms around my legs and howled. Gran shuffled closer, enfolded me in her arms, and rocked me from side to side.

When I finally cried myself out, Gran disappeared for a few minutes. She returned with a cool, wet flannel and two mugs of hot, sweet tea. She put the mugs on the low table and knelt on the floor in front of me. Without speaking, she wiped my face with the flannel and then held it against my sore, puffy eyes for a few minutes. Then she handed me my tea.

'Drink this, then we'll pack your things and get you to my cottage. It's just you and me now, Newson, and we have to look after each other. We WILL look after each other. We'll be okay. Eventually, we'll be okay.' She didn't sound very sure.

I looked at her incredulously. 'I'm not leaving here, I can't leave here. What if… what if they come back?'

'You can't live here by yourself, it wouldn't be sensible and it wouldn't be right. This is a family home and when a family needs it, they'll be very glad of it. Your parents aren't coming back, but if, for argument's sake, they did, they'd know to look for you at my cottage.'

I felt numb, as if someone else had taken over my body and were arguing in my place. 'You and I are a family, so we can live here. You can move in here with me, then when Mum and Dad come home, all of their things will be here waiting for them.'

'You know that's not our way,' Gran said gently. 'We don't hold on to things we don't have a use for, we share them so that nothing is wasted and everyone has what they need. This house is bigger than we need, and it's full of possessions we don't need.'

'But...'

'Your parents were so very proud of you, Newson. You were happy and content from the moment you were born, and you've grown into a sensible, gentle, caring young man. Going by your performance during testing last year, you'll be every bit as strong a Metal-Singer as your parents were Weather-Singers, and you're like them in every other way that counts too. You know what they would have done in your position, so my advice to you now and for the days, weeks and months to come, is this. Be the son of The New that your parents were so proud of and named you for. It's what they would want for you, for your own sake.'

All I could do was nod. A small part of me knew that she was right, but the larger part of me didn't want to admit it, to acknowledge that I was in a situation where she had cause to be. I clasped hold of my mug more tightly and looked around the living room, drinking in every detail of its contents and losing myself in the memories they evoked.

My gaze lingered first on the three armchairs arranged in front of the fire. For most of my life, there had only been two, but a third had appeared between them on my tenth birthday, when I was too big to squash in with either of my parents. It was a brighter red than my parents' chairs, but otherwise identical as had been their intent. I gulped a mouthful of tea and burnt my throat, the tears that filled my eyes as a result stinging my lower eyelids. I blinked them away and looked down at the sofa on which I was sitting. Memories of my father tickling me, my mother comforting me, both of them reading to me or listening to me read to them, all flooded my mind, forcing me to look up.

My mother loved to draw in both colour and charcoal, but kept most of her creations confined to her sketch books. The three that she had allowed to be framed and hung on the grey stone walls were there partly as a result of my father's pleading and partly due to their content; one was a portrait of my father, one was of me, and the third was a family portrait of the three of us.

'We'll come back tomorrow for those,' Gran said, following my gaze. 'When we've both had a good night's sleep, we'll come back and work our way around the house, and anything that's personal, that wouldn't be of use to another family, we'll take with us. Today, we'll just pack a bag with your clothes and anything you can't be without for the night, and get back to my – to our – cottage, where I'm going to run you a nice hot bath and make your favourite stew. Come on, sweetheart, bring your tea with you and we'll go and make a start on the packing.'

We left my family home less than three hours after I'd entered it. As I trudged down the cobbled front path, the echoes of my footsteps going the other way seemed to taunt me with their happiness. I'd had a great day at school – every day was great now that I only had a few weeks left before I would be leaving and starting my metal-singing apprenticeship – and I had been looking

forward to cooking the next dish on the list my mother had left for
me, not only because it was my favourite, but because I knew that
when she came home and saw all of the ingredients she had left
for me had been checked off her list and used in the appropriate
quantities, she'd know she'd been right to trust me to look after
myself. Now she would never know. In the space of a few hours,
my life had done a somersault.

A surge of anger caused my stomach to clench. How could my
parents have been so stupid? How could they have let this
happen?

I tripped on the same slightly raised cobblestone on which I
had tripped multiple times daily before I finally outgrew my
tendency to race everywhere at top speed, and heard my mother's
amused voice echoing in my head. 'I'll be calling you Purpleson
instead of Newson if you add any more bruises to your current
collection. Please, love, at least look where you're going if you
won't slow down?'

My stomach clenched again, only this time the spasm worked
its way up through my chest and neck to my face, causing tears to
fill my eyes and spill down my cheeks. I ground my teeth together
as a wave of pain, far more intense than any physical pain I had
ever felt, swept through me. I wanted to roar with it, to discharge
it in such a way that it could never come back, yet at the same
time, I wanted to hold on to it because the pain, the agony, was
full of my parents. It contained their laughter as my mother swung
me around before throwing me an arm's length to my father to be
swung around again; it contained them each holding one of my
hands as they walked me to school on my first day; it contained
them tucking me into bed and reading me stories, waking me up
with a smile and a kiss each morning, hugging me when I was sad,
celebrating with me when I was happy.

I tripped again and almost fell under the weight of my back-sack, which I had insisted on filling. Strong hands grabbed me and held me upright until I found my feet.

'I've got you.' Gran's voice was determined. 'Whatever happens from now on, I've got you.'

I swallowed hard and almost choked on everything that I should have let out. I didn't shout, I didn't scream, I didn't say another word as Gran guided me down the path, shutting the gate quietly behind her. I was vaguely aware of voices welcoming Gran home, asking if she and my parents had enjoyed their trip and offering help carrying our loads, but I don't remember what she said in response, only that her hands never strayed from my arms as she drove me along in front of her.

'Here we are,' she said, depositing me on her front doorstep and moving around in front of me to release the catch and open the door. She guided me into the hallway and I was immediately overwhelmed with memories of arriving with my parents for dinner, for lunch, with gifts for Gran's birthday, to celebrate Longest Night Festival with her. I could smell the meal she would always have ready for us, I could hear my mother voicing early appreciation for the food that we all knew would be delicious, and I could feel my father brushing past me on his way to the kitchen with our contribution of wine or dessert, usually both.

'Shoes off, love,' Gran said, 'then we'll take this lot up to your room.'

I was jolted back to the hallway that was devoid of scent apart from the slight staleness of an empty house, that seemed dimmer with just the two of us standing there, and that seemed colder than it ever had before, despite the warmth of summer bursting in through the open door.

My chest hurt. Every beat of my heart sent pain pulsing around my body. I couldn't contain it any longer. I sat down on the bottom stair and cried until I was sick.

When I had no more strength to cry any more tears, Gran said, 'Come on, I've run you a bath. Let's get you upstairs.'

I bathed and dried myself in a daze. By the time I had dressed in the pyjamas Gran left on the chair in her small and immaculate bathroom, and padded along to her spare room – my room now – she had unpacked my back-sack and the one of my father's that she had carried, put my clothes in the wardrobe and chest of drawers, and arranged the few possessions around the room that I had managed to bring.

I stared at the over-sized pine cone on the windowsill that my mother had found one day and turned into a puzzle, then at the small wooden animals arranged on the mantelpiece that my father had carved for me when I was small, then at the clock on the bedside table which my parents had commissioned Tyler – the Master Metal-Singer of our village – to make for me when I accepted his offer of apprenticeship following testing, as if seeing them all for the first time. They seemed so out of place here.

'Hop into bed,' Gran said, holding the covers up for me to slide underneath them, 'and I'll get some soup on the go, I think stew might be a bit heavy now you've been poorly. I won't be a tick, just snuggle down and rest for a bit.'

I walked past her to the windowsill and picked up the pine cone, then gathered the wooden animals from the mantelpiece. I arranged them all around the clock on the bedside table, and, feeling a little better now that my possessions were right next to me, got into bed and allowed Gran to tuck me in as my mother hadn't for years. She kissed my forehead and bustled out of the room.

I snuggled down on my side and glanced at my clock, noting that it was nearly half past seven. I drank in every detail of my treasured gift, just as I had when it was first given to me; its hour and minute hands shaped like arrows pointing at the numbers with their delicately tapered arrowheads, its second hand shaped like a bow complete with the finest of drawstrings, its brushed metal casing, glass cover and circles of glass in the clock face that allowed a view of the clock's intricate inner workings. It was a work of art and precision that would last a dozen lifetimes. I had lost my parents, but I would always have my clock. I felt the tiniest bit comforted by the idea.

I jumped as the pine cone toppled over. I reached out and righted it as both my mother and I had done so many times in competition. Half of the time, I would find the exact spot on which to set it so that it would balance upright – a point to me – while the other half, it would stay upright for a time and then topple onto its side – a point to my mother. My mouth curved upward very slightly into the faintest of smiles. It was as if the cone were alive and trying to get my attention, to remind me of the memories it held of special times with my mother. I was glad I had brought it with me.

The wooden figures all seemed to be watching me as intently as I had watched my father while he carved them for me. He let me choose what each would be before he began, and involved me all the while he was carving, with questions as to where I had seen examples of the animal I had chosen that day, how big its head should be in relation to its body, how long its fur was, whether it was marked in any way, whether there were any other details I wanted him to include, and where I wanted him to carve his and my initials as the figure's creator and recipient.

I reached out and lifted each figure in turn. The badger had my father's initials on its belly, and mine on the underside of its tail. The fox had our initials on the underside of its back paws. The deer had them incorporated into two of its spots, and the rabbit into each of its ears. I picked up the horse last. It had by far the most detail because when the horse upon whom it was based had visited our village, I couldn't take my eyes off him.

He was so tall that my father couldn't see over his back as he stood talking to the Horse-Bonded sitting astride him. He was a glossy, bright orange but three of his legs were white up to the knee, and the fourth had a white band of hair around it just above the hoof. His mane was so long that it blew back over his Bond-Partner, obscuring him when the wind blew. His mostly orange tail had four white streaks in it and two black ones, and his forelock had a scattering of black hairs. His orange eyelashes were in bright contrast to the dark brown of his eyes when he stood with them half closed, as he did whenever his Bond-Partner was dispensing his advice.

The horse looked directly at me once, when I tore down our front path to catch another glimpse of him and slammed the gate behind me, right behind him. He spun around, his nostrils twice their normal size and his eyes appearing to protrude from his face as they fixed on me. He snorted in concert with his Bond-Partner's chuckle, then turned back the way he had been going before my clumsiness disturbed him. My father had captured his startled expression exactly as I described it, and I shivered as I always did when inspecting the figurine. I remembered feeling as if the horse had seen right into me and decided I wasn't a threat to him, not just because I was one of the villagers he was there to help, but because I was me – as if he recognised me.

I had felt a little silly when I told my father about it, and feared he would advise me against fantasising, but he merely nodded and said, 'He saw in you what your mother and I see in you. We've often wondered if we're just biased, but that's all the confirmation I need that we aren't.' He refused to elaborate on his comment and I wondered again what he meant. Now I would never know.

A flash of pain pierced my heart again and reflexively, I held the horse close to my chest as if it could make me feel better... and it did, just a tiny bit.

When Gran pushed the door open with the tray she was carrying, I hastily returned the horse to my bedside table and sat up.

Gran put the tray on my lap and stroked my forehead. 'I'm sorry I can't make this easier for you.' She sat down on the bed next to me. 'Is there anything you'd like to talk about now you're a little calmer? Anything you'd like to ask me?'

'Are you sure there's no way at all they're alive?'

'I'm sure.' Gran put a hand to her heart. 'I can feel it here. If my daughter were alive, I'd know. I joined the search team in case we could find their... their remains, but the moment I realised they had been gone too long, I felt a sort of emptiness. I knew she was gone.'

'And Dad?'

'There's absolutely no way he would have survived without her, he'd have thrown everything of himself into saving her if it were possible, you know that.'

I nodded and swallowed a mouthful of hot soup, then another. My stomach felt no less empty. Gran sat quietly with me while I ate, then put the tray on the chest of drawers by the door while she closed the curtains.

'You're all done in,' she said. 'Sleep now. If you need me in the night, call out or come in to me, I'll be right across the landing. Goodnight, love.'

'Goodnight, Gran.'

As soon as she had pulled the door to behind her, I grabbed the horse. Once he was under the covers with me, I reached out and touched every one of my other possessions to make sure they were still there. Each gave me a slight sense of relief from my predicament, and I wished there were more of them.

The portraits hanging on the wall of our living room flashed into my mind. I yearned for them. They should be here with me, where I could see my parents and myself with them. Tomorrow. Gran said we'd fetch them tomorrow with everything else I wanted. I'd hang them on the wall opposite my bed and then this room wouldn't feel so empty. I wouldn't feel so empty. So alone.

Tears leaked out of my eyes onto my pillow. I squeezed the horse in my hand and relived again the experiences of seeing his likeness in the flesh, then of describing him in minute detail to my father while he carved the horse who had become so precious to me. The memories calmed me. I wanted more. I wanted those portraits now.

I thought of Gran downstairs. She would never let me go and get them, I would have to wait until morning like she said. I held the horse in both of my hands and curled around him, hoping he would see me through the night.

Gran's weary footsteps sounded on the stairs. She plodded along the landing to the bathroom and there was splashing as she washed, then brushed her teeth. She trudged to her room, each footstep sounding heavier than the last. I was almost out of my bed in case she collapsed, when she whispered outside my door, 'I love you, Newson, sleep tight.' Her door creaked as she went into her room, then creaked again as she pushed it to. The springs of her bed squeaked as they took her weight, then there was silence. Complete, deafening silence.

I couldn't bear it. I reached out for the rest of the wooden animals, then the pine cone and finally the clock. I gathered them all to me under the covers, trying over and over to relive the memories they held – trying not to think of the portraits that held my parents' likenesses and my mother's talent, or of the added comfort they would bring. I counted the muffled ticks of the clock and tried to picture myself in my old bedroom, falling asleep to those same ticks having been kissed goodnight by my parents.

Hours passed but sleep wouldn't come. I needed those portraits. When I could bear it no longer, I pushed back the covers and carefully replaced my belongings on the bedside table. I tiptoed to the door and listened. Then I tiptoed across the landing and listened again. I could hear Gran's deep, even breathing. She was exhausted after her journey back from the coast and everything she had brought back with her; she wouldn't wake easily now that she was asleep. I trod as lightly as I could along the landing and down the stairs, and made not a sound. I put on my shoes and then stepped out into the moonlight, the front door making only the faintest of squeaks as I closed it behind me.

The village was deserted as was normal after dark in the summer; the working days were long and dawn came around quickly, so people grabbed as much sleep as they could, when they could. Even so, I kept to the shadows so that if anyone happened to glance out of a window, the moonlight couldn't give me away. When I reached the house in which I had grown up, my heart leapt into my throat as I hoped for a moment to see any indication that the past hours had been a mistake, that my parents had merely been lost or delayed and had made it back after all. The house stood in darkness, empty and forlorn.

I bit my lip and hurried up the front path. If I could just get those portraits, I would feel better. I didn't bother to be quiet as I unlatched the front door and went inside. The house felt weird. Empty, as if the life had been sucked out of it. I didn't tarry. I lifted the portraits off their hooks, tucked them under my arm and left as quickly as I could. I ran back to Gran's and was relieved to hear the breathing of deep sleep still emanating from her room when I paused outside it to listen.

I pulled the curtains of my room open enough for me to be able to see what I was doing, then located two pictures already hanging on the wall opposite my bed. I took them down and rested them against the wall, then hung the portraits of me and my father in their places. I got into bed and propped the portrait of the three of us up against the lamp on my bedside table. I lay down and gazed at my parents, both of them smiling as their hands rested on my shoulders. Finally, I slept.

The sun was halfway to its peak in the sky by the time I woke the next morning. To begin with, I had no idea where I was. Then my father's relaxed smile found me from across the room and everything came flooding back. The bright optimism for the day, with which I always woke, winked out and was replaced by a hollow emptiness in my stomach that had little to do with its rumbling.

Desperately, I switched my gaze to the portrait by my bed, then to my clock, each of my wooden animals and finally the pine cone. I focused on them intently until the emptiness didn't feel quite so absolute, then noticed that the door was standing wide open. Gran had been in my room. Panic flooded me. Had she seen the portraits? What would she say?

I leapt out of bed, took down the two I'd hung on the wall and replaced the original pictures, then gathered the one from my bedside table and put all three portraits under my bed.

'Oh, Newson, love, you're awake,' Gran said, standing on the landing with a basket of washing propped on her hip. 'I'm glad you had such a lovely long sleep. Will you come down for breakfast, or shall I bring some up to you?'

'Um, I'll get dressed and come down, thanks,' I mumbled, reaching for the door and pushing it to. 'I won't be a minute.'

'Just as you like, I'll get some porridge on for you.'

My heart pounded in my chest. I didn't think she'd noticed the portraits, but she had nearly caught me hiding them. I took them back out from under the bed and stared at them until I felt calmer. I needed them and I didn't regret taking them, but I didn't know how to tell Gran what I'd done. I'd have to race into the front room when we got to the house later, and pretend to pack them into my back-sack then. I put them back under the bed, dressed hurriedly and ran downstairs to find Gran stirring porridge on the stove.

'Can we go to the house once I've had that?' I said. 'I don't have to go to school first, do I?'

'No, you don't have to go to school,' Gran said, 'in fact, I see little point in you returning for the remainder of the term. I think it would be better if you took the few weeks that are left to settle in here and begin to come to terms with what's happened, before starting your apprenticeship. Are you sure you're okay to go to the house today though? There's no need for us to hurry.'

There was every need to hurry; I was sure that the more of my and my parents' possessions I had around me, the better I would feel. 'I'm sure,' I said quickly.

Gran set a mug of tea down in front of me. 'How are you… how are you feeling this morning, love?'

I took a sip of the hot, sweet tea. 'I don't know.'

'Because you don't feel anything, or because you feel so much, you can't put it into words?' she said gently.

'Both, I think.'

'You feel so much that you don't feel anything?'

I looked up at her tear-filled eyes. 'I guess.'

She nodded. 'That's how I feel too. I suppose going to the house is the best thing we can do.'

I bolted down my breakfast and then practically ran there with my back-sack stuffed full of other bags, while Gran hurried after me. I tore into the front room, quickly selected ornaments both that my father had made and which had been given to my parents as presents, and proceeded to stuff them into my back-sack.

'We're just going to take personal stuff, remember,' Gran called from the hallway. 'Anything that can be used by another family needs to stay here.'

I looked around the room. Everything in it had been made, commissioned, received or gathered by me or my parents and that made all of it personal. I picked up a cushion as Gran entered the room.

'If you gather everything you want into a pile, I'll pack it all,' she told me. 'Not that cushion, dear, we have plenty at home.'

I looked at the cushion in my hand. It was red and had a small tear along the zip line where Dad had pulled at a loose thread and caused the material to come apart. I remembered him winking at me and whispering, 'It'll be our little secret.'

'It's damaged,' I said. 'I don't mind, I'll have it on my bed. We can't leave damaged things here for other people.'

Gran held out her hand. 'I know where your mother kept her sewing kit, I'll mend it now, it won't take a minute. Aren't your mother's sketch books in that cupboard?'

I practically threw the cushion at her in my hurry to find the books. By the time she returned with the mended cushion, the sofa was covered with items I wanted. I hugged the cushion to me and watched Gran pack the items that she deemed acceptable for me to take, and put the rest – the majority – to one side.

'Where are the portraits?' she said when she had finished. 'I don't remember seeing them.'

'I knew you'd let me take them, so I packed them straight away with the ornaments. They're all very personal,' I said. My desperation for her to believe me didn't quite mask the rasp in my voice due to the lie constricting my throat. It didn't feel nice but it was necessary.

Gran looked up at me wearily. 'Okay, well that's this room done then. I'll replace the things that need to stay here, shall I, while you move on to the kitchen?'

'But...'

'Newson, I understand you wanting to keep everything in this house, I really do, but we don't have room for it all and you know it isn't the right thing to do. Have you had enough for today? Shall we take what we've packed so far and leave the rest for another day?'

'No,' I said quickly. 'I want to take as much as possible today.'

'Right then, off to the kitchen with you, love. It shouldn't take long as the pots, pans, utensils, and most of the crockery and cutlery will need to stay here. Okay?'

I tried to sigh but found that my chest was so tight, I couldn't, not properly. How could I leave so much of my parents here? Gran said she understood, but if she really did, she'd let me take what I wanted.

I searched the cupboards for anything I thought she'd let me have, and found only three mugs with my parents' and my initials on them, a chipped bowl that my mother liked to use, and a large jug my father had given my mother, full of flowers, for her last birthday.

I wanted the fork with the slightly bent prong, because Dad used to sigh every time he ended up with it, and Mum and I used to giggle every time we set the table and put it by his plate. I wanted the set of six identical mugs because Dad used to hide a marble under one of them, switch them around and then challenge me to identify the mug covering the marble. I wanted the set of six plates because all of them were used by the three of us during the course of each day. I wanted the frying pan in which Mum taught me how to prepare my first cooked breakfast, and the saucepan we always used to make apple sauce.

Every single item in every single cupboard had a memory attached to it. Every single item belonged to my parents. To me. And I wanted all of it.

'Is this it in here?' Gran said, bustling in with an almost full bag, to which she added the few items I had placed on the kitchen table. 'Well done, Newson, you've done famously. We'll head upstairs, shall we?'

Distracted by the thought of going through my room, where I had a much stronger argument for taking pretty much everything, I followed her out of the kitchen.

It turned out that my argument wasn't as strong as I had thought. Apparently, anything I hadn't handled or used for more than a year should be made available to younger children of other families.

'You've seen how little storage space you have in your new room, we have to be practical,' Gran said. 'Put everything you want to take on the bed, then I'll help you do a secondary sort through as we pack what you'll be taking.'

'But this is all my stuff, it's all personal and you said I could take anything that was personal.'

'Anything that is personal to you now. That mobile was right at the back of the wardrobe and I'm willing to bet you can't even remember it hanging over your bed when you were a toddler. Your mother should really have turned a lot of this stuff out years ago. If you'd had younger brothers or sisters, it would have long since been passed down to them, but because you didn't, she allowed sentimentality to cloud her judgement.'

'But Dad carved the birds on that mobile, I'd recognise his work anywhere.'

Gran sighed. 'Okay, I'll pack the mobile, but please, be reasonable. I can't fight you over every single item we don't have room for.'

It was late afternoon when we left the house, staggering under the weight of the bags we carried. I buried the misery of leaving my parents' home and all of its contents under the relief of taking everything we had packed back to my new room, and picturing where I would put each and every item so that wherever I looked, there would be memories to comfort me.

I left Gran to accept the condolences of the villagers we passed. At each mention of my parents, I focused even more intently on remembering in turn each of the items I was carrying and where I would put them.

The second we were through the front door, I said, 'I'll take everything upstairs.'

'Okay, love, I'll get on with making us both some dinner, you must be starving, I know I am.'

I was, now I came to think of it, but my hunger was secondary to my need to get my possessions arranged around my room. I raced up and down the stairs until all of the bags were on my bed. I pulled the portraits out from underneath it and returned them to where I had positioned them during the night, then started on the ornaments that had been in the living room.

By the time Gran came up to tell me that dinner was ready, the windowsill was rammed full of ornaments and childhood toys – each arranged so as to be visible to me from the bed – and the mantelpiece was loaded with books. I had arranged more pictures on the floor, below the spots where I wanted to hang them, and Gran's pictures were stacked by the door.

'My, you have been busy,' Gran said, glancing around and then eyeing the bags full of more stuff still to be unpacked. 'Did we really bring all of that back with us?'

'It looks good, doesn't it, it'll look even better when I've finished arranging everything else.'

She looked at me somewhat strangely. 'Um, yes, I suppose it does. Come down now and eat.'

'Can we go back to the house tomorrow? We still have my parents' bedroom to go through.'

Gran put a hand on my shoulder. 'I had a look in there today while you were in your room. There's nothing there for you, Newson. If you think about it, their room was pretty bare; they preferred to display their pictures and ornaments downstairs where they spent most of their time. All they kept in their room were their clothes, some toiletries and a portrait your mother did of you when you were a baby. I packed the toiletries and picture. I thought it would be nice to put it on the living room wall here?'

I shook my head. 'I want it in my room. And I want to go through their clothes, some of Dad's might fit me soon.'

'They'll fit someone else now, love,' Gran said gently. 'It's what your parents would have wanted. I know how much you're hurting, goodness knows I do, and I can see that having your things around you is a comfort to you, but if you take things you don't need from the house, you'll be depriving someone else who does need them. I'm afraid it's a case of doing what's right in place of doing what's easy.'

Anger burst into life in my stomach and reached for my throat, constricting it and preventing me from screaming at her that I did need everything from the house, that it was all I had left of the parents I would never see again.

'Come on now, downstairs,' Gran almost pleaded.

I followed her obediently, still seething. I forced down the meal she had prepared, helped her to clear away and then went back up to my room, all without a word. I spent the evening unpacking and arranging more of my things, then when Gran called up that it was time for bed, I transferred the unpacked bags from my bed to the floor in front of the wardrobe, and got into bed fully dressed. I had no intention of trying to sleep when I knew for certain it would be impossible.

When the door creaked open ten minutes later, I pretended to be asleep. I waited until the springs of Gran's bed told me that she had retired to it, then waited another fifteen minutes. A brief moment of guilt dissipated my anger at her as her sad, pale face flashed into my mind. But then I remembered her refusal to allow me to take anything else from the house – things I needed and would always need. My guilt vanished leaving only hopelessness, emptiness, in its place.

I pushed my door until it clicked shut, lit the lamp on my bedside table, then quietly set about continuing to unpack the rest of the bags. When I had finished, my treasures covered the top of the chest of drawers, lined the walls at floor level, and even took up the surfaces of both the head and foot of my bedstead. Wherever I looked, I could see and feel memories. Memories that hurt, memories that made me laugh – memories that helped me to feel as if my parents were with me; as if they hadn't left me.

I undressed and got into bed. I continued to gaze around at all of my things for a while, then blew out my lamp and snuggled down to sleep. It wouldn't come. All I could think about were all of the things I had wanted to take from the house that Gran hadn't let me. I relit the lamp and drank in the sight of my carefully arranged possessions again, hoping to feel the same relief from grief and loneliness that they had given me before. It didn't happen. They weren't enough, I needed more.

I dressed in dark clothes, picked up the largest of the now empty bags from the pile on the floor, let myself out of the house and tore back to my old home. I knew exactly what I wanted.

I burst into the moonlit living room and took the mended cushion, then the poker from the companion set by the fire, which held memories of Dad telling me I was a big enough, sensible enough boy to poke sticks into the heart of the fire under his supervision. I took the fork with the bent prong, the set of six mugs and the saucepan I had coveted earlier, from the kitchen, cursing that I wouldn't be able to fit the set of plates and frying pan in the bag too; I had to leave room for what I wanted from my parents' room. I thundered up the stairs, past my room to theirs.

I opened their wardrobe door and cursed again at the darkness within. I didn't want to risk lighting a lamp in case anyone else happened to be as sleepless and in need of being out of bed as I, so I resorted to feeling for the hangers and lifting the clothes into the relative light of the moon that, thankfully, poured in through the window.

I selected shirts and pullovers of my father's, and a few dresses of my mother's that held particularly fond memories for me. I rehung the remainder of the clothes back in the wardrobe as best I could, packed the clothes and then headed for my mother's bedside table. Unbeknown to Gran, Mum had commissioned a new wedding band for my father, to celebrate their upcoming wedding anniversary, and had taped it to the underside of the topmost drawer. I remembered her giggling as she showed me where she had hidden it, the excitement in her eyes as she pointed out the elements she had asked Tyler to incorporate into its design which had particular significance to the two of them as a couple, including the stylised initials of my and their names. The band could be sung into something else by the Master Metal-Singer – or by me, in time – but it wouldn't be. It was mine.

I heaved the bag onto my shoulder and tiptoed down the stairs as if doing so were an important part of keeping the secret shared only by my mother and me, as if my father were still there and could leap out at any time and ask what I had been doing in their bedroom. My heart felt a little lighter, my footsteps too, as I made my way back to my grandmother's house. My house, I corrected myself, then swallowed down the pain of doing so.

I stopped outside Gran's room to check she was still asleep and was reassured by the sound of soft snoring. I hung my parents' clothes in the depths of my wardrobe, and hid everything else I had gathered under my bed, pausing to handle each item before putting it in place. I was sad that I wouldn't be able to see my new acquisitions, but comforted by the knowledge they were there. I changed into my pyjamas once more and was asleep within minutes of my head hitting the pillow.

## Chapter Three

*I* was aware of a presence nearby as I came to.

'Morning, sleepy head,' Gran whispered as I opened my eyes.

'Um, morning. How long have you been sitting on the end of my bed?' I sat up and nervously ran my fingers through my hair.

'Oh, about an hour. I was surprised to find you still asleep when I poked my head around the door just after dawn, and even more surprised to find you hadn't moved when I came up again a few hours later. Then I noticed the results of all your nighttime efforts.' She looked around the room and back at me. 'If you were having trouble sleeping, you could have woken me, you know. I'd have made you a hot drink and we could have talked until you felt sleepy, or played a game or something.'

'You were tired,' I said, 'and I was happy doing this. Have I really slept in for that long again?'

She chuckled as she got to her feet and threw open the curtains. 'See for yourself.'

I blinked and rubbed my eyes as sunlight blasted in. 'I have to get up, there's so much to do.'

'There isn't really, love. I thought we could go for a walk today? Take a picnic with us and enjoy the weather while we can? You won't have much spare time once you start your apprenticeship.'

I shook my head. 'Thanks, but I can't, I have all these pictures to hang on the walls, and I have to hang the ones of yours I took down wherever you want them.'

'Well, that won't take long. You can do it while I get the picnic organised and we can leave in, say, an hour's time?' She glanced at the clock by my bed. 'That's if you can see the time, you've really fitted a lot of things into the space you have in here, haven't you? How about storing some of it under the bed? I don't think there's anything under there.' She started to bend down to have a look.

'No, there isn't, I checked,' I said quickly, my heart thumping as I leapt out of bed. 'Okay, fine, you go and get the picnic sorted and I'll crack on with hanging the pictures so I can be ready in an hour.'

She smiled. 'It's lovely to see you so enthusiastic. Thinking about it though, you'll be wanting some breakfast before you start, and you need a bath, so I think we'll aim to leave in an hour and a half, shall we?'

I held the door open for her. 'Yes, okay, fine. I'll be down for breakfast when I've had a bath.'

Gran allowed herself to be ushered out of the room. I closed the door, almost panting with panic at the thought that she had nearly found everything I had stowed under the bed. I lay flat on the floor, pulled out the cushion and saucepan, and held them to me for a while until I felt calmer. Then I replaced them, glanced

around my room to make sure everything was where I had
arranged it, and made my way to the bathroom.

'This is better, isn't it?' Gran said once we had left the village
behind and were walking through open fields towards a high ridge
that we knew offered views of the surrounding countryside for
miles in every direction. 'They meant well, Newson, each and
every one of them, but that was hard for you.'

Hard? It had been excruciating. Since we hadn't appeared to
be in a hurry as we had when moving possessions from one house
to another, each and every person we met on our way out of the
village stopped us in order to commiserate with us both at length.

'At least it's over and done with,' Gran continued. 'They
offered their condolences and help, I assured them we're
managing, and that means no one will bother you once you're out
and about on your own.'

'So, no one will talk about it anymore? Mum and Dad will just
be forgotten?' I said.

'No, never that. It just means that you and I will be left to
grieve in peace.'

'It doesn't feel very peaceful.'

'So, tell me, how does it feel?'

'I don't feel anything most of the time. Other times, I feel
panicky but mostly just empty. Lonely.'

'I know I'm not your mum or your dad, but you do have me,
love. And your friends, you have a lovely set of those. I know
they'll be glad to see you when you're ready.'

'How will I talk to them now? We don't have anything in
common.'

Gran paused to shift the position of her back-sack slightly.

'You've grown up together, you have everything in common. None of them will be apprenticing as Metal-Singers, but it'll be good to talk about your apprenticeships once you all start in a few weeks' time, won't it?'

'They all have parents,' was all I managed to say. I swallowed down the pain that tried to announce itself, until the emptiness returned. I put my hand into the pocket of my shorts and clutched the horse figurine I had secreted there. I lost myself all over again in my memory of meeting the horse who inspired its creation, and of watching my father immortalise him for me.

'Newson?' Gran's voice brought me back to the present.

'Huh?'

She stopped and put her arm around me. 'I said it will get easier. I know it doesn't feel like it at the moment, but in time, it will. In the meantime, I'm here for you.'

I put my arm around her and hugged her back. 'I know. I'm here for you too.'

'So then, we'll get through this. Now, do you want to carry on up to the top of the ridge, or shall we picnic here?'

'Let's go up to the top.'

'I hoped you'd say that. Come on then.'

We sweated and panted our way up the steep side of the ridge, then stood side by side, breathing in the view when we reached its summit. Without speaking, we slowly rotated around one another so that we could take in the full beauty of the surrounding countryside.

The tiniest movement caught my eye in the distance. I squinted and pointed. 'I think... I think there's a herd of horses over there.'

Gran lifted her hand to shade her eyes and also squinted into the distance. 'I can't see them, my eyes aren't what they were, but I'm glad for you, Newson. Unbonded horses are a rare sight.'

'Bonded horses are a rare sight,' I said. 'They don't visit our village much, do they?'

'Maybe they don't feel they need to. We're pretty well sorted most of the time.'

'Maybe if one had come before Mum and Dad left for the coast with you, they'd have told them not to go, that they should stay at home with me.'

'That's not the kind of advice they give, love. They don't look into the future and tell us what to do to stop awful things happening, they help us with existing problems, ones that seem too difficult to work through. We tell them the problem and then they give us their advice through their Bond-Partners.'

'Are they always right?'

'Yes, always. You know from school that The New wouldn't exist without them, that the Ancients would never have survived had horses not helped them. The advice they give nowadays is every bit as good as the advice they gave our ancestors.'

'I could really do with one showing up now.'

'Can I help? You can ask me anything.'

'I want to know how to get you to understand that I need the things in my old house.'

Gran sighed. 'I do understand, Newson. I understand that you think you need them, that it's very hard for you to let them go to someone else, but the thing is, life is hard sometimes and we shouldn't use that as a reason to act selfishly. Do you remember our conversation last night?'

'You told me I have to do what's right instead of what's easy,' I said dully. 'So that's it?'

'Yes, I'm afraid it is.'

I put my hand into my pocket and took hold of my horse while squinting into the distance. The real horses were no longer in sight. I felt a yearning to get back to my room, to the rest of my possessions. I wanted to hold each and every item all over again and block out the panic that was beginning to rise in me again.

'I want to go home.'

'But we've just got here. Let's have lunch and then we can go straight afterward if you still want to?' Gran shrugged out of the straps of her back-sack and let it slide to the ground with a grunt. She took a handkerchief from her pocket and wiped sweat from her forehead with a shaking hand.

Concern for her punctured my anxiety and pulled at my heart. 'Okay.'

I couldn't eat quickly enough, and I couldn't get back soon enough. It wasn't until I was in my room, surrounded by my life so far, that my heart stopped pounding against my rib cage as if it were trying to get out.

I pulled out the cushion from under my bed and sat, hugging it. It was only when Gran called me down for dinner that I was jolted back to myself. I leapt off the bed and threw the cushion back underneath it almost in one motion, knocking the bedside table as I did so. Everything atop it shifted and many of the items fell over. I carefully righted and rearranged them all so that they were in the positions in which I wanted them, before going downstairs.

'Were you having a nap?' Gran said. 'Sorry if I woke you, but we both need to get back in the habit of eating regularly, we've been a bit all over the place the last few days.'

'Um, no, I was just thinking.'

'That's probably a good thing. Shall we play a board game after dinner? Or we could go for another walk?'

'I'd like to do more thinking in my room, thanks.'

I was aware of Gran's eyes on me as I selected my first forkful of vegetables. Then she said, 'If you're sure. I'll be down here if you change your mind.'

'I won't. Um, thanks for dinner.'

Her voice softened. 'You're welcome, love.'

Sleep evaded me yet again that night. I had spent all evening going through everything in my room until I felt calmer, more secure – but I didn't feel calm or secure enough. I pictured the frying pan sitting in the kitchen cupboard of my old house, and the plates I had coveted when I was sorting through what to take, and knew what I was going to do.

Once the frying pan and plates were secreted away beneath my bed, I slept – but only that night. The following night, I had to fetch a few more items from my old home in order to sleep. Every night thereafter for nearly two weeks, I promised myself that my late night dash to fetch more things would be the last. That the cutlery, crockery, cooking utensils, towels and clothes I took back to my room would complete my collection of memories and fill the emptiness that constantly threatened to overwhelm me. That the time would come when I had enough reminders of my previous life, as I had come to think of it, for me to be able to sleep without gathering more. But no amount was enough.

Then came the bombshell. A family had arrived in the village looking to settle, and would be moving into my old home.

'Newson, are you alright?' Gran said, putting a bowl of cereal in front of me. 'I'm sorry I've had to tell you when you haven't long been awake, but I wanted to give you as much time as possible to process it before you go out. You're due to go and see your Master in a few hours, remember?'

Of course I remembered. Tyler wanted to see me to go through the details of my apprenticeship before I started the following day.

The day when, it seemed, I was just supposed to go back to normal as if nothing had changed.

'Newson?'

I just looked at her, my whole body rigid with panic. Had I got everything I needed? I didn't think so. How would I get to sleep now? At least it would mean Gran wouldn't go back to the house and notice anything was gone other than that which she had said I could take. A family. People would be living in my parents' house. My house. They'd be sleeping in my parents' bed and in my bed, the bed into which Mum and Dad had tucked me and kissed me goodnight when I was small. I needed that bed, but I couldn't have it. Not now. Not ever. My parents were gone forever.

I got up so quickly, I banged into the table and milk slopped over the side of my cereal bowl onto the scrubbed wooden surface. I ran for my room, for safety. Once there, I threw myself onto my bed and grabbed my horse. I leant over the side of the bed and retrieved my cushion, hugging it and my horse and rocking backward and forward.

There was a knock at the door. 'Newson, may I come in?'

I still couldn't speak.

The door opened slowly and Gran almost tiptoed into my room as if worried she might scare me with a heavier tread. She lowered herself onto my bed and let out a long, deep sigh.

'I watched the Rock-Singers building that house,' she said. 'They finished it the day before the wedding, and the Carpenter and her Apprentices delivered the furniture, the Tailor's Apprentice delivered the curtains, and we all contributed food to stock the cupboards so it was ready for your parents to move straight into. It's going to be strange for the whole village, seeing a new family living there, and it's going to be painful for you and me, there's no way around it.

'I thought we had more time. It's usually months before an

empty house is taken over, often years. But Sally has moved back here with her husband and two children so as to be near her sister, and it makes sense for them to take the house rather than have to wait for the Rock-Singers to build them a new one. Letting them have it is the right thing to do.'

I shook my head hopelessly and hugged the cushion even harder.

'How is that cushion here?' Gran said. 'I thought I asked you to leave it at the house for the new occupants?'

A different type of panic took hold of me. How could I have been so stupid as to keep hold of it when she asked to come in? What would she do? Would she take it from me? Would she search my room for anything else I might have taken without her permission? Would she take it all away from me?'

I found part of my voice and managed to squeak, 'You did, I found it in the bags when we got home – it must have got mixed in with everything else by mistake.'

Gran looked searchingly into my eyes. They hardened slightly and I was sure she was going to take the cushion. Then they softened. She sighed again. 'I suppose that must have been what happened. Okay, Newson, you keep it. I'll arrange for the Tailors to make a replacement and deliver it to Sally. The sofa will look a little strange with one of its cushions missing, won't it.'

She never took her eyes off me. I never wavered. I couldn't, but a deep sense of shame came over me as her dark brown eyes, so like my mother's, bored into me, pushing her words from a few weeks earlier ahead of them. *You know what your parents would have done in your position, so my advice to you now and for the days, weeks and months to come, is this. Be the son of The New your parents were so proud of and named you for. It's what they would want for you.*

I was a thief and a liar, and Gran knew it. I was a

disappointment to her and to my parents' memory. My shame opened the door to the pain I had been holding at bay over the past weeks. But I couldn't feel that, it was too much, it would sweep me away. Anger blossomed in its place and quickly became fury.

'You're worried about the sofa?' I said, and then shouted, 'THE SOFA?'

Gran jumped. 'Well I…'

'You want the sofa to look perfect for the new family, after you've given it and EVERYTHING ELSE to them because it's the right thing to do, because it's what my parents would have wanted – well did they always do the right thing? DID THEY? They left me here to go and help the Weather-Singers on the coast and they never came back. Was that the right thing to do? To leave me to grow up without them? Was it the right thing for the Weather-Singers to do, to take all three of you away from me rather than just managing on their own? What if you'd stayed with Mum and Dad and died with them? I'd have been left completely on my own. WAS RISKING THAT THE RIGHT THING TO DO? But I have to do the right thing? I'm the only one who can't make a mistake, who has to do the right thing ALL THE TIME? It's not fair. None of this is f…fair.'

'And none of it's easy, but yes, it was the right thing to do,' Gran said softly. 'Accidents happen, but we can't all stay at home, too scared to do anything in case something goes wrong. We all help one another whether it's easy or not, because if we don't, we'll be on a fast track back to The Old. A horse told me that a long time ago through her Bond-Partner, and I've never forgotten it. I instilled it into your mother and I'm proud of her for never forgetting it, for always acting according to it.'

'And you're ashamed of me.' I set my chin, waiting for her to confirm it.

'I could never be that, love. You're a fifteen-year-old boy

trying to work his way through something very difficult. But work
through it you will, I know it.'

'But what if I can't?'

She patted my hand. 'You're your mother's son. You will.'

But I didn't.

When Gran told me that she'd run into Sally, who was thrilled
to not only have been given a house just days after her family's
arrival in the village, but to have so few kitchen items to
commission in order to have a full complement, and Gran had
asked what it was that she needed and found out there were items
missing that she knew had been there, I lied to her again. I told her
I'd seen movement in the house several times while it was empty
and had thought it my imagination, but maybe someone had been
in there after all.

When I began my metal-singing apprenticeship and turned out
to be every bit as strong a Metal-Singer as Gran had predicted, I
didn't use my strength to work through the orders more quickly; I
used it to make two of every order. I secretly kept each duplicate
so that the pain of having my creations taken away from me was
lessened, and I could continue collecting possessions that made
me feel secure enough to sleep now that I could no longer take
things from my old home. I told Gran I had been instructed to
make two of everything as practice, and to keep the duplicate for
my qualification portfolio even though we both knew that the
small items I was making that early in my apprenticeship were
unlikely to be included.

When I had a bad day and, after arriving home, needed the
comfort of wearing one of my father's shirts, I lied to Gran again
when she asked if it was Dad's.

She always knew when I was lying, and I knew she knew, but
neither of us ever said anything. I saw the flash of disappointment

in her eyes every time I did it, quickly replaced with a hope that was never rewarded.

By the time I was older and trusted with singing larger and more complex items into existence from the metal delivered to my Master's workshop by the Pedlars, my bedroom was groaning with contents, which began spilling out onto the landing.

'I know, it's a pain,' I said when Gran complained. 'I had to be an Apprentice Metal-Singer, didn't I? Tailors can shove their creations under their beds, Bakers can eat theirs, Healers just have notes to store at home, and Earth-Singers, Weather-Singers and Tree-Singers don't even have those. Once I'm qualified, I won't need to store things for my portfolio and all this stuff can go.' I clenched my fists at the very thought of parting with any of it, but resolved to deal with that situation when it arose – which of course it never did.

As always when I was lying, Gran held my gaze, and as always, she trusted that I would come around, that I would live up to being the person she and my parents had always believed I would be.

The years passed. I had no friends, having never been able to find a way to bear my schoolfriends when their very presence reminded me of what they had, and I had lost. I just had Gran, my apprenticeship and my ever growing number of possessions.

When Gran was called away to the coast to help their Weather-Singers again, she of course went and I of course didn't cope with her going. I worked even more furiously so that I had even more stuff to take home with me at the end of each day after Tyler had left the workshop, until she was back home and my terror of her failing to return was assuaged.

When I qualified as a Metal-Singer, I continued to make two of everything and bring the duplicates home. I told Gran that we couldn't possibly part with any of my metalwork as any or all of it might come in useful someday. I couldn't face clearing any of it out of the house even when Gran had a nasty fall as a result of tripping over a fireguard at the top of the stairs, and landing almost at the bottom.

I heard her yell and instantly ran for a Bone-Singer, Tissue-Singer and Herbalist. Terrified that they would insist I clear some of my belongings from the house, I lied to all three regarding what had happened, and about why there was so much clutter in our home – I told them that I had so many orders to fulfil, I was carrying on working at home at the end of each day and many of the resulting items were waiting to be collected – and Gran didn't correct me.

I began to notice the dull, disappointed expression that she wore when she looked at me, on the faces of many people I spoke to, but whatever they thought of me as a person, I was well-regarded as a Metal-Singer though I couldn't find it in me to care about either.

When Gran fell at home for the second time, I wasn't there. A message reached me at what was now my workshop – Tyler having retired the previous year – from the passer-by who had heard her screaming from out in the street and had called the Healers. When I arrived home, it took me some time to negotiate my way past the gates lining the hallway, one of which had toppled over and become entangled in the others, and squeeze past a collection of shovels into the living room, upon whose sofa lay Gran.

Mellow, the village Herbalist, was applying a dressing to Gran's leg while Gran sipped a foul-tasting medicine from a small bottle. Sarl, a Tissue-Singer, stood up from the low table on which she had been sitting next to Mellow, and clambered over a box of cutlery to stand in front of me.

'Newson, this has to stop,' she said in a low voice.

'I know, she's doing too much. I have told her,' I replied, unable to look Sarl in the eye.

'Not your gran's behaviour, yours,' she replied. 'You have to clear this house of clutter, it's not a safe environment for her to live in, or for you, for that matter. She had a deep gouge in her leg, which I've healed as best I can, and also concussion. No one else will say it, but I have no choice… your gran's biggest problem is you. We all felt for you when your parents died and we've watched you struggle ever since, but it's been nearly ten years now. You're not a kid anymore, you have to stop hoarding and lying, and start putting your grandmother first.'

I grabbed hold of another gate in order to remain standing on legs that suddenly felt as if they were barely there. I tried to rally by saying sarcastically, 'Don't tell me. I have to do the right thing.'

'That should go without saying, but I don't think you're capable of it. You need help, Newson, but no one can help you unless you ask for it – unless you want it. I'm begging you, for your gran's sake, ask for it. In the meantime, this house needs to be made safe. I'm going to arrange for some of your neighbours to come and take all of this metalwork to your workshop, where it can be distributed to those who actually need it instead of tripping up elderly ladies. I'll start by taking this.' She turned and bent down to pick up the box of cutlery.

Panic lanced through me and then within a split second, turned to anger. I grasped her wrist and growled, 'Don't you dare.'

'You're hurting me,' she hissed, not relinquishing her hold on the box. 'Let go, I'm taking this before your grandmother can fall over it again. Don't you want her to be safe?'

I did. I absolutely did, but I couldn't let Sarl take the cutlery because then I wouldn't be safe.

'You can't use all this stuff as a barricade against the world,

Newson.'

I wanted to laugh. A barricade against the world? If only it were that simple. I needed my things to barricade me from aspects of myself. 'Let go,' I said again. 'I'll sort this out myself.'

Sarl relaxed her grip on the box and stood up. 'See that you do, or I'll have to arrange for your gran to live somewhere else.'

I felt dizzy, as if I were standing still but the room, its contents and everyone else were spinning around me. Take Gran? No. I wouldn't allow her to be taken from me too.

'Thank you, Sarl, Mellow, for your help, but Newson and I can take it from here,' Gran said weakly.

Mellow fished in her bag and put another four small bottles on the table. 'Drink one of those every few hours and you'll be fine, but you must rest. I'll be back to change your dressing tomorrow.'

'There's no need, Newson can do it,' Gran said. 'Thank you for everything you've done, but we can manage now.'

Mellow and Sarl both looked from Gran to me, their eyes hardening in the process. 'Remember what I said,' Sarl said to me. 'Sort yourself, and this lot, out.' She and Mellow squeezed and clambered their way to the hall and then out of the house.

I sat down on the low table by the sofa. 'I'm sorry, Gran.'

Her eyes were sad, tired, in fact almost empty when she looked at me. 'I know you are, love. It's never too late to change things for the better you know.'

It wasn't too late for me to be better, was what she meant. I was relieved when she closed her eyes so that I didn't have to see the disappointment, the absence of hope within them anymore.

She died in her sleep that night. When I say died, I think that really, she just didn't have the strength to carry on living with me. In surrounding myself with possessions in order to protect myself from the pain of loss, I lost the one who had come to mean the most to me of all.

# Chapter Four

*G*ran's friends tried to help me. They brought me food and asked me to join them on walks, for meals and at social gatherings when they realised that dropping in to offer their company at my house was impractical. I gratefully accepted the food they brought but refused their invitations; I needed to be with my and Gran's things. Gradually, I was left alone, my only contact with people being at my workshop when they came in to commission or collect items. I could see the pity in their eyes, hell, I could feel it as it oozed out of them and all over me. I worked like a man possessed to fulfil their orders and make my habitual duplicate, because I was a man possessed – by guilt much of the time, loneliness some of the time, and my old nemesis, emptiness, the rest.

Five years passed, during which I filled Gran's room with my metalwork, then the garden. Whenever I passed Sarl or Mellow in the street, they would stare at me – Sarl angrily, Mellow with sympathy – and I would feel their eyes boring into my back once I was clear of them. Every time, Sarl's words would come back to me. *No one can help you unless you ask for it. Unless you want it.*

I wanted it, but I didn't dare to ask; I knew that if I did, that "help" would come in the form of being persuaded to let go of everything I had gathered in the fifteen years since my parents' deaths. Everything that had helped me to cope with living with their loss and then Gran's. So I didn't ask, not even when a Horse-Bonded visited the village with his horse, Risk.

I heard the commotion when they arrived. I was in my workshop, singing silver into a necklace that a villager had commissioned for his daughter upon beginning her apprenticeship, when shouts of excitement sounded in the street outside. They were joined by more, and by the sounds of laughter and sandals slapping against the cobbles as people ran past.

I went to the door and peered down the street to where a slim man with greying hair sat astride a sleek black horse who was advanced in years, judging by the white streaks in her mane and forelock, and the white flecks in her coat. I felt a strange urge to run to them, to wrap my arms around the horse and hug her as I had dreamt of doing so often to the only horse I had met before, while having to make do instead with clutching my small, wooden horse... which, come to think of it, I hadn't seen during the many years it had been since I was last able to get into my bedroom.

I took a step forward but then hesitated. If everyone in the village could see what a mess I was, the Horse-Bonded would too, and if he and his horse offered help, I didn't know if I would be able to refuse... and if I couldn't, I would have to part with all of my things. I backed into my workshop and closed the door firmly. Then I dragged one of the metal benches I had finished the day before in front of the door, and pulled the blind down over the window.

I tried to get on with some work but couldn't. By the time the hubbub had died down outside, I was sitting in the far corner of the room from the door, my knees drawn up to my chin, eyes shut and dripping with sweat.

I waited until it was dark – thankfully the nights were still drawing out so I didn't have too long to wait – and then shot out of the back entrance to my workshop and bolted home empty-handed for the first time ever. I shut my front door and spent some time barricading myself in with the numerous gates still stored in the hallway. I had food in the kitchen, to which I could just about clamber, so I decided to stay in the house until the Horse-Bonded and his horse had gone, however long that was.

It turned out to be just over a week, three days into which came a knock at the door. Heart pounding, I stayed where I was on the sofa – the only place in the house I could sit or lie down to sleep.

'Newson, are you okay?' It was my neighbour, Anni. 'Newson,' she called again, 'no one has seen you for days and we're all worried about you. Please let me know you're okay, or we'll have to come in and check?'

I couldn't have that. I called out, 'I'm fine. Just having a few days off work.'

There was a pause. 'Okay, well, do you need anything?'

'No thanks. I'll be back to work as soon as… as soon as I can.'

'Alright, well, please do let me know if you need anything.'

I left it a few minutes and then knelt on the sofa and peered out of the grimy living room window. I couldn't see anyone but climbed my way out into the hall and pulled an extra gate in front of the front door just in case.

Three more days passed with no sign or sound of the crowd that I knew would gather when the Horse-Bonded and his horse left the village. I spent my time reading, sleeping and going through as many of my possessions as I could access, each of which helped me to feel a little calmer about the continuing presence of the village's guests.

I was having a mid-afternoon doze on my seventh day of confinement when a loud knock on the front door jolted me to wakefulness. I immediately curled up on my side and wrapped my arms around myself.

'Hi, Newson, my name is Devlin,' a man called out. 'I'm just here with my horse, Risk, to ask if we can be of any assistance at all?' His voice was kind and every part of me wanted to go to the door and meet him and his horse, and accept their offer. Every part except for the fear that roiled around in my stomach and taunted me with what would happen if I did.

'I understand you've had a difficult time these last fifteen years,' Devlin called out, 'and I'm sorrier than I can say that neither I nor any of my peers have visited here in all that time; you're a long, long way from The Gathering here, you see. But Risk and I are here now, and we'd really like to help if you'll allow us to? We can, you know, or rather Risk can. She's getting on a bit now so this will be our last trip away from The Gathering, and our only chance to meet you.'

I put my fist in my mouth and bit down hard on it, drawing blood, to prevent myself calling out to him.

'Okay, well, I'm afraid we'll be leaving tomorrow. We're staying at Mellow's, so if you change your mind, please do come and see us.'

There were the sounds of hooves clopping on the cobbles of my front path, then the gate squeaking open and shut. Then there was silence, which I broke with my sobbing.

I stayed where I was, not trusting myself to stay away from Devlin and Risk, until the next morning when finally, a multitude of voices called their farewells to the Horse-Bonded and his Bond-Partner. I waited another hour to be safe, then squeezed my way up to the bathroom as quickly as I could to relieve myself and wash. I grabbed some food and hurried to my workshop, lifting a hand to those who called out how good it was to see me on my feet again. I threw myself into my work, convinced that I could bury the memory of the past week under the mountain of orders waiting for me.

It didn't work. I felt the loss of Devlin and Risk, the only two who could have helped me, almost as keenly as I had felt the loss of my grandmother. Were they to arrive in the village again, I knew I would react the same way towards them as I already had, but that fact neither altered nor eased the utter hopelessness that engulfed me. I was a lost cause. Soon, my home and garden would be so rammed full of everything I needed around me, I would be unable to get into either. I would be homeless. A thirty-year-old man who had no choice but to live in his workshop until that also became too full to enter. I had let everyone down; my parents, Gran and all of the villagers who deserved a fully functioning Metal-Singer instead of a deranged, selfish one who had crammed his home with resources that should have been made available to them.

I felt a little dizzy all of a sudden. No, not dizzy exactly, I decided, more disorientated. It was as if I were being compelled to turn around and walk – no, run – into the wall of my workshop. I wondered if I had finally gone mad or developed some kind brain disorder; that would explain a lot.

I put both of my hands on the workbench and leant on them, trying to regain my sense of balance. It didn't help. I closed my eyes and breathed in and out slowly. That didn't help either, in fact the sensation got worse. I opened my eyes and turned around to face the wall. I felt a little less disorientated. I walked towards it as my whole body seemed to want to, and when I got there, put my hands against the cool, grey stone. The slight relief I had felt

while walking disappeared. I needed – no, not needed, was
required – to continue walking in the direction in which I was
facing.

Required. By whom? Who was doing this to me? Had Devlin
and Risk returned to the village? Was it Risk who was affecting
me this way? I pictured her in my mind, standing out on the street
when she and Devlin had arrived. They had left the village in the
same direction, the opposite direction to that in which I was now
facing and wanting to run ever more urgently. It wasn't Risk. As
she faded from my mind, a brief glimmer of understanding took
her place. But it couldn't be. Surely?

The tugging on my body and mind increased – for tugging was
what it was. My glimmer of understanding became certainty, then
hope and then overwhelming, blinding fear. I was being tugged by
a horse. That was always supposed to be a good thing, something
that was celebrated by the person who had been chosen by a horse
to be their Bond-Partner, and their family, their friends, their
whole village. But I didn't have any family or friends. I just had
my stuff, which I needed. All of it. I wouldn't leave it.

I don't know how long I stood with my hands on the wall,
trying to push myself away from it – from the urge to run through
or at least around it to get to the horse who was attempting to draw
me to them. I gritted my teeth and sweated as if I were trying to
lift something I wasn't strong enough to lift, for that was how it
felt, trying to resist the horse who had chosen me as their Bond-
Partner.

Bond-Partner! My attempt at a smile became a grimace. I
couldn't be one of the Horse-Bonded; they helped people, they
looked after people. I could do neither of those things for myself,
let alone anyone else. I let people down. I stole, I lied, I put my
own needs above those of anyone else, even my grandmother, who
had died rather than carry on living with her disappointment. No, I

would be a useless Bond-Partner and whichever horse had chosen me was mistaken. I wouldn't go to them. I wouldn't tell anyone I had been tugged. No one need know that a horse had called me to them and I had refused to go. I would carry on with my work and no one would be any the wiser.

A memory flashed through my mind of learning at school that when a person was tugged by a horse, they had no choice but to answer the call. In the panic that followed, I tried to bury what I knew just like I buried everything else I didn't want to confront – by focusing on things I owned. Physical things gave comfort as readily as emotions took it away.

I tore myself away from the wall and made my way unsteadily back to my workbench, where I grabbed hold of a trowel in one hand and a hand fork in the other, both of which were nearly finished. I focused on the trowel, which needed a little more curvature. I tuned into the metal… or at least I tried to.

Since my very first attempt to tune my mind into the lump of metal put before me during my testing for aptitude for metal-singing, I had been able to do it immediately, instinctively. But when I tried it this time, it was as if my mind were being bent away from the metal, not even allowed to reach it, and pulled ever more strongly towards the wall.

I focused hard on the trowel and tried again, with the same result. My old friend, panic, was my companion once more. I threw the trowel and fork down on my workbench and fled my workshop for the safety of home.

I slammed my front door behind me and hauled at the gates there, barricading myself in once more. They tangled together and I was left trying to pull four of them past myself at one time in the already tight space. My panic gave me the strength I needed and I managed it, but I ripped a trouser leg and scraped some skin off my arm in the process.

The gates weren't enough, not for this. I reached for a metal bench further along the hallway and jammed that in front of the gates, then stacked box upon box of door handles, cutlery, jewellery, tools, fishing hooks, arrowheads, pokers, axe heads – endless items that were useless to me in terms of their intended function but invaluable in the use to which I had put them – until I deemed myself sufficiently protected from that which I was unable to confront.

The second I stopped building my barricade, I realised that it was nowhere near sufficient. My head began to pound with the effort of standing still when my whole body and a good part of my mind, it seemed, would have me running for the far distant hills. Without meaning or wanting to, I turned towards the kitchen. Towards the back door that led out into the garden. I almost smiled with relief. It was impossible to get out that way without risking life and limb. I thought of the enormous heap of entangled, rusting metalwork and instantly felt a little calmer. It would protect me.

But it didn't. It transpired that nothing could; the more I tried to stay in one place, the stronger, the more unbearable became the pull on my mind. I staggered into the living room and curled up on the sofa as I had when Devlin and Risk were outside, but was soon trembling with the effort of remaining still when I should have been moving towards the horse who remained adamant that I would be their Bond-Partner. When I could stand it no longer, I climbed my way back to the kitchen and occupied myself by heaving yet more boxes and metal items in front of the back door, all the while feeling as if I would vomit from the effort, but unable to stop and risk being overcome by the urge to move it all away again so that I could leave.

When I had exhausted all of my strength, I busied myself with making a stew. My hands shook, my stomach roiled and occasionally heaved, but I wouldn't be deterred. When the stew was ready to eat, I couldn't face it. I spooned it into a container and left it on the side for later.

I looked around for something else to do and immediately regretted my lapse in activity as the tugging increased even more in strength. I grabbed hold of the oven door handle to prevent myself from attempting to scramble over everything I had placed in its way. The pull on my mind was too strong. My possessions had protected me from everything life had thrown at me so far, but they couldn't protect me from this.

I cried and I yelled and I threw stuff, which rebounded off other stuff and came to rest amongst even more stuff. The tugging decreased slightly. Was that it? I wondered. Did I just need to cry and scream and shout, and the horse would realise they had made a mistake and leave me alone?

I yelled some more and threw anything I could easily dislodge from the surrounding pile, onto everything else. The tugging increased in strength again. It was no good, I couldn't stand against it. The tugging decreased again. Because I had begun to give in, I realised. The only way I could stop the unbearable was by doing the unthinkable.

Leave? I couldn't leave, not without my things. I needed them. The tugging grew so strong that I felt as if my insides were following it while my outer shell stood hanging on to the leg of a chair that was sticking out from the pile.

'OKAY, I'LL COME,' I yelled. 'JUST GIVE ME SPACE TO THINK HOW I'M GOING TO DO IT, WILL YOU?'

The pull on my mind immediately decreased to a steady, low-level reminder, a suggestion even, of the direction in which I would need to head when I left.

Panic overtook me again. When I left? What was I thinking? The pull increased again. When I left, I told myself. There was no way around it if I wanted to stay sane. What passed for sane in my world, anyway. I glanced around. I would take as much stuff with me as I could. My handcart! I'd had the village Carpenter make it so that I could bring home large items from my workshop. I had made a lean-to under which to store it at the side of the house, so I'd be able to load it easily and I'd carry even more of my stuff on my back. But what to take?

The tugging increased again and continued to increase until I hurried towards the narrow pathway between everything stacked all the way up the stairs. Then it remained steady but didn't decrease; I wasn't to be given time to ponder. In the absence of time to think through what to pack, I threw things out of my way until I could get into my bedroom, where I repeated the procedure until I reached my bed. I pulled out a large back-sack that had been my father's, and swiped my arm across the bedside table, sweeping everything atop it into the back-sack along with a load of dust. My clock hadn't ticked for years, the pine cone was brittle and on the verge of disintegrating, and my wooden figurines smelt musty, but I couldn't leave them behind.

I picked up random items and dropped them in my back-sack, hurling everything else that was in my way to either side as I cleared a path to the wardrobe. Once I had managed to open one of the doors sufficiently to reach an arm in, I grabbed a whole load of clothes I hadn't seen in years, many of them my father's, and rammed them into the back-sack on top of everything else.

I made my way back downstairs, packing as many of the smaller items that lined my way as possible, as I went. I left the sack on the bottom-most stair and began removing the barricade I had thrown against the front door. By the time I had finished, I was weak with hunger but I couldn't stop. I flung open the front door, ran to the handcart, threw aside its tarpaulin and dragged it in front of the house. What to take?

The tugging increased again, reminding me not to think. I threw a couple of gates into the cart; they would come in handy. For what, I couldn't think just then, but they were certain to be needed at some point. The boxes that had formed part of my barricade followed the gates into the cart. When it was almost full, I clambered to the kitchen and fetched some containers of water. On my return to the kitchen, I upturned one of the countless boxes of cutlery I had amassed. I filled it with crockery, pots, pans and cooking implements, then upturned a box of scissors and filled that with food. I paused briefly to eat half of the stew I had made what felt like days earlier, then put the tub containing the remainder on top of the rest of my food.

I looked around. Was there anything else I would need? Panic made my legs feel weak. I needed everything. The pull on my mind increased to an unbearable level once more, giving me no choice but to grab the two boxes and head for the open front door. I wedged the boxes in between some others, pulled the tarpaulin over the cart and its contents and affixed it securely. I fetched my back-sack from the house, unable even to look at everything else I would be leaving behind, due to the dizzying, nausea-inducing pull on my mind which only decreased a little once I had shut the front door.

I heaved the sack onto my back, positioned myself between the handles of the cart and gritted my teeth as I lifted them to hip height. The pull on my mind remained steady. I followed it.

'Newson, where are you going?' Anni hurried along next to me as I staggered away from my home, pulling the cart behind me.

'I'm being tugged by a horse,' I said between my teeth, 'and I have to go to it.'

'You're… you're what? Newson, are you sure?'

I grimaced. 'You think I've finally gone mad and I don't

blame you. I just know that if I don't follow this pull on my mind, I'll finally lose it. I don't want to go but I don't have a choice.'

Anni put a hand on my arm. 'Newson, stop a minute. Please, just stop.'

I shook my head. 'I can't. The horse won't let me.'

'But even if you are being tugged, this isn't how it's done,' Anni said. 'This isn't how you're supposed to leave on your quest to find your horse. We should be giving you a Quest Ceremony, we should be providing you with everything you'll need on your journey. You need to give us time to organise that for you, and to send word that we'll be needing a replacement Metal-Singer.'

'This horse won't wait for all that,' I replied. 'It doesn't trust me with time to stop and think.'

'Newson, I'm worried about you.' Anni's voice shook. 'I've tried to look out for you. I haven't done a very good job of it, I know that, but I've tried. You don't look well and I'm worried that if you leave like this, with a load like that, something bad will happen to you.'

'I can't leave it behind. Thanks, Anni, for caring, but I'm not your problem. I'm no one's problem anymore, everyone in the village can heave a sigh of relief.'

'That isn't what will happen. You're a brilliant Metal-Singer and a... and a decent man with a few problems. We all care about you and you'll be missed. Will we ever see you again?'

'I don't know anything other than I have to keep moving that way.' I nodded my head in my direction of travel.

'Well, if you're being tugged, I hope your horse can help you to be happy.'

Happy. I knew there was a time when I had felt that way, but for the life of me, I couldn't remember it. 'Bye, Anni.'

'Fare you well, Newson.' Anni dropped back and let me go.

I was aware of other people passing me by as I continued

onward and out of the village, but I kept my eyes down and my focus on pulling my cart while following the tugging. I was only given the mental space to think about doing anything else once the sun had sunk behind the hills in the distance. I dropped the cart handles and fell to my knees on the grassy plain I had been traversing, then cursed as sand worked its way into open wounds on my hands which, some hours ago, had been blisters. At least it had remained dry, the spring breeze having kept away the rainclouds that would have made my journey all the more difficult.

I shuffled back to the wheel of the cart and leant against it, panting. When I had my breath back, I reached behind myself into the cart for a canister of water. I poured a little over my hands, washing the sand out of my sores, then wrapped my hands in strips that I tore off an old shirt, in order to keep the wounds clean. I pulled myself to my feet and found the tub of stew and a spoon. I ate the stew cold, drank my fill from the water canister, then sank back down to the ground and looked around.

There was nothing but grass and small bushes for miles. It would be dark and cold soon, and there would be animals emerging from their dens and burrows to graze and hunt in the darkness. I couldn't have them near me or my stuff.

I was exhausted but I dragged myself to my feet again and pulled on more clothes from my back-sack, then lifted the gates out of the cart. Why did I only bring two? I could make a barrier around myself with them and the cart, but what about all my stuff on the cart? That flaming horse had made me leave so much useful stuff behind – hell, all of it was useful. All of it made my life more bearable, and now I was without most of it. My ever faithful panic announced itself anew. I rummaged around within my back-sack until I found my wooden horse.

I was immediately transported back fifteen years to when I had

spent my first night at Gran's house, as it had been then. I
remembered the comfort the horse had given me in those early
days, the memories that had soothed me. The steady pull on my
mind increased very slightly and then decreased again, almost like
a recognition of my memories. That was exactly what it had been,
I realised. The horse was using the strength of the pull it was
exerting on my mind to communicate with me; to respond to my
memories of the horse who had inspired the figurine in my hand.
The strength of the pull increased and decreased again – I was
right! The horse had just confirmed it!

I focused on the memories more intently. I remembered the
horse's appearance, his easy relationship with his Bond-Partner,
and how he had seen right inside me, how I'd felt as if he'd
known I wasn't a threat even after I'd alarmed him, because he
recognised me. Was it he who was tugging me? No, he'd be a very
old horse now, and anyway, he already had a Bond-Partner. So,
who was it, and why?

The tugging increased and decreased again. It didn't matter
who and why. I had no idea how I knew that was what the
communication meant, but I knew. All that mattered was that I
found my horse. But I would have to survive the night first.

I found reserves of strength, which I would have sworn I
didn't possess had I not been in my current situation, to pull the
many boxes of metal items out of the cart. I stacked some along its
underside so that no animal could reach me that way, then used the
rest to keep the gates upright around me. I didn't think there
would be animals of large enough size to scale my barricade, this
close to the village, and I drew comfort from the sight of my
possessions around me. Thoughts of the horse who was tugging
me combined with exhaustion to help me along the remainder of
the pathway to sleep.

# Chapter Five

$\mathcal{J}$ woke with a start. A cold breeze had stripped my face of its warmth and was chilling me to the bone. I jumped as the chirping that had woken me sounded again from a nearby bush. I sat up, scaring the birds who had perched there into flight. What was I doing outside? Where was all my stuff? I looked wildly around myself and then jumped to my feet, grabbing hold of the side of the cart to steady myself as memories of the previous day came flooding back. I winced at both the pain in my hands and the sight before me; this cart, these boxes, a couple of gates, were all I had.

Something was poking me in the ribs. I put my hand under my outer garments, to the pocket of my shirt, and retrieved the horse figurine. Immediately, the pull on my mind, which I realised had decreased to a level where I could almost ignore it, increased until it occupied the emptiness left by all of the possessions I had been forced to leave behind. Part of me was comforted by the foreign sensation, the rest was outraged. What right did anyone else, even a horse, have to force me away from my home, my things, my life?

The pull on my mind increased until it was uncomfortable again. Well then, I would just have to load up the few belongings I'd been granted enough time to gather, and make my way onward, wouldn't I?

I lifted my box of food and one of the water containers out of the cart, then began taking my temper out on all of the other boxes as I hurled them back in. By the time there were only the gates left to pack into the cart, there was no room for them, such was the disorganisation of the pile of boxes already within. There was no way I was leaving the gates behind. Cursing, I pulled half of the boxes back out, managed to wedge the gates in, then repacked the boxes with a little more thought. I ate some cereal from my food box, drank from the water canister and then repacked them too, securing everything underneath the tarpaulin.

I unwrapped my hands and checked the state of my opened blisters. They didn't look too bad so I rewrapped them, shouldered my back-sack and took hold of the cart handles again. I winced at the pain from which the wrappings on my hands couldn't protect me as I began to pull the cart, then yelled as it snagged on a particularly dense tussock of grass, dragging the dressings across my wounds. I threw the handles back down.

'YOU SEE WHAT YOU'RE DOING TO ME?' I shouted to the horse in my head. 'I'm in pain because of you – because you wouldn't just let me be.'

The tugging decreased significantly, then increased again. What was that supposed to be? Guilt? Sorrow? Sympathy? Regardless, it was no help to me.

Despite myself, the tiniest part of me registered that it was more than a help; it was a connection. But I didn't want to listen to that part. I winced as I reorganised the dressings on my hands, then wrapped more strips of torn shirt around them for extra cushioning.

I dragged my cart all morning, shouting and cursing often at the horse who was making me do it. The hills for which I was very obviously heading seemed no closer by midday. I was determined to reach them by nightfall in the hope they would give me extra protection from the biting wind that had blown out of the early morning breeze, so I made myself a quick sandwich, downed a little more water and trudged on to the throbbing rhythm of the pain in my hands.

I weaved around and between small rocks and dense tussocks of grass in an attempt to avoid my cartwheels catching on them and consequently my hands, but there were many that avoided my scrutiny and caught me anyway. I yelled louder each time and once even considered offloading some of the cart's contents. The panic that seized me caused me to pull the cart even harder before I could contemplate doing such a thing again.

By the time I reached the hills, an hour or so before nightfall I judged, blood had soaked through the wrappings on my hands, my jaws ached from gritting my teeth, and every other muscle within me ached from dragging the cart. I kept going until I had rounded the closest, smallest hill and could no longer feel the wind, then dropped the cart handles. Having been bent over all day in order to take the strain of carrying and pulling my loads, I couldn't stand up straight.

I allowed my back-sack to fall to the grass, reached into the cart for some food and water, then sank to the ground myself. The pull on my mind decreased to an almost pleasant level, as if the horse were happy with me for some reason. I was too tired to think on it further. I ate, drank and washed my hands clean of blood. I rewrapped them in clean dressings and put them under their opposing armpits and clamped down hard on them to try to quell their throbbing. I thought that I probably needed a Herbalist, maybe a Tissue-Singer too, but I also knew that my chances of receiving help from either were zero unless I happened to come across one in my path; the horse wouldn't stop tugging me until I was with it, until we were bonded, if everything I had learnt at school was right. I had a feeling it was.

I clamped down harder on my hands and contemplated building a barricade around myself once more. I couldn't bring myself to move a muscle other than clamping down on my hands even harder. The panic that wanted to convince me I wouldn't be able to rest, to sleep without being surrounded by my usual wall of belongings, couldn't find the energy within me to amount to more than a brief moment of concern before I was sound asleep.

The following day was even tougher. I woke late, feeling as if I had barely slept and surprised that I had, considering the level of pain in my hands that announced itself as soon as I was conscious. I peeled off their dressings and washed them again, then rebound them with fresh strips of shirt. I didn't get a chance to feel sorry for myself for their poor state of repair before the relentless pulling on my mind resumed.

I breakfasted quickly and steeled myself to pick up the handles of the cart. When I was all set, I bent down between them... but couldn't bring myself to close my hands around the cloth that bound them, let alone around wooden handles whose constant companions were weight and friction.

I stood up again and looked back at my cart. Could I unload some of its contents? Hide them somewhere and come back for them when my hands had healed? I reeled at the thought. No. That wasn't possible. Pulling the cart was. Painful, but possible. I didn't allow myself to think any further; I bent down, grasped the handles and, gritting my teeth, lifted the cart and pulled it into motion.

I glanced up to where the tugging on my mind was directing me, and was relieved to see that I could pass between the next two hills, the ground appearing relatively level except for the rocks and grass tussocks I had already grown used to avoiding. My leg and back muscles screamed at me as I began to move.

Many times over the next few hours, I reconsidered unloading some of the cart's contents. Each time, the protests of my mind were worse than those of my body and I continued slowly, painfully, onward. When the ground began to slope upward, I couldn't bring myself to lift my eyes from the grass immediately ahead of my feet, and confirm what my body and the weight of the cart were telling me; there was now a hill between me and the horse who refused to stop its persistent demand of me.

I wouldn't be beaten, I told myself. I would do this one step at a time and I would be triumphant when I arrived at the top complete with my stuff.

*You are complete without it.*

I jumped so violently at the thought that appeared in my mind, I lost my grip on both handles. The cart slid back away from me as I fell face first into the grass, the weight of my back-sack ensuring that I landed heavily and couldn't easily get up. I managed to lift my head and look up towards the top of the hill, but there was a large boulder directly ahead of me into which I would have walked head on had I not been distracted.

I pulled one of my arms out of its back-sack strap, then managed to turn slightly to one side so that the sack slid off me. I wriggled free of it entirely and, gasping, pushed my knuckles into the ground and staggered to my feet.

The hill was dotted with bushes, boulders and the odd tree,

none of which obscured the grey horse standing on its brow, highlighted by the sun's rays. She was watching me. How did I know she was a she? I asked myself. Because I did, as surely as I had known that the thought which had appeared in my mind was hers and not mine. As surely as I knew that I was the object of her focus even though I couldn't make out exactly in which direction she was staring.

*There is much that may not be explained other than by trusting how you feel. You have made a promising start.*

'To what?' I said. Then ventured tentatively, *To what?*

*To our time together. To your learning. We will continue.* She turned and walked away, dropping out of sight within only a few strides.

'WAIT!' I shouted, and began to hurry after her feeling strangely unencumbered. I stopped. My stuff! How could I have forgotten my stuff?

I turned back towards my abandoned back-sack and the cart that had rolled back down to level ground. Then I faced uphill once more. She was walking away from me, I could feel it, and I needed to follow her, to reach her, to bond with her so that I'd never feel alone again. She was no longer tugging my mind but she didn't need to; she was right there, a subtle presence that was with me, that felt comforting – but that I needed more of. I needed to be with her as much as I needed my belongings.

I ran to my cart and hauled it the distance up the slope which I had already travelled, grimacing at the pain in my hands but accepting it as necessary if I were to be with my horse. But when I put the cart down in order to pick up my back-sack, it rolled back down the slope. I cursed myself for an idiot as I heaved the back-sack into place, then hurried back down to the cart on shaking legs.

I dragged it only four strides further up the hill than I had the first time, before my legs buckled beneath me. I tried to keep hold of the cart and shrieked as its weight took it back down the slope, the dressings from my hands with it. All the time, I could sense my horse walking steadily away from me.

I couldn't let her leave me. If I didn't catch up with her now, would she ever allow me to in the future? Would she sever her ties with me and just leave me, like my parents had, like Gran had?

Part of me registered surprise that my horror at what I was about to do was less than my fear of losing my horse. The rest of me organised my body to begin lifting boxes out of the cart and stack them by a boulder, along with one of the gates. I paused to consider whether to leave or take the tarpaulin, but not for long. I quickly covered my abandoned items with it, securing it to the ground to ensure its protection endured until I could return.

I threw my back-sack into the cart, reapplied fresh dressings to my hands, ground my teeth together and dragged the cart up the hill. I tried to, anyway; I'd taken no time to replenish my body's strength since my previous attempts and I didn't make it as far as I had before, even with a half load which once again rolled back down to the bottom of the hill.

I yelled out to my horse to wait for me but she continued onward without hesitation. My newly-fledged sense of her seemed to be weakening. All I could do was stand still, looking between my cart and where I had last seen her. I would have to abandon all but my back-sack.

'NOOOOOOOOOO!' I yelled over and over until I was hoarse. If I lost my stuff, I would lose my protection from the emptiness that had threatened to consume me for the past fifteen years. Then what would I have? Nothing. No reason to live, just an empty stretch of nothingness that utterly terrified me. But I would have her.

I latched on to that thought. If I had my horse, I would at least be able to manage without my stuff until I could persuade her to return to it with me and help me transport it. Relief flooded through me. That would work; she could pull my cart for me if I could catch up with her and bond with her properly, if I could make her see how important my belongings were to me.

I hastened back down to the cart, emptied half of the contents of my back-sack into it and then stuffed as much food into the sack as I could before selecting a half-full water canister. I would carry that; after having dragged the cart so far, it would be easy. I repacked the cart and secured the tarpaulin over it. I hoisted my back-sack into position, took hold of the water canister and began to climb the hill for the final time.

It was steeper than it looked and I was more exhausted than I would admit to myself. My strides shortened and my footsteps slowed. When I tripped over a root and dropped the water canister, it rolled back down the hill and I was too tired to go back down and fetch it. I consoled myself with the thought that my horse would bring me back for it very soon, and trudged on, trying to hold away my panic at the knowledge that she was steadily increasing the distance between us.

When I finally reached the top of the hill, she was nowhere to be seen. I was alone with just my back-sack and what was now excruciating pain in my hands. Further, my sense of my horse was still thinning, as if it were a thread that had been stretched to its limit and could snap at any moment.

I glanced back down the hill to where I had left my things and felt a little calmer. I could still go back to them. Flaming lanterns, I could go back home and regain everything I had left behind. But then I looked into the distance to where I could just about sense my horse to be, and remembered how it had felt to have her thoughts in my mind. I knew there was no going back.

The longer I stood still, the more panicky I felt, so I took one last, longing look down the hill before hurrying down its other side after my horse.

My fatigued legs gave way twice. The first time, I was saved by a bush in my path, into which I collapsed and rested for a few minutes until I could find the strength to push myself back up to my feet. The second time, I fell heavily on my side and couldn't get back up. Further, I suspected that I had sprained my ankle. I wriggled out of the back-sack's straps and pushed myself onto my knees, but when I managed to stand up, resting my injured leg, I couldn't lift the back-sack. I needed water and rest, but could have none of either.

Sobbing, I pulled the food out of my back-sack, followed by the rest of its contents. With shaking hands, I repacked my clock, the portrait of my parents and me, my collection of wooden animals, the remains of my pine cone, a few clothes and most of the food. I bound my ankle as best I could in the arm of the shirt I had been shredding to bind my hands, then, unable to bear the sight of the rest of my belongings strewn over the hillside, left them there without a backward glance.

Was it my imagination, I wondered, or was the thread that joined my horse and me no thinner for my having stopped? Had she stopped too? Was she finally going to wait for me? Maybe I could go back for some of the things I'd just unpacked? Maybe she'd come back and help me carry them? Immediately, she was on the move again, I was certain of it. I limped painfully onward.

I was relieved beyond measure when I reached the bottom of the hill – thankfully a longer, more gradual descent than my ascent had been – to find a stream running along the valley. I almost fell into it face first, and quenched my thirst. Then I washed my face using the bindings around my hot, throbbing hands, and finally removed my boot, sock and bandage, and sat with my ankle in the cold water.

When I checked my sense of my horse, I found that the thread between us was no thinner than it had been; she had stopped too, I was sure of it this time. Galvanised by the knowledge, I tore some bread off a loaf, wrapped some slices of ham around it, and quickly ate my inside out sandwich.

I got to my feet with the help of a fallen branch from a nearby tree and, using it as a staff to help take the weight off my injured ankle, carried on my way, hoping to close the distance between myself and my horse. Exasperatingly, she began to move too. How was I ever going to catch up with her? I couldn't allow myself to think that I wouldn't; I had left everything behind for her so I had to.

By the time I finally stopped limping my way over, around and between countless hills, the sun had long since sunk behind them, having burnt my face. My ankle was throbbing as much as my hands, one of which was dripping with blood from where I'd been grasping the staff, and I hurt just about everywhere else. On top of that, I was faced with a night without either my horse or my possessions, aside from those few that I carried on my back.

I slid down my staff and allowed it to fall to the ground. I jumped as the end of it splashed into water – as luck would have it, I'd come across another stream. I scowled, immediately discounting my previous observation; luck had played no part in the proceedings of the past few days. If it had, I would have been safe and sound at home, not lost, injured and alone.

I managed to allay the panic trying to rise in me by arranging my clock, pine cone, portrait and figurines around myself. I ate, drank and then just about managed to find the strength to wash. When I woke the next morning, I was still lying on my stomach by the stream, my head hanging over its shallow bank.

I tried to move, but every part of my body protested so I stopped. I was soaking wet, I realised, and extremely cold.

Thankfully, the hills that had caused me so much hardship now sheltered me from any air movement that would have chilled me further, but nevertheless, I needed to move, get dry and warm. And, I realised with a flash, I needed to check on my things. Fear gave me the strength that was missing during my previous attempt to move. Slowly, painfully, I wriggled back from the edge of the stream, then rolled onto my side and drew my knees to my chest. I rolled onto them and rested for a moment, then straightened so that I could turn around whilst kneeling down. The pain that wracked me somewhere deep inside eclipsed that which riddled my body.

My clock had been cleaned of its skin of dust, and soaked through so that droplets of water ran down the inside of its glass face. The portrait was ruined; my parents and I were a grey mess. The pine cone had finally fallen apart, and of all the wooden figurines, only the badger remained. My back-sack was under a tree a short distance away, presumably having been dragged there and then abandoned by whichever animal had dispersed my figurines.

It was as if the rain had trickled not just into my clock but into the gaps in my façade of a man just about managing to cope with life. Further, whoever or whatever had trampled on my pine cone and made off with my figurines had rammed it home to me once and for all how fragile was the protection I had tried to erect around myself – the protection that was in any case no longer there.

I crawled, shivering, to the clock and managed to persuade my almost frozen fingers to pick it up. I hurled it against a tree where it smashed, all of its constituent parts dispersing into the long grass. Then I collected the badger, crawled to my back-sack and hugged both to me knowing that neither was enough. I was alone.

The second I admitted that which I had avoided

acknowledging for half of my life, I allowed in that of which I had been terrified for every bit as long.

I saw my parents' faces as they smiled at me, shared a look with one another that meant I was in trouble, watched over me while I read to them or did my homework. I heard their voices as they sang to me, laughed with me, consoled me, congratulated me, cuddled me. I even smelt the soap my mother liked to use, and the unguent my father used to rub under his nose when he had a cold.

The pain of loss filled my lungs and wrenched at my heart, strangling it so that I thought it would stop beating. It clenched my stomach until I wretched. It pounded so hard inside my head that I wanted to knock myself out rather than carry on feeling it. I cried silent tears, barely able to breathe and partly hoping that I would cease to as grief stripped me of my will to live, just as I had always suspected it would.

But as seconds turned to minutes and then to hours, I continued to draw in air, and, though I shivered violently with my body's efforts to get warm, my breathing very gradually deepened and evened as I cried myself out. My stomach rumbled as it unclenched. The pounding in my head eased, giving me the space to realise that the sense I had of my horse had strengthened despite her being no closer in distance to me.

*You should change your garments,* she informed me.

Anger flared within me, banishing the remainder of my pain. *I'm in this situation because of you,* I told her. *Of all the things you could have done to help me, telling me to change my clothes is the best you can come up with?*

*You are in your present situation because you allowed a childhood fear to dictate your thoughts and behaviour. You may begin to rectify your error by tending to your body. Then we will tend to your mind.*

# Chapter Six

*I* sat up and allowed my back-sack to drop to the ground beside me. I gingerly inspected the badger that had become nestled within the dressing on my hand. He was none the worse for wear. At least someone had come out of the previous day unscathed. I put him in a side pocket of my back-sack and attempted to secure the fastening, but my hands were shaking too much with the cold that had at least dulled their throbbing.

I sighed, my anger fleeing as I realised that my horse was right. The sun was up now and actually had a little warmth in it, but my wet clothes were hindering my body's attempts to regain a comfortable working temperature. Since it seemed I had survived that which I had been so sure I wouldn't, I should change my clothes. I managed to grasp and release the drawstring that held my back-sack closed, and felt about within it. Its contents were dry. I pulled out a change of clothes and slowly, wearily, painfully, removed my damp ones, laid them out in the sun, and donned their replacements.

My stomach rumbled noisily. I fed it in a daze, exhausted

again now that I was devoid of emotion. I persuaded my aching body to crawl to the stream so that I could drink, wash my hands and dunk my ankle until it was too numb to be painful. Then I rebound my hands and ankle, crawled back under the tree and slept.

I woke to the sounds of birds cheeping in the branches above my head. The sun was halfway back down to the hills, telling me that I had slept through the rest of the morning and half of the afternoon. My heart lurched and I looked around desperately for my back-sack, then calmed as I realised that my hand was resting atop it.

*You do not need it in the way you believe you do.* She was still no closer to me, nor indeed any further away.

*Yes I do. It was my father's and it contains clothes, food and my ornament.*

*I am aware of that which it contains.*

*So then you'll also be aware that it's all I have left until I can return for the rest of my stuff.*

*Which you also do not need. You have proven that to yourself.*

*And how have I done that, exactly?*

*You believed you could not survive without it. You are surviving without it.*

I frowned, confused, and retrieved the badger from the pocket of my back-sack. *That's because I still have this, and my back-sack, and... you. I have my sense of you.*

*You reach for the pattern to which you have adhered for so long merely because it is familiar. You have released the pain which you used your possessions to avoid feeling. You need neither those which remain nor me.*

*Well, why did you tug me then? It can't possibly be because you need me.*

*There is much we can achieve together.*

*I may be stating the obvious, but don't we need to be together in order for that to happen? You left me.*

*At no time did I leave you.* I was surprised by the sense of kindness, of patience, of… honesty that accompanied her thought. She wasn't defending herself against my accusation, but simply stating a fact.

I rallied. *Well, I don't see you anywhere. I can feel you're some distance away. How are we supposed to bond properly when we're so far apart?*

*We bonded in truth before either of us were born. We have never needed physical proximity with one another or indeed physicality itself for that to remain the truth.*

There was so much about her statement with which I wanted to argue, but one aspect dominated the remainder. *We don't need to be with one another to be bonded? How can that be? The Horse-Bonded always travel with their horses, they're never apart from them.*

*That is a situation and not a prerequisite for sharing a bond.*

*But I've left everything for you. I need to be with you.*

*You are everything you need. You know this now but it will take time for you to admit it to yourself.*

*Please come back, or at least let me catch you up?*

She didn't reply. Further, she seemed smaller in my mind, as if at any moment my sense of her would fizzle out and she would disappear completely.

I tried to stand up, to make my way to her, but my ankle was too swollen and painful to support me. I sank back to the ground, catching sight as I did so of the sodden pulp within its frame that my family portrait had become. I was surprised by the sadness I felt. Not scared, not filled with a compulsion to grab whatever I could in its place, not empty… not even alone, now I came to think of it; just sad.

*You do not need it in the way you believe you do.* Her thought didn't come directly from her this time, but from where it had lodged within my mind. *You are everything you need.*

The thoughts scared me, so I pushed them to one side and crawled back under the tree. I unpacked my back-sack and took stock of what I had; one ripped, partially missing shirt, two others, a spare pair of trousers and two pullovers were all the clothes I had in addition to those currently drying in the sun. There was enough food for five, maybe six days if I ate meagre rations. And I had a small, wooden badger. It wasn't much.

I waited several minutes for the panic that never came, then my thoughts switched to my ankle. I couldn't walk on it – flaming lanterns, I couldn't even stand on it – and I knew from when Gran had once sprained her ankle that the quickest way for it to recover would be to rest it. She had been immobile for almost a week and then advised to stay off her feet as much as possible for a further week after that, but I was pretty sure her ankle had been more swollen than mine. So maybe if I rested for three to four days, I'd be okay to continue as long as I had my staff? And that would give my hands time to heal too?

I looked about myself for the staff and spotted it where I had dropped it on my arrival in what, I realised as I took in my surroundings properly for the first time, was a beautiful spot. The stream tumbled down from between two hills to my right, and disappeared around another to my left. The tree above me was heavy with leaves and white blossom, a nearby bush was bright yellow with blooms, and the first flowers of spring dotted the surrounding hillsides. I had shelter, water and food, so I supposed if I had to be stranded somewhere for a few days, here was as good as anywhere.

But what then? I didn't know where I was, how to get back to my stuff, or how to reach a horse who didn't want to be reached. I had no means of hunting or cooking meat, and the food I had brought with me would run out before I was likely to come across the nearest village. It was all hopeless. I was hopeless.

Listlessly, I separated a small ration of stale bread and slightly mouldy cheese from my food store, and nibbled them. When I needed water, I crawled to the stream. When I needed to relieve myself, I crawled behind a bush a short distance away. Otherwise, I dozed the afternoon away beneath the tree while birds fluttered between the branches above my head, insects buzzed around me, some of them landing on me for a short while before deciding I had nothing to offer, and the stream splashed and tinkled past me on its way to goodness knew where.

The longer I remained still, the more rabbits hopped around nearby, but they were gone in a flash if I made even the tiniest movement. When one thumped his hind feet on the ground, I opened my eyes and sat up with a start, hoping that my horse had come for me. As the rabbits fled back to their burrows, a shadow passed over the ground. A buzzard circled for a few minutes and then flew on.

When darkness fell, I ate another small ration of food, dunked my hands and ankle in the stream until they stopped throbbing, rebound them and settled down to sleep.

Two days passed. When I woke with the dawn chorus on the third, I remained lying with my head on my back-sack, listening to the birds conversing above my head. Two sleepy, questioning cheeps were answered by one that sounded equally unsure.

*Is anyone else awake?* I imagined them saying. *Is it light enough to move around?*

*Maybe, what does everyone else think?*

The stream seemed to answer them by quietening slightly, as I had noticed it did on the previous two occasions I witnessed night giving way to day – or was that just because the flapping, chirping and rustling of animals coming back to life made it appear that way?

My stomach growled somewhat painfully. I supposed I should eat. I sat up and smiled as the rabbits that were grazing and hopping around nearby remained where they were. I was glad that my hands were feeling so much better as I had to really grasp hold of the remainder of my loaf in order to tear off a chunk to eat with a helping of strawberry preserve. I brushed the resulting crumbs from my lap and birds dropped out of the branches to peck at them, one even landing on the toe of my booted foot. I watched them bounding from crumb to crumb on their impossibly thin legs, and marvelled at how tiny, how vulnerable, and yet how perky they were. I missed them as soon as they had taken flight.

When I unbound my ankle, I found that it was almost back to its normal size. Black, blue and green, but looking a whole lot better. Did I dare risk my hands by attempting to pull myself up the staff so I could test its strength once I was upright? I decided that I would… and then found myself regretting my decision, not because my hands were adversely affected, but because the rabbits all shot back to their burrows; apparently, on my feet I was a far more frightening proposition than when sitting.

A swift snatched a biter from the air an arm's length from my shoulder and I smiled again. I was never on my own out here, not really. Why had I never realised that before? I shrugged as I touched my toe to the ground and put a little weight on it. My ankle ached rather than took my breath away with the sharp pain I had experienced before. I tried to put my foot down flat but couldn't completely. I could limp with the aid of the staff, but I risked damaging my ankle further.

Rabbits popped their heads back out of their burrows and, eyeing me cautiously, began to slowly emerge and nibble at the grass once more. I envied them for being able to just eat what nature provided so easily for them. A thought occurred to me. Maybe I could too? Then my food store would last longer and I could wait here until my ankle had healed more.

I leant on my staff and hopped on the spot as I gazed around. Where before I had seen bushes and flowers, now I saw a potential food source. But how to know what was edible? I remembered being taught at school that the Ancients used their intuition to know what was safe to eat after leaving the processed food of the cities behind. Could I do that? Could I be the son of The New my parents had thought me to be?

My heart ached when I thought of them, then settled as determination rooted itself within me. I had let them down. I would try to be a son of The New, and if I poisoned myself in the process then I was no great loss to the world. Where to start though? I had spent a great deal of my life holed up in either my workshop or my home, and had no idea what any of the plants that surrounded me were except for the grass.

I stared at some nearby flowers. They were bright yellow with a multitude of narrow petals that tapered at their ends. I had seen the rabbits nibbling them, so they couldn't be harmful, could they? I lowered myself to one knee and picked a flower. I sniffed it and felt no alarm. I pulled a single petal off and put it on my tongue. Still no sense of alarm, just a feeling of rightness. Rightness? I didn't even know what I meant by that, exactly, just that eating the flower would be okay. So I did… and I decided that I was fine.

I waited for half an hour to be sure, then picked a leaf from the innermost swirl that had surrounded the flower. It was slightly bitter, but not so much that I wanted to spit it out, or felt concern. The outermost leaves, however, were tough and unpleasant. I spat out the two I'd put in my mouth and made a mental note not to eat any more.

The yellow flowers of the nearby bushes tasted slightly sweet and nutty, but the spiky leaves were a no go. The young leaves of the cleavers – which I did recognise due to having had them stuck on my back by a friend at school – that had tangled themselves around and within the bush were delicious, but the older ones were chewy and a little woody.

I limped to my back-sack, emptied it and looped it over my arm so that I could collect more of the plant parts I had identified as being edible. By lunchtime, I had enough for what would have been a salad bowl, had I had a bowl. I added some small pieces of cheese and some meat jerky, then settled down to eat it feeling pleased with myself. I listened to the birds, watched the rabbits and took in the sight of the veritable food pantry that surrounded me as I ate. I felt strangely – very strangely – peaceful.

When a thumping sound reached my ears, I looked around to see which rabbit was creating it, and what it had identified as a threat; I couldn't see any birds of prey and I didn't think foxes would be around at this time of day. Strangely, I couldn't see any of the rabbits thumping or looking even remotely alarmed.

Then she rounded the hill to my left. The rabbits in her path moved out of the way of her feet but didn't race away to safety. The birds continued to flit about their business and the stream continued to trickle past as my horse entered the tranquillity of our home as if she were a long time inhabitant rather than a visitor.

She was beautiful. She had looked grey from a distance, but now that she was closer, I could see that the grey surrounded a multitude of white splodges of varying sizes. Her mane and tail were silvery white and she moved with a graceful elegance, but it was her eyes that held my stare as she closed the remaining distance between us. They were large, dark and bright but more, they were wells of the kindness I had sensed in her thought to me. I was glad I hadn't been close enough to see them before; had I been, her sudden departure would have completely devastated me.

*You have discovered that you have the ability to look inside yourself,* she informed me. *You have admitted to yourself that you are all that you need. You have released your pain and the greater part of your dependence on physical items. You have yet to release your addiction to tragedy.*

*My... what? How am I addicted to tragedy? I had it forced on me.*

*Your parents' deaths affected you deeply. Your grandmother's loss weighs on you still but you have released much of the pain of both. You have no need to create tragedy where there is none.* Her thoughts carried nothing but kindness, patience and truth, just as they had before. She wasn't scolding me but I felt chastened nevertheless. And a little silly. Try as I might, I couldn't argue with anything she had told me.

I glanced at my back-sack which I had repacked with my clothes, the small wooden badger and the meagre remainder of my food. I had dived into it three times a day for the food, but hadn't once thought about its other contents since accepting that I was stranded in my little beauty spot. Further, the remains of the clock, pine cone and portrait were still where they had met their demises, also undisturbed by me. How had I not registered those facts before?

*You do not need them in the way you believed you did.*

My initial irritation at her repeating counsel she had already given me, and which I still didn't understand, was instantly smoothed by her continued kind patience. *Meaning?* I asked her.

*A stock of food and clothing renders your physical existence somewhat easier. The rest of the items you valued had uses at times but none were essential for your survival as you supposed. In truth they were a distraction from your purpose here. No longer. Your time here has been well spent.*

I sensed her satisfaction and was reminded of the previous

time I had felt it from her; when she first communicated with me and told me that I had made a promising start to my learning. I shivered as understanding of the situation dawned on me.

I managed to get to my feet so that I could look her straight in the eyes, rather than up at her. *You abandoned me so I'd try to follow you, so I'd learn what you've just told me I have. But what if I hadn't learnt it? What if I'd never got over losing my stuff? What if I hadn't learnt to use my intuition like the Ancients did? What if I hadn't learnt how to find food for myself? Would you ever have come back for me or would you have left me to die here?*

She gazed back at me, both her eyes and my sense of her assuring me that she wasn't capable of telling me anything other than the truth. *I merely responded to your energy as it presented itself to me. I did that which you needed me to do.*

*Why couldn't you just have stayed with me while I realised I didn't need all my stuff?*

*You would have transferred your need for possessions to a need for me. The pattern would have remained in place with equal strength. It is much weaker now but we will need to ensure that you do not allow it to regain a hold on you.*

*We? You're going to stay with me now?*

*I was always with you. When you feel comfortable enough to walk we will continue on our way.*

*To The Gathering?*

*That is a suitable destination.*

*I've heard it's a long way away from here.*

*It is where it is. We are where we are. At some point the two will coincide. Until then we will practise being all we need.* She wandered over to the stream and drank, then began to graze, leaving me standing on one leg, propped up against my staff, unsure what to do with all of the information she had given me.

I resorted to a custom that afforded me comfort by its familiarity. *My name is Newson,* I told her. *Do you have a name? What do I call you?*

*You are Searching For Truth. You may name me as I have named you.*

I had no idea what she meant... yet I did. A small grain of something deep within me responded to the name she had given me, and began to swell. It was unfamiliar and felt out of place, yet I knew I wanted more of it; I wanted to hold onto it, to focus all of my attention upon it and let it become all of me because, strange as it felt to me, I could sense strength within it – something I had never felt before in my life.

*There is strength in truth.* Her thought drew me in to her being as much as did the kindness in her eyes. *You should lower yourself to the ground for you will end up there regardless.*

I obeyed her immediately, my body responding to her thought as if it were my own.

*Name me for that which you sense within me,* she instructed me.

She was everything. She was all around me and within me. She was an infinite mass of truth and honesty that was so pure, I found myself wanting to cry. There was no room for conflict within her – how could there be when the way ahead of her was so simple, so obvious? A word blazed within me, hurting me with its opposition to everything I knew myself to be. Integrity.

She released me as soon as I had her name. *Integrity,* I thought to her... and caused myself a mountain of pain. The sense of wholeness, of completeness and strength about her – as if she could never be threatened by anything because her consistency of character wouldn't allow it – only highlighted in the greatest possible way to me what a fractured, pathetic excuse for a man my fear and selfishness had made me. I had made Gran's life a misery and caused discomfort and hardship to everyone else unfortunate enough to have crossed my path since I lost my parents. I was a disgrace.

*Judgement of the past has no place in these proceedings.* Integrity's thought was as honest and kind as before. *Experiences that are deemed negative are as valuable to the learning process as those deemed positive despite neither judgement having any basis in truth. It is truth to which we will dedicate ourselves from this point forward.*

*But how can I forgive myself for all the pain and trouble I caused my grandmother? I couldn't help it but I did it nevertheless. She died because of me.*

*The peculiar emotion in which you are currently indulging has no basis in truth. Neither of your assertions have basis in truth. We will dedicate ourselves to neither.*

She was right – I knew it, I could feel it in her thoughts – but how could she possibly be? *Guilt? I have no reason to feel guilty? And I COULDN'T help it, and Gran DID die because of me.*

*You acted out of fear until you realised the alternative. You and your grandmother agreed before either of you were born that she would help you to learn everything you have. She learnt much in return and she passed when she was ready. That is the truth. Everything else is a distraction from it.*

*It's absolutely not that simple…*

Integrity continued as if I hadn't interrupted her. *We will dedicate ourselves to sensing the truth of every situation and acting in accordance with it however difficult or uncomfortable.*

Her thought reminded me of advice I had received a long time before. *Gran told me to always do what's right instead of what's easy, but I couldn't do it.*

*You were consumed with the preservation of self. When aligned with truth that can be useful. When aligned with fear it is*

*more likely to be less preservation of self and more harm to self as*
*you have already discovered. We will dedicate ourselves to truth,*
she repeated.

*How will we do that? And by we, I mean I. You're just being*
*kind, making out there'll be any effort on your part.*

*We have already begun. In searching for food you found the*
*truth within yourself and acted upon it. When I gave you your*
*name you sensed its truth and grasped hold of it. When you named*
*me you realised that truth is all I am and everything you have the*
*potential to be. All we need do now is hold to the beginning we*
*have made and discount anything that isn't true.*

*You make it seem so straightforward.*

*Straightforward is an appropriate description. From the*
*options before us in every situation we will choose the one which*
*is true and then move straight and forward towards it. We will*
*dismiss the options to either side of us however tempting they may*
*be for they will not be true. What feels true to you in this moment?*

I considered. *I feel happy. Content. I've eaten and I've slept*
*but I need to rest my ankle so it carries on healing.*

*So rest.*

*There's something else.* I could feel it nagging at me inside and
when I focused on it, my stomach clenched. *I need to look*
*after you.*

*Truth affords peace and not discomfort. Identify the source of*
*your disquiet,* I was instructed.

*I'm worried about you, about whether you have everything*
*you need.*

*Do you sense any evidence to the contrary?*

*Um, now you come to mention it, no.*

*Then identify the source of your disquiet. With honesty.* There
was so much kindness and patience attached to her thought that I
didn't feel scolded, merely free to do as she asked.

*I'm... well, I guess I'm worried about me and whether I have everything I need. Which is you. And if you're not okay then I won't have you.*

*Your initial admittance is true. It will serve you to work your way through the remainder.*

I shuffled backward until I was resting against the tree trunk, and thought whilst watching her graze as if that were all that was occupying her.

Finally, I ventured, *You want me to say that in truth, I don't need you, don't you?*

*I would that you admit the truth and then choose it to the exclusion of all else.*

*Okay, well I guess I've already proved I don't need you, but I feel like I do. Now you're here, I can't think of anything happening to you, of you falling ill or getting injured or going off without me to find other food.*

*You are allowing yourself to focus upon the part of your old pattern that yet remains within you. You are choosing fear instead of the truth which now also resides within you. Remember that this is a straight and forward process. You are Searching For Truth.*

I felt panic beginning to bubble up within me. I wanted to run to Integrity, to pull her close to me, to tie her to me somehow so that she would always be near me, always be okay, always be the mountain of strength I could sense her to be. But the name she had chosen for me, the name she had just called me, reached deep inside me to where the grain of truth that had begun to swell when her thoughts touched it before, swelled further. I found the truth and moved straight and forward towards it, just as she had advised. Even then, I found it hard to admit; I couldn't seem to frame the thought and make it real.

Eventually, I resorted to blurting it out. 'I don't...' I gasped. 'I don't need you. I don't need to keep you near me for you to be okay. For me to be okay. You have everything you need and will do unless I sense otherwise. I should rest.' I gasped again, feeling utterly exhausted.

*That is the truth,* Integrity announced. Her sense of triumph gave me a boost, which quickly dissipated as panic took hold.

'I'm not going to be able to do this,' I said. 'I feel like I need to sleep for a week just because I managed to admit something I already knew. I can't go through that every minute of every day.'

Integrity flicked her tail at a biter but appeared otherwise unperturbed. *It bodes well that you have realised the task we have ahead of us. When you encounter difficulty you need only reach for the truth of our bond for there you will find the truth of everything else. We will remain here until your body is healthy for that will signify that your mind is strong enough to leave. Searching For Truth. Rest now.*

# Chapter Seven

*I*ntegrity was right, as I came to learn she always would be. I should have been walking normally within two weeks of spraining my ankle, but it was three before it had fully recovered, or, more accurately – and as Integrity reminded me whenever I railed about the time it was taking – before my mind was strong enough to allow it to fully recover. In the meantime, the truths to which I had admitted were frequently tested.

When my food ran out, I had no choice but to turn to my inner guidance for help so that my foraged pantry never ran empty, and I learnt to trust that my intuition would keep me fed and safe. Integrity challenged me much more. She refused to be bound to any assurances as to her whereabouts or proximity to me; she would stay near me for a while, then wander further away in order to source different herbs, with no guarantees as to when, or even whether, she would be back. Sometimes she would be nearby when I went to sleep but absent by the time I awoke. Other times she would be several hills distant when I went to sleep and little closer when I awoke.

Each and every time I was tested, I went through the same panic, the same need to be near her. Each and every time, she called me by the name she had given me, prodding my soul to stir and remind me both of the person I was and the one I had the potential to be. And each and every time, my soul searching caused me to land in the same place of admitting that I was all I needed.

I became quicker at working through the process, but not quick. Nevertheless, as I became more confident at negotiating it, my ankle gradually strengthened until I could walk on it without needing my staff.

When I woke to find Integrity in sight for the first time in four days, I was barely given time to rejoice in my relief at not having to go through my ritual of panic, searching and admittance before she announced, *It is time for us to move on.*

*Straight and forward?* I asked her with a grin.

She lifted her elegant head from the grass and gazed at me. *Straight and forward. Come.* She spun on her hocks and trotted away.

I got to my feet much too quickly and staggered against my tree as my blood pressure struggled to stabilise. *Hang on, wait for me, I haven't eaten and I need to pack my stuff.*

*None of which is necessary.*

'INTEGRITY, WAIT!' I yelled as if it would make the slightest difference. *Eating is necessary, as are my clothes, which are currently hanging all over the glade.*

*We will eat as we go. The clothes you are wearing will be sufficient.* She disappeared around a hill in the distance, leaving only a cloud of dust and a sense of honesty in her wake.

It had been dry and the weather showed no sign of breaking, so she might be right. I sighed. She was right. She wouldn't have told me an untruth. I glanced around the spot that had been my home for the past weeks and felt a flutter of fear at the thought of leaving the remainder of my stuff there. I looked back to where the dust was still hanging in the air after Integrity's passing. I didn't have the time to work through my process.

*Searching For Truth. Come and find it.* A sense of anticipation, of excitement, even, accompanied her thought, making my heart flutter.

I settled for diving for my back-sack, empty aside from the badger in its side pocket, and hurrying after Integrity. I shrugged out of the pullover that had kept me warm during the night, and stuffed it into the back-sack through whose straps I forced my arms as I broke into a slow, careful jog. My ankle felt stiff but not sore, so I continued until I rounded the bend around which Integrity had disappeared, to find her grazing there. She raised her head suddenly and I swear there was a glint in her eyes as she turned away from me at a trot once more.

'Slow down, I'll twist my ankle again if I have to run after you,' I called after her.

*That is not the truth.*

*Of course it's the truth, look at the ground.* It was covered in cropped grass, completely devoid of tussocks, rocks, stones – any hazards I could see. *There'll be rabbit holes everywhere,* I insisted. *Many of them are invisible until you fall down them.*

*Feel which way is true for that which you need to experience and you will move with strength and confidence. Doubt yourself and you will find every rabbit hole that I have evaded.*

*Feel? How do I do that?*

*The same way you explore which plants are safe to eat.*

I thought about the feeling of rightness that assured me my senses of smell and taste were accurate in letting me know which parts of which plants were edible. *Okay, but I can't do that at speed, I'll have to feel my way slowly. I can't keep up with the pace you're setting.*

*Searching For Truth.* Her thought triggered the part within me that knew what she was about. I hadn't looked for the truth, I had come up with my own and stated it as fact. So I could feel my way at speed? I dithered on the spot, wanting to go after her, to trust her and the feeling of rightness that assailed me as soon as I recognised the truth, but afraid to injure my ankle again.

*The choice between truth and fear will present itself to you over and over. One will strengthen you. The other will weaken you,* I was informed as Integrity disappeared around yet another hill. *Choose fear and you are more likely to injure yourself no matter how carefully you tread. Choose our bond and you will progress.*

I could sense that she was still trotting. She carried no worries, no concerns for either her safety as she traversed the burrow-infested countryside, or for mine. I knew what I had to do, but I couldn't seem to make myself do it; every time I thought of running after her, I was wracked with a phantom pain in my ankle, almost as intense as that which I had felt when I injured it.

As the seconds ticked by, the pressure I felt myself to be under intensified along with the pain that I knew couldn't really be there. I waited for Integrity to call me by my name again, knowing it would give me the strength to do as she wanted. The address never came. I sensed that most of her attention was taken up by feeling her way; joining the inner sense she had of her surroundings with the information provided by her physical senses so that she moved confidently and effortlessly onward.

She wasn't going to give me any more help. The realisation hit me hard. She was leaving me again, just like everyone always did, like she already had so many times. Only this time she was leaving me to my own mind too. She had told me that she'd never do that, that she'd always be with me, that whenever I encountered difficulty, all I had to do was to reach for the truth of our bond... I frowned as her exact counsel from a few weeks earlier came back to me, echoed by that which she had given me only minutes before. *Choose our bond and you will progress.*

It was all suddenly very simple. I focused on my sense of Integrity but instead of merely using it to know where she was, what she was doing and how she was feeling, I reached out to her and drew everything she was into myself. Her truth eclipsed my fear, blasting it out of my mind as if it had never been.

I began to run. We were strong, confident and joyful as we tore across the countryside. I couldn't see Integrity and I didn't need to. We were two parts of the same whole, moving with trust and a level of energy I had never before felt in my life.

*We are being true to who we are and why we are here. Being any other way is literally exhausting.* I couldn't decide whether the thought was counsel from Integrity or my realisation. It didn't matter; it made no difference to the effect, which was that I ran all morning without once going down a rabbit hole or even landing on ground that was anything other than level and welcoming to my tread.

When I finally caught up with Integrity, the hills were far behind us and she was grazing some lush grass near a shallow but wide river. Her dappled coat gleamed in the sunshine that was carrying a comfortable warmth, her white tail swishing repeatedly at the biters that warmth had brought to life. I'd never been very close to her before, sensing that she wouldn't allow it, but now I ran straight for her.

She watched me slow my final steps, her dark eyes kind and knowing. It was as if everyone I had ever loved gazed out of them – my mother, smiling at me, my father, nodding at me with a wink, my grandmother, forgiving me for my mistakes, and

Integrity herself, welcoming me to the bond that had solidified between us.

I threw my arms around her neck and hugged her. She whickered and then gently nuzzled my back while I clung to her, laughing as I released the past and embraced the present.

The two months that followed were among the happiest of my life. Integrity and I walked and ran side by side whenever the mood took us. When it didn't, she grazed while I foraged, slept or bathed in convenient bodies of water, and she slept when she deemed me alert enough to watch over us both.

To begin with, it was Integrity's sense of The Gathering's location that guided our direction. As time went on and I became more adept at sensing which way was true for what we needed to experience, I followed my own truth instead of that contained within our bond.

Integrity constantly challenged my ability to find and choose the way forward. When we came across rivers whose depth and ferocity couldn't be accurately judged from the bank, she left me to choose where to cross. When we had gone for hours without coming across water, she left it to me to decide whether to remain on our current course or divert to where I felt there might be water. When the weather turned, she left it to me to decide whether to continue onward or find shelter and wait out the storm. When mountains reared up before us, she insisted that I choose where to traverse them. It mattered not that I had never seen a mountain before and knew nothing about the conditions we were likely to face, or that all I had with me were the clothes on my back, a back-sack and a wooden badger. She was as sure as ever that if I chose the path that was true for us both then whatever happened would be exactly that which was necessary.

And she was right. Whether it took a few minutes to decide where to cross the less ferocious-looking rivers, or many minutes to tear my attention away from the pounding of my heart in my chest, trust our bond and choose where to cross the wide, turbulent ones, I got us across them all with minimum difficulty. I always found water before either of us became dehydrated. The overhang of rock, to which my truth led us, was large enough to keep us dry and protect us from the storm that buffeted our surroundings until it blew itself out.

By the time we found ourselves negotiating a narrow, rocky track that took us around the side of a mountain, I was short of breath from the vista before us rather than from the terror I had expected to feel when I first sensed the path we should take. From my place deep within the truth of my bond with Integrity, all I could see was beauty, all I could feel was wonder. When the temperature plummeted at nighttime, I curled up between Integrity and a boulder, on a bed of sparse grasses interwoven with mountain flowers, and slept soundly until it was my turn to watch over us both. My mind was strong. My body was strong. I was beginning to believe that I might be invincible.

But then we came across a forest. I was high on the success of negotiating an environment as inhospitable as the mountain range – from which we were now descending – and happily picking my way alongside Integrity down a far more gentle, albeit rocky, slope than we had encountered during the previous few days, when I spotted the dark green of trees in the distance. They beckoned to me, promising me easier foraging than I had recently been afforded, and I increased my pace moments before realising that I felt a little uneasy. I stopped and rested against a boulder, frowning.

I looked all around myself and couldn't see anything of which to be afraid. I reached for my bond with Integrity, expecting my disquiet to disappear as it always did when I could bring myself to choose its antithesis… and reeled as I found that it remained.

I spun to look at Integrity, who had also come to a halt. *It's you who's worried. Why are you worried? Ahhhhh. Woeful. There could be Woeful in the forest.* I looked back down the slope and where before I had seen opportunity and welcome, now I saw a threat to my horse. Fear clenched my stomach and lanced at my heart. Had I been alone, the biggest danger to me would have been a stray Woeful talon if its owner tried to take my back-sack from me in the hope of finding food. The danger to Integrity was mortal. Were a Woeful to catch her scent and hunt her, she would be hard pressed to escape, hindered by the slope and closely growing trees while the Woeful swung easily through the branches.

Anger added itself to my fear. How dare anyone threaten Integrity? She was gentle and kind and beautiful – what right did anyone have to take her life and her body?

*The right afforded by the agreement already in existence between a predator and its prey before the hunt ensues,* Integrity informed me.

*What agreement?*

*Discarnate souls agree that they will interact in countless different ways and for countless different reasons once they are incarnate. The interaction between predator and prey is one of those many agreements and the outcome of a hunt will be true to that agreement.*

My mouth dropped open. *This is about truth? Death is about truth?*

*Everything is about truth. You have eaten the flesh of countless*

*animals. Consider the fact from your place within our bond. Do*
*you feel as though you acted inappropriately?*

I paused to consider. *No. But that's different, we're talking*
*about you being the prey here.*

*It is the same regardless of who is the predator and who is the*
*prey. It is time for you to choose our way forward once more.*

I turned to walk across the slope. *We're not going down there,*
*we'll go this way and when there are no more trees below us, then*
*we'll go down.*

It was a minute or two before I realised that Integrity wasn't
following me. I turned around to see her standing calmly watching
me.

*Why aren't you coming?* I asked her. *You told me to choose the*
*way and I've made my choice, we're going this way.*

*I will follow so long as you choose the way that is true.*

*And that's this way. How can it be true to our path to put you*
*in danger?*

*If you do not know then you have neither searched for nor*
*found the truth.*

*I don't need to search for it, Integrity, I already know that*
*there's no way I'm taking a path that puts you at risk of dying.*

*Choose our bond as you have at every turn thus far and I will*
*follow you.* Integrity rested a hind leg and lowered her head
slightly. She was only intending to flaming well have a snooze.

'Integrity, come on, please come this way?' I called out to her,
hoping to jolt her into movement.

She remained where she was. I could still sense her unease at her
proximity to the trees but could further sense that she had no
intention of removing herself from its cause. Okay, fine, I'd do this
the way she wanted me to. I reached for our bond and allowed it to
become all of me so that fear couldn't influence my choice... but my

heightened sense of everything that was Integrity only magnified the disquiet I felt from her. So then my choice to avoid the forest was true for us both. Hopefully she would follow now that I had gone through the process to know for sure which way was the right one.

*Avoidance of fear does not equate to the identification of truth. You know this.* Integrity's thought was as gentle and patient as ever.

*When it's my fear, then sure, I know that, but this is yours. Your fear can't be ignored.*

*I do not suggest that we ignore fear. In order to ignore an emotion one cannot help but give it credence. Fear such as I am experiencing is merely the instinct of my kind to be wary in an environment where an agreement between predator and prey may come to fruition. It is within me but has no involvement in the identification of the way ahead that is straight and forward. This is the most difficult decision you have made yet but remember that you are Searching For Truth. Find it within our bond and focus on it to the exclusion of all distractions.*

Her use of my name immediately sparked the knowledge that the straightforward way to The Gathering was directly down the slope and through the forest to the hills beyond. I judged that we were probably only a week's travel away from our destination, but the thought of working our way through the forest made it seem like a year's worth. How could the rightness of the path we should take feel so wrong?

*Focus on it to the exclusion of all else.*

*I can't. I've never seen a Woeful in the flesh, but I've seen pictures of them and they're terrifying. The thought of one of them hunting you…*

*Is one you should question. Is it true or have you conjured it for yourself? You already know the answer. You have identified it*

*but are refusing to focus upon it to the exclusion of all else. You
are weakening the strength you know you can possess.*

*You're my strength,* I protested.

*That is not the truth.*

*But without you, I couldn't have left my stuff behind, I couldn't
have done any of what I've done these past few months. I can't go
forward and straight without you.*

*That is the truth. When you are ready to take the straight and
forward path I will be ready to take it alongside you.*

I made my way back to where my horse stood, and perched on
a nearby boulder staring at the forest below. Were there any
Woeful down there? If so, how many? I shivered at the thought of
even one scenting Integrity and taking her from me.

My stomach rumbled noisily and a griping sensation reminded
me how sparsely I had eaten over the past few days, how much I
needed to get down into the trees to forage. I glanced at Integrity.
Not at her expense. It was only then that I noticed her ribs were
protruding ever so slightly through her rapidly emerging summer
coat. She needed to graze properly too. I knew the path we should
take, so why was I still sitting there when we both needed food
and water? Because I was frightened of losing her. But if we
didn't find water soon I would lose her anyway. I went around and
around in circles, knowing what to do, where to go, but unable to
make myself take the first steps.

Integrity dozed on.

The sun's rays, stronger now that summer was nearly upon us,
began to glance off the surrounding rocks so that I had to squint in
order to continue staring at the distant trees. Integrity sighed and
shifted from one back leg to the other. She couldn't rest properly
here. We had to go somewhere, we had to leave, but Integrity
would only follow if I took the path I didn't want to travel.

When the sun began its descent through the sky, I began to

panic. The only thing worse than taking Integrity through the woods would be doing it in the dark.

I jumped off the boulder and said to Integrity, 'Okay, you win, we're leaving.'

She stretched her neck upward and then stretched each of her hind legs out behind her in turn. Her dark eyes were bright and expectant as she waited for me to resume our journey and as soon as I did, she took her place at my side. Her unease continued but did nothing to slow her steps further than the difficult footing ensured.

*You're absolutely sure you want to do this? You won't let me choose any other route?* I asked her.

*The truth is never in doubt.*

I doubted it constantly during the hours it took us to journey through the forest. I jumped at every sound from above us, whether it was the sudden rustle of leaves catching a breeze, branches creaking as squirrels and the heavier birds both launched from, and landed on, them, or angry squawks as one animal's territory was invaded by another. Integrity, on the other hand, gave the appearance of being relaxed despite her unease causing her to have a heightened awareness of her surroundings. She browsed the lower branches and drank deeply when we came across clean, flowing water. She even paused to scratch her back under a branch growing at the right height.

When the gloom of the forest began to lighten in front of us, I hastened my pace, my fear of losing Integrity strangely increasing the closer we were to safety. I didn't see the tree root that tripped me, or the one on which I landed with my other foot and subsequently slipped off, causing me to wrench my previously injured ankle.

I clamped a hand over my mouth so that I wouldn't yell out and possibly attract the attention of the Woeful I was increasingly sure must be waiting to pounce on Integrity before we left their haven, and paused only momentarily to pick up a branch on which to support myself so that we wouldn't have to slow our pace.

It was only once we had left the trees and found ourselves at the top of a grassy slope, that Integrity observed, *You have given yourself cause to once more be dependent upon a physical crutch.*

*I don't get it,* I replied. *I followed the right path.*

*Out of fear and not truth. You weakened yourself and your body was injured as a result.*

I limped away from her, wanting to increase the distance between us and the trees. *Why is it so wrong that I want you to be okay?* I was relieved to hear her footsteps thudding softly along behind me.

*That will always be the case regardless of circumstance. It is not that you want me to be free from harm so much as you do not want to suffer my loss.*

I stopped in my tracks and immediately winced at the feel of weight through my ankle as I inadvertently put down the foot to which it was attached. *That's not... I mean, I don't...*

*The truth,* Integrity reminded me.

She was right on both counts and I knew it. I thought I had come so far during the months we had been bonded but when it came down to it, I was still the same selfish person I had always been. I raised a hand to her cheek as she stopped beside me. *I'm sorry. You shouldn't have chosen me as your Bond-Partner, you deserve so much more than I can offer you.*

Integrity leant into my hand and blew gently on my face. *We have visited this subject briefly. You are now ready to accept more of the truth. I did not choose you so much as fulfil my side of our agreement to work together in this incarnation. There is much we can achieve together. You are more sensitive than most humans of this time. Your ability to sense the truth will allow you to be of much support to those whose roles it is to elicit change. We merely need work together so that you will choose to do it no matter the circumstances.*

*But we wouldn't have been able to work together if a Woeful had killed you,* I insisted. *Regardless of my selfishness in being afraid for your safety, that is still true.*

*I would never have made an agreement to be prey to a predator when doing so would have interrupted my agreement to work with you. I was never in any danger despite the instinct of my kind warning me that I could be. You had all of the truths necessary to walk confidently through the forest if you had chosen to focus on that which you knew rather than that which you feared. It is of no matter. When we revisit the issue you will have the opportunity to choose differently.*

I stepped away from her in horror. *Revisit the issue?* 'Revisit the issue?' I repeated out loud, my voice a squeak. 'We're going to put ourselves in the path of Woeful on purpose?'

*We cannot help but do so. Your choice on this occasion has created a ripple of energy that will attract a situation in which it can rebalance. There is no reason to choose fear now or when the situation occurs.*

*You have to be joking.* I knew she wasn't.

*We will have time to strengthen the likelihood that you will choose to see the truth of the situation when it arises,* Integrity informed me and marched onward to The Gathering.

*I'm going to delay our journey again,* I told her as I limped after her, clutching my new staff. *As soon as we're away from here and we find a place where we have water and plenty to forage, I'm going to have to rest up for a week or two.*

*Focus your attention on strengthening your mind and you will require less time than you suppose,* was her response as her tail swung left and right ahead of me.

She was right again, of course. Once we had rested comfortably on the bank of a large lake that glistened peacefully in the sunshine, well away from the forest, and had both eaten our fill of the glories that nature provided us both, I found that the pain in my ankle had lessened considerably. To begin with, I told myself that it was the cold water of the lake, in which I had immersed it for several hours, that was providing me with relief. When only faint bruising was visible the following day and I was able to limp around without my staff, however, I was forced to admit the truth of the situation... and found that the pain lessened even further.

*There's strength in the truth,* I observed to myself as if learning the phenomenon for the first time.

*Remember that as best you can when you are among your own kind once more,* Integrity advised. *It will not be easy.*

*Like any of this has been easy?*

*It has merely been preparation for the challenge that awaits us.*

*Which is?*

*Choosing the pattern that we are in the process of establishing within you over that which is comfortable for you in its familiarity. The presence of your fellow humans will remind you of your old pattern and tempt you away from the new one. It will serve you to be aware of the fact ahead of time.*

I sighed. *Noted. I thought being at The Gathering was supposed to be helpful to newly bonded pairs, not make things harder?*

*It will ensure the illusion of difficulty and as such be of significant assistance. Searching For Truth you have done well. When the challenges you will face increase in difficulty you can be assured it is because you are ready for them. Your energy will attract that which it needs to rebalance in any given moment.*

*I don't find that even remotely reassuring.*

*I sought not to reassure but to assure.*

*And the difference is?*

*The former is an admittance of fear. The latter is a recognition of strength.* The kindness and complete honesty of her thought gave me heart, despite her insistence that she attempted no such thing.

*Come on then, let's go, shall we?*

By way of reply, Integrity turned and walked in the direction of The Gathering.

So many times over the days that followed, I wanted to turn and run from the path I knew to be true for us both; the thought that the challenges I had faced since Integrity tugged me were merely an easy lead in to what I would face at The Gathering scared me almost witless. Every time I faltered, Integrity would drop her head and graze until I chose the sanctuary of our bond and had the strength to continue onward.

When we dropped out of the hills onto a dirt track, I knew we were close to our destination. My footsteps slowed and I had to reach a hand out to Integrity's shoulder to support myself as I felt liable to stumble and injure my ankle yet again.

*You need merely make the same choice that you have proven countless times you are capable of making,* Integrity informed me and speeded up so that in order to continue taking support from her, I had to speed up too. *Every time you make it you carve an easier path for yourself to make it again. The past days have felt difficult to you but have ensured the following days will be easier.*

A thought struck me. *You scared me on purpose with your*

*warning of how hard I'm going to find it, so I'd spend this time*
*practising sticking to the truth.*

*You were ready for the challenge. You have succeeded at every*
*turn and will continue to do so. Choose the way that is straight*
*and forward again and your ankle will return to strength.*

I breathed in and out deeply, recognising now that the time I
always felt most uncomfortable was the split second before I
chose rightness over falsehood, and knowing that once I did, I
would feel relief from the churning in my stomach, the tightness
in my throat and the pounding at my temples.

I sighed and walked easily again beside Integrity. I kept my
hand at her shoulder though, enjoying the warmth of our physical
connection, and feeling that I would need it when The Gathering
came into view. I was totally unprepared for the sight when it did.
Integrity and I had followed the track between some very steep
hills and when it dropped sharply away in front of us, we both
stopped to take in that which was before us.

There were people everywhere, hurrying between grey stone
buildings that were larger by far than any I had seen before,
working in some of the fields, riding horses in and between
others… the horses! It had never occurred to me how many
Horse-Bonded there were and therefore how many bonded horses
there must be, let alone that so many of them would be here at the
same time. The fear that had begun to pull me away from my
strength at the sight of the people, receded at the sight of those
horses. Integrity took a step forward at the exact moment I did.
We belonged here.

I amazed myself by how quickly that knowledge faded when
we were far enough down the hill for me to be able to hear the
voices of the closest Horse-Bonded.

'I can't do this,' I said aloud. 'I don't know who I am now. I
won't know what to say, what to do, how to be.'

*You are Searching For Truth as is everyone else here in one way or another. Continue practising and you will continue to find your true self. Then you will know what to say and do so that we may achieve that which we are here to achieve.*

Her use of my name helped me exactly as she knew it would. The way ahead that had seemed frightening and overwhelming only moments before was now clear in front of me.

*I need to be helpful when I would have been selfish, I need to be kind when I would have been harsh, and I need to be honest when I would have lied,* I affirmed to us both. *Whatever happens, I need to act with integrity and I have you to remind me what that means.*

If only it was as easy as I made it sound.

## Chapter Eight

*I*ntegrity and I continued on down the hill to where a path led between two of the stone buildings – which were even more massive than they had appeared from above – and onto a cobbled square surrounded on all sides by more buildings. There was only one other gap between them, at the corner diagonally opposite the one at which we stood, which I presumed led to the fields.

A horse whinnied in the distance and Integrity whinnied back, making me jump. I looked up at her in surprise; in the months we had been together, the only sounds she had made were the odd whicker or snort, and those of her footsteps. She had missed being with other horses, I knew it as surely as I knew that I hadn't missed being with other people. Shame flooded me. How had I never considered what her needs might be, what she had given up in order to find me and stay with me to help me? How was it that I didn't know where she was from, what her life had been like before I met her, how old she was, even?

Because I was selfish. Our relationship was all about me and my problems, my needs.

*That is not the truth,* Integrity told me.

I began the process of finding it as I had practised so many times, but was distracted by a woman's voice. 'Well, hello there, beautiful!' A delicate hand appeared under Integrity's nose. She sniffed it and then nuzzled it gently as its owner, a slim woman with grey hair cropped close to her head stepped past my horse and in front of me, her other hand outstretched. 'Hi, I'm Turi, and judging by the bewildered look on your face, you're newly bonded. You're also dreadfully thin, if you don't mind me saying. You've obviously had something of a journey here?'

I just stared at her.

She chuckled. 'You don't need to speak, I know exactly how you're feeling. You've barely recovered from the shock of being tugged in the first instance and the bonding process in the second, you've learnt so much from your horse in the short time since you bonded that you have no idea whether you're coming or going, and now you've landed here where the sound of human voices is grating on you after having become used to the peace and quiet of silent communication. All you want to do is turn around and run for the hills.'

I opened my mouth and closed it again without issue, but at least managed to shake Turi's still outstretched hand.

Her eyes crinkled at the corners as her smile broadened. 'Don't worry, I can't read your mind, I've just been exactly where you are, as has every single person here. Being newly bonded is mind-bendingly wonderful and completely overwhelming at the same time. You need time to adjust to your new situation and status in life, not to mention to being here, and you'll be given all the time you need, don't fret.'

A man and woman whom I judged to be of similar age to me

walked past with a wave and a smile, neither stopping to introduce themselves, confirming her assertion. I relaxed a little.

'That's it, you'll be okay,' Turi said knowingly. 'Might I know your and your horse's names before I show you both around?

'Um, yes, I'm...' I cleared my throat. 'I'm Newson and this is Integrity.'

Turi smiled again and stroked Integrity's nose with the back of her finger. 'Is she indeed. Right, well, let's show your beautiful girl to the paddocks so she can choose one, then you can get yourself cleaned up and settled in a bedroom while I go and prepare some food for you. You look as if you could eat solidly for a week and still have room for more. Come on, this way.' She turned and walked away, accompanied by Integrity.

I remained where I was. 'I... I thought I'd be sleeping near Integrity.'

Integrity and Turi both turned and looked back at me.

'Don't worry, you will be,' Turi said. She pointed to the building to my left. 'That's the accommodation block, where there are lots of empty rooms for you to choose from, in fact you might even get one on the ground floor as I think Ineurin was planning to leave today, so his'll be free.' She turned and pointed towards the gap at the far corner of the square. 'Two out of the four paddocks just on the other side of that gap are empty, they're always made available to newly bonded horses so that their partners can get to them quickly when they have a panic.'

She came back to me and patted my arm. 'Don't look so horrified, I told you we've all been where you are. When I got here with Equal, I was nigh on hysterical at the thought of being separated from her. Everything I thought I knew had dissolved to nothing and I had no idea who I was other than that I was Equal's Bond-Partner. I swear I really believed that if I let her out of my sight, I'd just fizzle away to nothing. You'll find yourself again,

Newson, just a different self from who you were before. By the time the next new Bond-Partners arrive here looking like the two of you do, it'll be you standing here and telling them everything I'm telling you.'

'You don't know me,' I said. 'You don't know how I can be.'

She patted my arm a final time and turned to walk back to Integrity, saying over her shoulder, 'I know you're Horse-Bonded, and that's all any of us here need to know. You're among friends, Newson. Come along.' She and Integrity walked away, leaving me no choice but to hurry after them.

*I seem to have spent a good deal of our time together looking at your rump,* I complained to Integrity as I drew alongside her.

*There are times when I would follow you and times when I would have you follow me.*

*What you mean is, there are times you need to push me in front of you and times you need to pull me along behind you so I'll do what I'm supposed to. I get it, I'm a nightmare and a selfish one at that.* I remembered the process I had begun before Turi interrupted it. *You don't think I'm selfish, that our relationship is all about me but I don't have time to look for the truth.* I proved my point by being distracted from the subject again by all of the people smiling and greeting me as they passed the three of us.

*You cannot spare the time to avoid it,* Integrity informed me. *The truth is not something in which to engage only when you are otherwise unoccupied. The more you live by it the quicker you will become at recognising it.*

I sighed and began the process once more. As soon as I was immersed in our bond, I realised my error. I was indeed selfish, but our relationship was not all about me; Integrity wasn't being diminished by being bonded to me but rather was enjoying being my teacher, my partner, my friend. It was as if something were changing within her in concert with the changes occurring within me.

*I am fulfilling my potential*, she agreed. *I cannot do that without you just as you cannot fulfil your potential without me. We are partners.*

A smile stole across my face as I felt our mutual understanding strengthen our bond further. *Partners.*

I realised that we were both stationary and Turi was standing a short distance away, leaning on a gate.

'Ahh, you're back with me,' she said. 'You look altogether happier.'

I blinked. 'Sorry, I was just...'

She held both hands up. 'Working things through with Integrity, I know. Well done. Now, these are the two paddocks which are available.' She pointed to the first on the left and the second on the right. 'Which paddock would Integrity like to use, and would she like company? Equal is in with two other horses down near the river, but she's happy to come up here and... oh, never mind, she's on her way, it seems that she and Integrity are ahead of us.'

As if to prove the point, Integrity let out another loud, shrill whinny, then turned to the paddock on our left, trotted a few steps and jumped into it over the fence. She continued trotting until she was in the middle of the paddock and then dropped her head to graze the lush, green grass.

Turi chuckled. 'I love it when they don't bother with gates. Some horses won't countenance jumping in and out of the paddocks they've chosen and will call for their Bond-Partner to sort the gates, but others, like Integrity and Equal, tend to see gates as a nonsense. I do see their point.'

We both turned at the sound of hooves drumming on the dry, hard-packed earth that ran either side of the stony track, to see a chestnut mare with only a snip of white on her muzzle to break her colour, approaching at speed. I marvelled as she slowed only marginally, turned and almost sat down before leaping into the paddock Integrity had chosen.

Turi giggled. 'There is literally nothing she won't jump, I swear she'd give the buildings a go if she thought it necessary.'

Equal came to a stop a few strides away from Integrity. When my horse closed the gap between the two of them, they sniffed one another's noses and then both squealed and stamped in the same instant. My alarm was immediately quashed by another giggle from Turi and my sense of Integrity's delight. Another stamp and squeal were followed by both mares spinning around and lifting their hind legs as if they would kick one another. Equal reversed towards Integrity, who cantered away. Satisfied, Equal cantered after her and then the two of them proceeded to canter around the outside of the paddock before stopping side by side to graze.

'Well, now that Equal has satisfied herself that Integrity is indeed a more refined paddock mate than the two stallions she was in with, just like she supposed when she sensed her presence here, we can all relax,' Turi said with a grin. 'And Integrity chose the closest paddock to where you'll be sleeping, isn't that great?'

It was anything but. I could manage to be apart from her, though, I told myself; Integrity had ensured our separation enough times that I knew I could do it. I felt a wave of admiration and affection for my horse as I realised exactly how premeditated all of her actions had been since the first moment she allowed me to see her. I sensed that her attention was fully on her field mate and on selecting which grasses to eat; she had no intention of helping me or giving me any reason to stay with her, and I suspected that if I didn't devote myself to reaffirming the fact that I was all I needed, she would jump back out of the paddock and take herself further away.

'Er, yes, great,' I spluttered.

'Let's go and bag you the room Ineurin's been using then, so I can leave you and get some food organised. How fortunate is it that, as head of the kitchens, I was the first to come across you? Just so you know, food is usually only available at mealtimes unless there are extenuating circumstances, so that those of us on kitchen duty can maintain some sort of order, but in my position, I can bend the rules.' She winked at me and then frowned as she caught sight of my back-sack. 'That looks empty. How long is it since you've eaten?'

'The food I brought from home ran out nearly two months ago. I've been eating regularly, just not food that's particularly filling.'

'Two months?' She clapped her hands to her cheeks. 'And you have no hunting or cooking equipment with you, so you've only been eating plants? In spring? How are you still alive? Just what kind of Quest Ceremony did your friends and family give you? An invisible one?'

I found myself chuckling even as I frowned, feeling strange. 'I didn't give anyone the chance to organise a Quest Ceremony for me, so it was more of a non-existent one. And I'm alive because of Integrity. Because of integrity.' Turi gazed at me in silence, I assumed wondering why I had apparently repeated myself though in fact, I hadn't. 'Because of my horse and everything she's been teaching me,' I clarified.

'She taught you to know which plants to eat?'

I grinned ruefully. 'If only. She put me in a position where I had to learn for myself; where I had to trust that I know what's right. Then she took every opportunity on the way to make sure I practised doing it. I don't think it'll ever come easily to me though, I'm not a very nice person.' I stopped talking, surprised at having made such an admission to a stranger.

'You seem perfectly decent to me,' Turi said. 'No one is perfect, least of all those of us the horses have chosen to improve, but we all try our best to learn what they're trying to teach us. We muddle through and when we look back, it's always a nice surprise to realise how far we've come.' She turned and began to walk back to the buildings, and I was surprised to find myself following her.

'You all struggle too?'

'Of course,' she said over her shoulder. 'Why do you think we all live here together so much of the time?' She didn't wait for an answer. 'It's so that we can give one another moral support while our horses are pushing us to become better human beings. As you've already discovered, it's not easy and can be overwhelming at times.'

'Yes! It is!'

Turi paused until I was alongside her, and grinned at me as we entered the square. 'Like I said before, you're among friends here, Newson, and if I may, I would like to count myself as your first. Integrity will have all of the answers you'll ever need. She'll push you when it's necessary and she'll support you when necessary, but if you ever need to talk about anything, laugh about anything, cry about anything, even – and you will – then I'm here for you.'

'I'm not good with people,' I said. 'I'm completely self-absorbed. I've been bonded to Integrity for months and I don't know anything about her at all.'

'Well I don't normally admit it, but since our friendship appears to have jumped straight to a level of disarming honesty, I have an inferiority complex,' Turi said. 'You'll notice that I tell everyone I'm head of the kitchens whenever the opportunity presents itself, and also when it doesn't. We're supposed to rotate between the different chores that keep this place running, but whoever is rostered to do the job of Overseer is always kind enough to put me in the same position – and I mean kind to everyone else, not to me – because if they don't, I can't help myself from loudly criticising every morsel of food that passes my lips, not because there's anything wrong with it but because I need everyone to think I'm the best cook here.

'I've tried to be the best rider, to have the most immaculate horse, to be the most knowledgeable about horses, but Equal has thwarted me at every step until where she's concerned at least, I'm happy to just be her Bond-Partner. I'm getting better at not being such a know-all about everything else, but my progress is slow and obviously non-existent where the topic of cooking is concerned. There. That's me, and here we are at the accommodation block.' She was almost panting as she reached for the door. She yanked it open with such force, she over-balanced and fell back against me. 'Blimey, I don't know my own strength.'

'You get it from being truthful,' I said, and felt slightly strange; lighter, somehow. I held her until she was stable on her feet and turned to look up at me.

She cocked her head to one side and grinned. 'I recognise that expression. You've just had one of those moments, haven't you? When you realise how far you've come from the person you were? I'm happy for you.'

So was Integrity, I could feel it. She gave only the faintest sense of her satisfaction that I was progressing as she knew I would, but it was there.

'Thank you,' I said as I followed her into the building. 'From the sound of it, you've come a long way too.'

'Not far enough, but I try, and everyone here knows it so they put up with me. Ahh, perfect, see that door wedged ajar? That means Ineurin has indeed cleared out of the room and left it available for someone else – you.' She pushed the door wide open and replaced the wedge, then beckoned me inside. 'Is this okay? The sheets on the bed will be fresh ones.'

The grey stone walls and thick wooden mantelpiece reminded me of my bedroom at home. The fact that the room's only other contents were a wardrobe, an armchair, a log basket and companion set by the fireplace, a bed against one wall and a small bedside table and lamp, all of which were clearly visible and accessible, was as clear a reminder of everything I had left behind as was possible.

'Newson?'

'It's fine, yes, thank you.'

'Great.' She stepped back out into the corridor and pointed further along it. 'There are bathrooms and toilets down there, and in the cupboards alongside them you'll find clean towels, soap, bath salts, whatever you need to feel human again after your travels. If you leave your door wedged open, I'll send word to one of the Tailors to drop over a load of clothing for you so you'll have something clean to wear when you get back.' She looked me up and down. 'I'm pretty sure I have your measure. I'm off to prepare you the first decent meal you've had in months. Come over to the kitchen in about an hour, okay? Just ask anyone in the square and they'll point you in the right direction.' With that, I was alone.

I could hear people moving around, talking, laughing, shouting in a few cases, in the rooms above and around mine, as well as outside, and despite being enclosed within four walls, I felt vulnerable. I shrugged out of the straps of my back-sack and fumbled within it for my lone possession. When I found it, I placed it in the centre of the mantelpiece, into which I noticed had been skilfully carved a horse's head.

I stood back and observed the carving and the badger above,

which looked as tiny and exposed as I felt. I snatched it back and placed it on the bedside table. That was a little better.

A door slammed and Turi yelled down the corridor, 'Newson, your clothes will be here shortly. I forgot to ask if there's any food you don't like?'

I hurried to the doorway and called back, 'No, I'll eat anything.'

Turi raised a hand and hurried back out onto the square, leaving the door to slam behind her again, which jolted me into action. I headed for the bathrooms but when I reached the first of them, turned and hurried back to my room. I snatched the badger off my bedside table, returned it to the side pocket of my back-sack, and pushed the sack as far under the bed as it would go so that it wasn't visible. No, that wouldn't do, whichever Tailor came with my clothes could still find and take it. I grabbed it and hurried back to the bathroom, hurling it inside before choosing some bath salts, soap and a towel from the nearby cupboard. I returned to the bathroom and locked myself inside with my things.

*You need them not,* Integrity whispered in my mind.

I glanced down at where my filthy back-sack was propped against the sparklingly clean, white bath. I noticed for the first time that it was practically threadbare in places – the irony was not lost on me that apart from the straps and two side pockets, its integrity had all but disintegrated. I should chuck it, I decided. But first, I should take it back to my room.

I unlocked the door and poked my head out. Finding the corridor empty, I hurried back to my room, returned the badger to my bedside table and furtively put the back-sack on the chair as if I were returning stolen goods. I hurried back to the bathroom and locked the door behind me, feeling relieved that no one had seen me, and ridiculous for worrying about it when no one would have known what I was doing or why. Yet I felt better for having done it; better for being alone in the bathroom with only that which I needed in order to have a bath. *Thanks, Integrity.*

*You chose well.*

I turned on the bath taps, hurled in a generous amount of bath salts, then busied myself with peeling off clothes that were almost as threadbare in a multitude of places as was my back-sack. Once I was naked, I inspected my body and was surprised to discover the truth of Turi's observation; I was indeed lean. But strong. I had never before seen all of the muscles that were now visible, and when I looked into the rapidly fogging mirror on the wall, my eyes stared back at me with a strength that made me appear a stranger to myself.

*When you eat only food that feels completely right you are afforded a level of energy and strength far beyond that which the food in question might suggest,* Integrity informed me suddenly, making me jump.

*So you're telling me to only ever eat plants?*

*It is not so much the food itself that is in question but whether it is right in any particular moment. That which will give you maximum benefit one day may be that which will hinder you on another. You have become in the habit of asking yourself what you should eat and the condition of your body reflects your success at trusting your answers. I merely suggest that you continue the practice regardless of location and circumstance.*

*Now you tell me, I've already told Turi I'll eat anything.*

*The situation will present an opportunity for both of you to progress.*

I groaned and turned off the taps, prepared to quickly dress and rush to the kitchen to tell Turi… what, exactly? That I wanted to look through the food stores and select my food for myself? She was already bending the rules by cooking me something outside of the set mealtimes, I didn't think she'd let me break them entirely.

And I was filthy, she'd no doubt told me to have a bath before going to the kitchen for her sake as well as mine. I sighed and turned the taps back on.

When I returned to my room wearing a towel around my waist and carrying my filthy and – I had realised once I was clean – smelly clothes, I found that not only was my bed covered in piles of clothing, but my back-sack was missing and a brand new one hung from an arm of the chair on which I'd left it.

My first instinct was to panic. The back-sack had been my father's. Aside from the badger, it was all I had left of him.

Integrity was quick to pull me up. *That is not the truth.*

I calmed as her honesty reminded me of my own. I had my memories. They were a part of me as no physical item ever could be, they helped to make me who I was, and it was impossible to lose them.

*Thank you. Again.*

Integrity reverted her attention to her physical surroundings, which involved an increasing number of biters attempting to land on her, the huge choice of grasses and herbs from which she was enjoying selecting those that took her fancy, and Equal squealing at a stallion in the neighbouring paddock.

I inspected the back-sack and found it to be of a similar size to my father's, well made and sturdy. I sorted through the clothes on my bed and selected underwear, socks, a pair of light brown trousers, a cream shirt and a pair of brown boots before putting the rest in the wardrobe. It seemed that Turi indeed had my measure, as everything fitted perfectly. Despite myself, I couldn't help feeling a little more secure now that my wardrobe was full. I made a mental note to ask Turi whom I needed to thank for everything.

'No thanks are necessary but they'll be appreciated nevertheless,' she told me once I had found my way to the kitchens. 'You'll be wanting the Tailor's workshop. It's just along from the Saddler's, who'll want to see Integrity tomorrow morning at the latest, so she can start work on her saddle. I'll show you where both are once you've eaten. For now, take a seat and prepare to be amazed.' She put a bowl of steaming soup on the table, along with a spoon. 'Vegetable soup. I thought I'd ease you in gently.'

I sniffed a spoonful to see how I felt, as I had grown used to doing. 'You won't have had better, I can absolutely assure you of that,' Turi said a little stiffly.

'I'm not meaning to be rude or ungrateful, I just have to check whether it's what my body wants right now,' I told her. The distraction caused me to lose the sense of the ingredients I'd had. I sniffed the soup again.

'You said you'd eat anything,' Turi said. 'I ran all the way back to your room especially to check, and that was what you said.'

'I know, I'm sorry about that. Integrity told me that in order to be strong, I have to only eat food that's right for my body, so I have to check each time.'

'And is it?' Turi said, her mouth hardening.

'If you'll stop interrupting while I'm trying to check, I'll tell you,' I shot back. Turi sat down and glared at me.

Anger and discomfort prevented me from being able to concentrate on my task. *Integrity, what do I do? Should I just eat it? I can't do this while she's staring at me.*

My horse repeated her earlier counsel by way of reply. *The truth is not something in which to engage only when you are otherwise unoccupied. The more you live by it the quicker you will become at recognising it.*

I sighed and glared back at Turi until she looked away. Then I focused all of my attention on the smell of the soup. It smelt good. It smelt right. I took a sip from the side of the spoon. It was fabulous, there was no other word for it. I polished off the spoonful and said, 'Thanks, this is amazing.'

'I told you it would be,' Turi said, her voice softening. When I was close to finishing, she rose and went to one of the many stoves that ran along one wall of the enormous and apparently well-equipped kitchen. She returned with a large plate, which she placed in front of me along with a fork. 'Rabbit stew. I'd normally leave a little time before the first and second courses, but by the time you've assessed whether this meets your approval, you should be about right.'

An image of my rabbit friends who had kept me company when I had been injured popped into my mind, and my stomach turned over. I looked up at Turi, ready to apologise for refusing it, but then the smell of it wafted up my nose. It was exactly what my body needed. I polished it off, followed by the plate of seconds that a rapidly defrosting Turi fetched for me.

I was just sniffing a spoonful of apple crumble when a stream of people began to wind their way among the workbenches towards Turi. My friend introduced me to them one by one, interrupting my assessment of her crumble each time, and then set them about the tasks of preparing the evening meal. When the first to have arrived, a young woman dressed in bright yellow breeches and shirt named Florence, witnessed me returning to sniff my spoonful for the ninth time, she called out to me to ask what I was doing.

'He's checking to see if my crumble is good enough to pass his lips,' Turi said.

'Wow, Newson, you're braver than I am,' Florence said with a chuckle. 'I'm surprised our head cook hasn't emptied the bowl over your head already.'

'His horse told him to do it,' Turi said, 'so if you'd like to get on with your work?'

Florence grinned at me. 'Your horse is called Integrity, isn't she? Kim told me after she pointed you this way earlier.'

'What of it?' Turi said, putting her hands on her hips.

'It means that I hope the crumble's good.' She held up her hands at the expression on Turi's face. 'Turi, come on, you know I'm only teasing. Newson, if you don't want it, I'll have it.'

Their discourse gave me the time to choose. The crumble smelt very good, but it didn't smell right; my body didn't want it. How could I tell Turi that in front of her workforce? If I lied and ate it, I'd be going against everything Integrity had instilled into me. If I told the truth, I'd humiliate my friend. What to do for the best? I felt very hot all of a sudden.

'I'm actually really full,' I spluttered. 'The crumble smells great, could I have some another time when I haven't had seconds of your stew?'

'Result, I'm starving.' Florence whipped away my bowl before either I or Turi could protest.

Turi watched it go and then looked at me with hurt in her eyes... which then glazed over slightly. I got to my feet, wondering if she were going to faint, but then she refocused on me and managed a weak smile. She came around the table and sat by my side, whispering, 'According to Equal, we're good for one another. Our patterns clash and apparently that's a good thing for both of us. It doesn't feel like it to me at the moment, does it to you?'

A bead of sweat dripped from my brow onto the table. 'What do you think?'

A smile tugged at the corners of Turi's mouth. 'I think you're going to say a lot of things I don't want to hear, and you're going to make me increasingly hysterical, but I also think we're going to be the best of friends.'

As it turned out, she was right on all three counts. My honesty challenged her insecurity and her insecurity challenged my honesty, but as I settled into The Gathering, it was to one another that we turned when we had need.

I easily took to the chores to which I was assigned in any given week, and was relieved to be given a space in the Metal-Singers' workshop so that I could do just about the only thing that was familiar to me in my new existence. But when I found myself smuggling duplicates to my room of some of the smaller items I had been commissioned to create – two door hinges, a bolt and a hair clip – it was Turi to whom I found the courage to admit my failing, giving me the strength to smuggle the items back to the workshop. She immediately made me feel better by admitting that she had needlessly corrected three of those rostered to help her in the kitchens that day, not because they were doing anything wrong but because she had needed to hear the sound of her own voice.

As the days, weeks and months passed, we got into the habit of discussing our struggles whilst grooming our horses, feeding them or clearing dung from the paddock they continued to share, a choice that we were both aware they had made for our sakes more than theirs.

I always made time to watch Turi when she and Equal had a session with Mistral, the Master of Riding, who was a man of similar age to her but with the bushiest eyebrows I had ever seen. To begin with when I watched them, it surprised me that Turi appeared to be a completely different person when she rode; the friendly yet prickly, outspoken woman I knew was replaced by a meek and nervous rider each and every time. The mystery resolved itself once my saddle was ready and I began to have lessons with Integrity, however.

Having seen many of the other Horse-Bonded riding their horses since my arrival, I expected to find it easy, especially since I considered myself fit and strong, trusted my horse implicitly and was at my most comfortable when I was with her. As soon as I was on her back, though, I felt as exposed and vulnerable as I had when I found myself alone in my room for the first time. I felt under pressure to be as accomplished a rider as everyone else, but was surprised to find my body sluggish and uncoordinated when I tried to make it do as Mistral instructed, and shocked that Integrity moved as heavily and with as little apparent grace beneath me. I felt self-conscious, which only compounded the amount of pressure I felt myself to be under.

*You know what he wants us to do, can't you help me out a bit?* I asked Integrity as I attempted in vain to use the relevant parts of my body to signal to her my intention to make the circle, on which we were currently wobbling, gradually smaller.

*I am providing you with the assistance you need regardless of whether it is that which you desire. When your attempt to control your body comes from your true self and not from that which fuels your current efforts then the physical interaction between us will be as straightforward as everything else.*

'Just relax,' Mistral said, mirroring her advice, 'and it'll come. You're not doing anything wrong as such, you just need time to practise co-ordinating the different signals you're giving Integrity so that they're in agreement with one another rather than fighting one another as they are at present. We'll meet back here at the same time every day and we'll just take our time so that you can enjoy learning everything Integrity is teaching you. Before you know it, you'll be off for a canter along the river bank with Turi and Equal. Isn't that right, Turi?' he called over to where she sat on the top rail of the gate of his teaching paddock. 'You and Newson will soon be racing the river.'

By the look on her face, her horror at the thought was on a level with my disbelief.

Mistral chuckled and said, 'You two are the unlikeliest of friends, but a great pair nonetheless.'

I dismounted. 'So say our horses.' I loosened Integrity's girth as I had been shown to immediately on vacating the saddle. 'What do you mean though?'

'Just that it's always good to see people striking up friendships that are as unlikely as they are comfortable. Turi isn't always the most popular person around here despite the size of her heart, so I'm glad you appear to have so much time for her – although considering the name you chose for your horse, it shouldn't come as much of a surprise. Take confidence from that choice, Newson, I do, it tells me that you'll work through the issues you're having with your riding.'

It was as if he could hear Integrity's counsel to me, though I didn't think it possible. 'Can I ask what your horse's name is?'

He grinned, his eyes sharp and penetrating beneath his shaggy eyebrows. 'Prudence.'

I grinned back. 'That's a relief. I thought for a minute that you and Integrity must be in cahoots behind my back, but you don't need to be able to hear her counsel.'

'Any more than you need to try being someone you're not,' he said, his eyes never leaving mine. 'You're a novice rider, Newson. Allow yourself to be that and you'll be taking that canter along the river in no time with Turi in your wake, whether she believes it at the moment or not.'

I nodded slowly. 'I didn't understand why Integrity and I had to come here, I thought there was nothing I needed to learn that she couldn't teach me, but I think I get it now. The horses give us the instruction and we give each other the practice, don't we.'

He laughed and clapped his hand on my shoulder. 'You're a very welcome addition to The Gathering, Newson, a very welcome one indeed. You'll help a lot of your fellow Horse-Bonded to practise what their horses are in the process of teaching them.'

I stroked Integrity's neck. 'Integrity told me a similar thing. She told me I'll be able to help those who are going to elicit change.'

Mistral raised one eyebrow so that the eye below was completely unveiled and appeared even more penetrating. 'Did she indeed. I can see why you'll be necessary to the process; it's never more tempting to lie to oneself than when presented with a choice between what's easy and what's right.'

His words reminded me of Gran. I bit my lip.

'I'm not the first to tell you that, I can see,' Mistral said. 'I'd be honoured if you'd think of me as your friend, Newson, I'm in need of hearing what I'd rather not as much as the next person. You'll find me good practice.' He winked, the gesture taking away none of the sharpness from his eyes.

# Chapter Nine

*W*e became firm friends, Mistral and I. He had a knack of knowing when I was struggling to find the right thing to say or do in a given situation, and of finding ways to help me. When the other parties involved were talking to me, challenging me or otherwise distracting me from knowing the response that would be the most truthful and helpful to give, he often appeared and intervened until I had the answer I needed. It was common for him to pause my lessons with him and raise his eyebrows so that his sharp eyes were fully unveiled and I could be in no doubt that he wanted me to take the time to find and be true to myself, rather than attempting to be someone I wasn't; so that, as he had predicted it would, my riding could continue to improve.

When I was deemed competent enough to take Integrity for a wild canter along the banks of the river at the far end of The Gathering, it wasn't only Turi and Equal who accompanied us – Turi's confidence having improved alongside my ability to be true to myself – but also Mistral and Prudence.

When the time came for Integrity and me to start travelling to and between the villages offering Integrity's counsel, Turi had reached the point where she could stand for someone other than herself to be head of the kitchens, and she and Equal came with us. I was glad of their company, for where I had slowly become better at immersing myself in the truth of a given situation so that I could behave in accordance with my horse's name when in the midst of the Horse-Bonded, doing it amidst the cacophony that always ensued when we reached a new village was overwhelmingly difficult to begin with. Turi stepped in every time, giving me the space to sense whom, of those offering me lodging, needed Integrity's and my company the most. I was comfortable when villagers came to ask for Integrity's counsel, but when they merely wanted to converse with me, I was liable to flounder and panic without Turi there to divert attention away from me while I anchored myself in my bond with my horse.

As time went on, I got better at doing so and slowly grew in confidence that I would always be able to sense the truth of a situation no matter the noise and distraction, but as the years passed, I grew ever more frustrated with myself that I couldn't seem to do it more quickly and without immense effort.

When I reminded Integrity that she had assured me the more I lived in truth, the quicker I would get at recognising it, she merely replied, *The pattern for truth grows stronger within you but requires more room than you are prepared to afford it. When you choose to release your previous pattern then the new one will be unimpeded.*

*What old pattern? I'm giving everything I have to doing and saying what feels right and true, however uncomfortable it makes me and everyone around me. I'm not even remotely the person I was when we bonded.*

*How did you feel when Turi and Equal chose to leave here without us?*

I fought hard with myself before I was able to be completely honest about Turi's departure a week previously. *Angry. Turi and I have been friends for five years and whenever we've left to go travelling, we've gone together. I've missed her.*

*You yet struggle when you feel that something has been taken from you. You have relinquished your dependency on possessions but you have yet to take the final step and release the belief that caused the dependency to arise. Until you do that your need for those you hold dear will act as a barrier to truth through which you must break every time you search for it.*

*The truth is that I am all I need, and I have to stop believing otherwise.* I slapped my palm to my forehead. *I know it, every time I realise it again, I know it, but I can't retain it. Why can't I retain it? Why am I so slow, such an idiot?*

*Traumatic events can lodge very deeply within the mind and the body and the soul. When they occur in childhood they become buried beneath layers of subsequent events and experiences so that their many hiding places are difficult to locate in order that they may be released. You have done both on multiple occasions but facets of the pattern yet remain. The time is approaching when you will have the opportunity to release it entirely but you require more practice in order to have the best chance of succeeding. Be patient and trust the path we have chosen to travel together.*

I tried to be patient. I tried to be honest and helpful at every turn, however much it took out of me to find and live that which I could feel came from my true self rather than the injured, angry, selfish part of me that continued to fight for survival. I slowly made more friends – true friends on whom I knew I could rely to support my attempts to behave with integrity at all times, even as I found ways to support them when I could see they were struggling to change in line with their horses' advice.

Adam and his horse, Peace, only ever resided at The Gathering during the winter, when the weather made the huge distances they travelled to the remotest of villages during the remainder of the year too difficult. It was always a huge relief to me when they returned. Almost twenty years older than I and loved and respected by all at The Gathering, Adam always sought me out, wanting to tell me of his travels and keen to hear any opinions I had to offer about the experiences he related to me. While always giving me an enormous sense that I was living my life as I should be and doing well in my constant attempts to find and be true to myself, he always seemed desperate for any insights I could offer that could help him with his own troubles, though I could never get a sense of what they were.

When a young bear of a man named Mason arrived with his mare, Diligence, the two of us struck up an instant rapport. I sensed much turmoil beneath his gentle manner, particularly during his riding lessons with Mistral; as with all of us, he could hide nothing of himself once he was astride Diligence, and his perfectionism hindered his attempts to be the rider he deemed that his horse deserved, every bit as much as my egotism hindered mine. Though I sensed it was futile, I did my best to echo Mistral's assurances to Mason that far from letting down his Bond-Partner, he was an able and sensitive rider, hoping that if he heard it enough from those he trusted, he would one day choose to believe it.

A number of years passed before Quinta and Noble arrived, Quinta every bit as anxious as her Bond-Partner was composed. Mason was the first to greet her on her arrival, and his gentle calm couldn't have been a more perfect antidote to her anxiety. I would have given her space to settle in before attempting to judge whether I could also be of assistance to her, but Integrity surprised me by jumping into Noble's paddock with him and insisting that I choose my sense of the right thing to do for Quinta when she visited her horse, over my initial observation that she would prefer not to have to talk to me. Quinta surprised me by being every bit as intuitive as I, if not more. She connected with Integrity immediately and as a result, I found myself knowing far more easily than with most, exactly what support she needed. In the process of providing that support and receiving much from her in return, she and Noble became almost as dear to me as was Integrity.

Of all of my friends, I found it by far the most difficult when Quinta and Noble left The Gathering without Integrity and me. With Integrity's encouragement and support, I used each and every time they left to practise recognising the pattern that still plagued me, and work through it until I reached the truth that I was fine without them. While I achieved it every time, I still never seemed able to move completely away from having to work at it and had to work even harder when, after seventeen years as two of those to whom I was closest, Mistral and Turi's Equal died within days of one another.

I recognised my reaction to their losses almost immediately; I knew that the anger and panic I felt, the urgent need to be with Integrity, the terror I felt for Adam who was away on his travels with Peace, the strong desire I had to plead with Quinta not to leave The Gathering any time soon, were the parts that yet remained of the old me. I knew I could choose to feel differently and I did, repeatedly, until I managed to grieve in a way that was more normal and healthy for the loss of my friends.

I managed to be there for Turi, to comfort her with the truth that in her grief she was having trouble remembering – that Integrity had begun referring to her as *She Who Is Equal* months before, when Turi had achieved the potential she saw for herself while bonding with her beloved mare, and, finally knowing the impossibility of being anything other than equal to everyone else, released the inferiority complex that had thwarted so many of her friendships. Equal trusted Turi to continue on without her, and Turi should trust her Bond-Partner that the time was right for her to go. When she admitted how lost she felt, I suggested that she stay on as head of the kitchens, since her time in the position combined with her new mindset made her an asset to The Gathering. While she was thinking about it, I circulated a petition which was signed and commented on by every Horse-Bonded in residence, all of them begging her to accept the suggestion, which she gladly did.

I even managed to support Feryl, the younger and less experienced of Mistral's two Apprentices, in his grab of the Master Of Riding position, knowing through my bond with Integrity that while he wasn't the better man for the job, he needed the position far more than did Mistral's first Apprentice.

But supporting Turi and Feryl was harder than it should have been, given that I had been practising thinking and behaving with Integrity – and therefore integrity – for so many years. I was beginning to tire, to believe, in my darkest moments, that I would never truly be Newson in character as well as in name. I persevered though, my Bond-Partner a constant source of strength and assurance that it would get easier.

When Adam and Peace returned to The Gathering for what Adam told me would be the final time, his and Peace's travels having finally come to an end, the joy I felt was short-lived; Peace died shortly afterward and Adam left The Gathering to retire in his newfound peace, inflaming the pattern within me from which I just didn't seem able to wrench free.

By the time young Amarilla and her Bond-Partner, Infinity,

arrived at The Gathering several years later, I was exhausted by my continued efforts, yet couldn't help but be both fascinated and intrigued by the two of them. At just sixteen, Amarilla was the youngest ever Horse-Bonded, yet her piebald mare, though only four years old, seemed to me to be the oldest bonded horse I had met. Where Integrity's eyes were dark and kind, Infinity's were pale blue and... bottomless. When she looked in my direction as I stood, observing her in her paddock just after her arrival, it was like being scrutinised by the sum of the ages. As a result – and without any help from my own Integrity – I found myself knowing absolutely how small I was in the grand scheme of things, and how silly was my need to cling to those I loved.

The relief of finding that knowledge so effortlessly eased – just for those moments while her gaze lingered upon me – the years of self-deprecation at my incredibly slow progress. It also gave me fresh energy to persevere with my efforts to live in truth to the exclusion of all else, as did Adam's sudden return to The Gathering as Amarilla's Master of Herbalism, and Quinta's declaration to Turi and me over breakfast the following morning, of her intention to remain at The Gathering now that those who would elicit change had arrived.

Her words jogged my mind. Those who would elicit change? Where had I heard that before? I wracked my brain until, as always, I frustrated myself by having to remember all over again where to go for the truth when I should never have left it. As soon as I was with thinking with Integrity, I remembered the counsel she had given me when explaining why we needed to travel to The Gathering. *There is much we can achieve together. You are more sensitive than most humans of this time. Your ability to sense truth will be of much support to those whose roles it is to elicit change. We merely need work together so that you will choose to do it no matter the circumstances.*

Quinta's eyes widened at the panic that filled me as I realised that I had finally run out of time to be the man Integrity had always been so sure I would be; those to whom Integrity and now Quinta had referred were here. They would need me to be capable of supporting them regardless of the circumstances, and I wasn't sure I was.

*They are catalysts for change,* Integrity told me. *You will not be immune to their influence.*

'Newson, are you alright?' Quinta asked me.

I pictured Infinity's stare when I had observed her in her paddock the day before, and remembered the change she had immediately stimulated in me. I grinned. Maybe this was the break for which I had been waiting, maybe Amarilla and Infinity would be as much help to me as I was determined to be for them. 'Yes, I think I am,' I replied. 'Amarilla…'

'Is here,' Quinta interrupted, nodding over my shoulder as she smoothed her hands over her hair to check it was still contained within its band.

I turned to see the slight, unassuming-looking teenager smiling shyly at those who greeted her on her way past the tables at which they were breaking their fasts, while following a tall, dark-haired and often dark-stared young woman, whom I knew to be called Rowena, towards the food table.

Turi, Quinta and I all got to our feet as the pair neared our table, and introduced ourselves to Amarilla.

There was no mistaking the added shine in Quinta's eyes as she grinned at Rowena and then shook Amarilla's hand, or the warmth in Turi's. When it was my turn, I found myself assuring Amarilla that she would meet Integrity very soon, because for some reason it felt important that she did – that she knew who we were and, by my horse's name, that we would help her.

When she moved on to greet someone she recognised from her

home village, the three of us sat down and Quinta said, 'Well, that was weird.'

I nodded my agreement.

'I thought Amarilla was perfectly sweet,' Turi said. 'I'm glad Rowena's taken her under her wing though, she looks like she needs a bit of confidence.'

'I don't mean that I think Amarilla's weird,' Quinta said, 'just my reaction to her – and Newson's apparently?'

I nodded again. 'To be honest, it's not her so much as her horse, and by extension, her,' I said.

Turi looked between the two of us in confusion. 'Huh? What's wrong with Infinity?'

Quinta smiled and leant against the back of her chair. 'There's nothing wrong with her, just the opposite.'

'It's like meeting the beginning of the end,' I said and blinked. Just picturing Infinity had caused me to instantly immerse myself in Integrity and speak that which I knew to be the truth.

Quinta's smile vanished and her eyes became thoughtful. 'Rowena, Adam and I have all been expecting Amarilla and Infinity for some time. I had no idea that you have too?'

'Not as such,' I replied. 'In all honesty, I'd forgotten until ten minutes ago that Integrity told me my ability to sense the truth would be needed by those who'll bring change. It was only when you said you'd be staying here now the two of them have arrived, and why, that I remembered. I can feel the effect of them being here already, can you?'

'I can feel it and I can see it in the way everyone's behaving,' Quinta said. 'You must have noticed that too, Turi? The confusion and excitement after everything Salom related in the square yesterday about Amarilla's journey here? At sixteen, she's the youngest person ever by a long way to have been tugged, she nearly died trying to find Infinity, then the two of them were hunted by a Woeful on the way here but escaped intact apart from Amarilla's broken arm, which she healed using bone-singing despite having had no training, because Infinity told her she could. And she's called her horse Infinity. The anticipation to see what that means is off the charts!'

'There has been more than the normal amount of gossiping in the kitchens,' Turi said thoughtfully, 'but I just told everyone to pipe down and get on with preparing dinner yesterday and breakfast today, otherwise none of us would have eaten.' She turned and watched Amarilla taking a seat opposite Rowena, her plate piled high with bread, fried eggs and tomatoes. She smiled at Quinta and me. 'Well at least she has a good appetite. By the sound of it, she's going to need all the energy that lot will give her, and more.'

I watched from afar as Amarilla and Infinity began to create waves at The Gathering where before there had only ever been the odd ripple. I was as shocked as everyone else when, after only a few lessons with Feryl, Amarilla made the decision to learn to ride on her own with the help of a few friends. Having already seen Feryl struggle many times in his position as the Master Of Riding, I felt moved to try to ease the fallout that followed, but when I looked at the situation with Integrity, it seemed the wrong thing to do.

*You do well,* Integrity assured me. *It is ever more important that your mind remains open to the truth and is not moved by the emotions evoked by change.*

I tried to remember that and adhere to her advice in the weeks that followed. When I thought of Infinity, it was easy. When I thought of Feryl, it was difficult, especially as I saw him

becoming more and more enraged. When Rowena approached me
to ask me to create metal bits, of all things, for Infinity, Rowena's
Oak, and another horse, Gas, whose Bond-Partner, Justin, had
joined Rowena in her efforts to help Amarilla to ride, I was
horrified. No bonded horses had ever worn anything in order for
us to ride them, except the saddles that were used for the horses'
comfort. But when Rowena told me it was Infinity who had asked
for such, I remembered Integrity's counsel again and agreed to
help.

It was Amarilla who arrived to help me measure the three
horses' mouths for their bits, bringing news with her that at the
urging of his Bond-Partner, Diligence, Mason had been up all
night making the bridles to which they would be attached. I
admitted the concerns I'd had, which rapidly faded away as the
news of Dili's involvement combined with the effect Infinity
always had on me, and I sensed the right thing to do. I had the bits
ready in no time, and when Feryl challenged me about my
involvement, I refused to admit fault. I felt sorry for him but I also
felt that the challenges he was facing were in his path because he
was ready for them, just as had always been the case for me.

We were approaching the end of one of the harshest winters
any of us could remember when Quinta said over dinner, 'We
should join them, you know.'

I followed her gaze to where Amarilla, Rowena and Justin sat
laughing with their friend, Shann, who had begun to ride with
them a few weeks previously. The four of them had endured much
ridicule from many of the other Horse-Bonded for their continued
rejection of Feryl's teaching, not to mention because Amarilla
frequently abandoned the chores we were all assigned, leaving her
three friends to take up the slack while she went and rode Infinity.
Whenever I thought about the situation, I felt sure there was more
to it than Amarilla just being indulged by her friends in laziness,

and Quinta, Turi, Adam and Mason heartily agreed with me. I stuck up for the four of them whenever the situation presented itself, urging our fellow Horse-Bonded to refrain from judgement and wait to see what happened, and came in for a large amount of ridicule as a result.

As time went on, I doubted myself less and less where Amarilla and Infinity were concerned, and really felt as if finally, I had reached the point where I knew right from wrong quickly and regardless of the discomfort my judgement afforded me. As such, I knew instantly that Quinta was right, and smiled as I felt the warmth of Integrity's approval of my decision.

'I agree,' I said. I remained seated, knowing that she wasn't referring to joining them at their meal. 'They've moved their horses to the furthest but one paddock so they can get their horses to the riding paddock without attracting an audience. If we're going to watch their riding sessions with a view to asking them if we can join in and have them help us learn to ride as they are, I think it might be an idea to move Noble and Integrity to the paddock the far side of theirs. They won't thank us for attracting the attention they're so keen to avoid.'

Quinta nodded. 'Noble's happy with that. It'll mean further for us to carry hay and water across the snow and ice, but it'll be worth it, and actually, there's a decent hedge down one side of those far paddocks, so they'll be able to spend more time outside the field shelter without that awful wind forcing them back in.'

'That's settled then.'

We helped Noble and Integrity to move paddocks the following morning. Noble, who was as small and dainty as his Bond-Partner, lacked the height to clear the gate and would have been forced to wait for Quinta to open it for him regardless of the conditions, but I was relieved that for once, Integrity waited with him; the ice that had formed on the path as a result of the snow having been thoroughly trampled had given her pause to consider whether sailing over the fence as she usually did was a good idea.

Quinta and I dragged a large, four-wheeled barrow behind us with two bales of hay and four water containers, as the four of us slipped and slid our way up the path, Noble and Integrity whinnying to Infinity, Oak, Gas and Shann's Spider as we passed their paddock. Quinta and I had a job to open the gate of the paddock beyond, as first the catch was frozen and wouldn't release until I rummaged around in the snow just inside the fence and found a rock large enough to hit and shatter the ice, and then the snow impeded the inward swing of the gate. By the time we got it open far enough for Noble and Integrity to squeeze into the paddock, we were both sweating despite the cold.

'Have I ever mentioned that...'

'You detest winter?' Quinta volunteered. 'Only about a hundred times every single year.' She rubbed the sweat off her face with her sleeve before it could freeze. 'I have to admit this one has been a stinker, but at least it seems to be on its way out. The wind isn't as harsh today and the snow's definitely softening in places. Hang in there, Newson, before we know it, everywhere will be green again, the birds will be soaring and singing, and the air will carry the delicious smell of spring. It's going to be an exciting year this year.' She tilted her head towards the four horses in the neighbouring paddock who were all lined up along the fence, waiting for Noble and Integrity to plough through the untouched snow and reach them.

Infinity diverted her gaze towards us and I was overwhelmed with a feeling of rightness about the decision Quinta and I had made to join the efforts of Amarilla and her friends, rather than just supporting them. I couldn't help but smile. It seemed that Infinity had been the missing part of the equation that I had been trying to balance ever since Integrity and I bonded. After all the years of trying to root myself in the truth that I could access so easily when I chose it instead of the many distractions that pulled me away from it, all of the frustration, the difficulty and the endless practice, I had finally reached a frame of mind where it came naturally. I was no longer Searching For Truth, I was He Who Is Integrity, I was sure of it; I was sure that the next time Integrity had cause to call me by name, that was the one she would use.

And not only that. For the first time in a long while, Quinta, Mason, Adam and Turi were here all at once. Having Mistral, Peace and Equal here would have made things perfect, but nevertheless, I was surrounded by those I loved. For the first time since before my parents died, everything was great and as Quinta had observed, the year that was coming when this infernal winter finally ended, would be exciting. Change was on its way and Integrity and I were well placed to see it through.

'Wow,' Quinta said as we pulled the paddock gate shut. 'Not only are you smiling, which is a rare enough event on its own, but you're smiling in winter. I mean, what are the chances?'

I laughed an actual laugh from deep down in my belly. It was a strange sensation but a very welcome one, as if all of the years of frustration and all the pain and anger I had ever felt just fell away from me. I felt light and... happy. 'As of this moment, they're high,' I said, 'and getting exponentially higher that it might happen again.'

Quinta leant on the gate and stared up at me. 'You're different, I can feel it in my skin. You're happy. Newson, I couldn't be more pleased for you.' She smiled and raised a hand to my cheek. 'You've always put so much pressure on yourself to do the right thing, and I know how hard it's been for you. It's feeling easier now?'

I placed my hand over hers. 'It's feeling easy, thanks to Integrity, you, Noble and the rest of our friends, and thanks to Infinity.'

The piebald, blue-eyed mare once more turned her gaze from our horses to the two of us.

'She draws you in, doesn't she,' Quinta said. 'I can't hear her in my head like I can Noble, but she affects me in a way none of the other horses do, not even your Integrity. I feel as if everything is possible when she looks at me, and I know everything is possible because she and Amarilla are here. We'll start watching them working together this lunchtime, shall we?'

'Absolutely. That means I'd better get on with sorting this lot out.' I lifted one of the water containers out of the barrow and hurled it over the fence to land in the snow by the water barrels.

'I'm up to date with my weaving orders,' Quinta said, 'so if you can just get the four of them in there, I'll clean the barrels and empty the water into them, then I'll get the hay to the field shelter. I know you're besieged with orders now that Luther and Chan have heavy colds and you're the only functioning Metal-Singer.'

'I'm not leaving you to do all this on your own, your lips are turning blue,' I said. 'Come on, we need to get ourselves moving again. You take the first load of hay to the shelter and spread the straw that's hopefully stacked there ready, so you're out of this wind. It might be less harsh than it has been, but it's still vicious. I'll sort the water and then bring the rest of the hay. Okay?'

Quinta rolled her eyes but smiled. 'Okay. And then I'll come with you to your workshop and fetch and carry for you so that you'll be ready to stop work at lunchtime. I won't come and watch the others ride while you're still slaving away.'

'Deal.'

Quinta climbed through the fence and reached for the bale of hay I heaved over the top of it to her. 'I'm proud of you,' she whispered as she took it from me. She smiled and turned to fight her way through the snow.

I was so full to the brim with happiness, I actually thought I might burst with it. I got the barrels clean and full of water in next to no time, blasted my way through the snow with the second bale of hay, and helped Quinta to shake up the remaining straw into a thick bed for Noble and Integrity once I'd distributed the hay into the hay racks that lined the walls of the field shelter. By the time we had finished, our horses were done greeting Infinity, Oak, Spider and Gas, and shuffled in through the straw to the hay racks from which they began eating hungrily.

I wrapped my arms around my horse's neck. Her coat was thicker than it had used to be during winter, and her neck thinner. It was twenty-three years since we bonded, and the years had taken their toll on her, but she still wanted to be ridden, still wanted to work with me, to help me see how we could help those she had always been adamant would appreciate our help. *Thank you, Integrity, for your patience, your honesty and consistency. I owe you everything.* I waited for her to call me by the name that would confirm I was the man I had tried so hard and waited so long to be.

*You owe me nothing,* she told me. *We have come far together as we agreed but we have further to go. Remember to be everything you know you can be when the level of challenge increases as it will.*

*Whatever happens now, I'll be fine, there's nothing that can make me be anything other than true to myself and to you.*

*Remember,* Integrity repeated.

I stepped back from her, a slight feeling of disconcertion

penetrating my elation. Why hadn't she called me the name I was so sure I deserved?

'Right, come on then, let's get back,' Quinta said, ducking under Noble's neck and then walking tall beneath Integrity's. 'They have everything they need, and you have a whole load of metal waiting to be sung into the orders on your worksheet.'

I blinked. 'Um, yes, sure.'

'Are you okay?'

I reached for Integrity, easily becoming everything I could sense within her. I could find no reason to be alarmed. 'I'm great. Yes, come on, let's get back into the warm.'

## Chapter Ten

Quinta and I took our lunch up to the riding paddock that our friends had chosen to frequent all winter, on three out of the following five days, only missing two of them because I really couldn't spare the time away from the Metal-Singers' workshop – which was still empty of Metal-Singers aside from me – and Quinta insisted on giving up her spare time to help me.

The first two riding sessions we observed left us a little confused as we failed to see what it was exactly that Amarilla, Rowena and Justin were trying to do. We did agree though that Oak seemed to be moving more elegantly under saddle than we had seen him do before, Gas appeared to be far more focused than was normal, and Infinity wore such a look of determination, it was impossible not to be drawn in and watch ever more closely to see what was happening. Shann sat on the fence alongside us and tried to explain, but it was hard for both of us not to chuckle when it became clear that he was almost as much in the dark as were we.

During the third session, I began to get a glimmer of what the three riders were trying to achieve as I witnessed Rowena repeatedly riding Oak from halt to walk to trot and back to walk and halt in fairly rapid succession. At the beginning of the session, Oak appeared to falter in his balance a little, leaning slightly forward during the transitions between the paces, but as the session went on, he was gradually able to be more consistent and retain his increased elegance throughout the transitions.

'He's more lifted in front,' Quinta said. 'I can see it now. Rowena's helping him to lift and sit his weight further back onto his hindquarters. How amazing that a horse of Oak's build and size can appear so light on his feet, I can't wait to try that with Noble. Can you see it, Newson?'

I nodded. 'I can. And I think I can see Justin trying to do the same with Gas. Amarilla's trying too with Infinity, but it's a lot harder for her. Fancy attempting it when she's still learning to ride, the girl has guts although judging by the look on Infinity's face, she wouldn't have a choice if she wanted one... which she doesn't. What they're doing is hugely important.' I knew it. I could feel it.

'So, you and your horses will be joining in tomorrow then?' Shann said cheerfully.

'I think I'd like a couple more sessions watching first, so I'm sure I really get what they're doing and how into my head before I start attempting it with Noble,' Quinta said. 'Are you sure they won't mind helping us? They look as if they have enough to contend with, riding their horses.'

'Of course they won't, they always made time to help me,' Shann said.

'Do you mind if I ask why you aren't riding with them now?' Quinta asked him.

Shann glanced surreptitiously at Rowena, who was at the far end of the paddock from where we sat on the fence, completely absorbed in her riding. 'I told them it was because I still don't get exactly what they're trying to do or why, and I don't, not really, but I'll make the effort to once it's a bit warmer. It's my hands, you see, they hurt with the cold unless I ball them up inside my gloves, and I can't hold a pair of reins like that. Don't tell Rowena, she already suspects that's the reason and if she knows for sure, I'll never hear the end of it.'

Quinta and I laughed. Always the joker, Shann was as light of heart as I had always been heavy, and had the gift of being able to transfer that lightness to those around him.

'You hate the cold, but though you won't ride, you still come to every session to give your friends moral support,' I said, knowing it was true.

Quinta patted his arm. 'You're a good friend to them. We'll keep your secret.'

'Spider will be happy to have a go once it's warmer,' I said, nodding to where the brown stallion stood watching his field mates at their work.

'Spider's eternally happy whatever he does,' Shann said. 'He knows as well as I do that whatever happens, it's all good. It's probably a good thing we're giving this lot a head start.' He flicked his eyes to the three riders. 'Once we get going, we'll only show them up.' His eyes held such a mischievous glint, Quinta and I couldn't help laughing again. 'Oh, thank goodness, it looks like they're calling it a day. We can see to the horses and get back in the warm like normal people. Are you coming again tomorrow?'

'We'll try, it depends on how much work comes in for Newson, he's still on his own in the workshop,' Quinta said.

As it happened, I had too much work to do. As strong a Metal-Singer as I was, I just couldn't get far enough through my orders to give myself any choice but to carry on working through lunchtime. I tried to persuade Quinta to take her share of the food she had fetched from the dining room, and go and watch the others ride without me, but she refused.

'Luther and Chan are almost well again,' she said. 'I'm pretty sure they'll be back to work in a few days' time, and then we can go and join the riding session every day. In the meantime, I'm helping you, otherwise knowing you, you'll work on into the evening as well as missing your lunchbreak. Now, where's your worksheet? I'll organise the items you've already made so they can be collected without you being disturbed, and then I'll gather the bits of metal you'll need for the remaining orders so they'll all be in line, waiting for you to sing them into something else.'

She didn't need to tell me how she would be helping as she'd done it twice already that week; she just wanted the time to start doing as she had said before I could argue.

'Thanks, Quinta. Again,' I said.

Her eyes widened as she read my worksheet on her way to where I had practically thrown the items I had made that morning. 'This is insane. Right, okay, so then I'll stay all afternoon as well. I've done my shift in the Weaver's workshop and I did a longer stint compacting dung logs than I was down for yesterday, so if I do a long one again tomorrow, I'll have contributed my hours.' She turned to me. 'Can you stop lobbing stuff onto the finished pile until I've organised what's already there? It's going to take me a while to sort it all out and label everything according to who ordered it, and I have no wish to get hit by a low-flying door hinge in the meantime.'

I grinned. 'No low-flying door hinges, got it. Where do you stand on hammer heads?'

She returned my grin. 'As it happens, I have an even greater aversion to those. Stop talking and sing.'

We got on as well together labouring in my workshop as we

always had in every other way. Thanks to Quinta's superior organisation skills, I got through my orders in two thirds of the time it would have taken me had I been alone, and not only that but I finished my working day feeling a lot less tired and a lot more content than I would otherwise have been.

'I can't thank you enough,' I told her as I handed her the final item, a small wheelbarrow.

'No, we all at The Gathering can't thank you enough for taking on the work of three people,' Quinta said, affixing a label to the wheelbarrow. 'Right, that's everything. And there's the dinner bell, great timing.'

'You carry on, I'll see you there in a bit,' I replied. 'I'm going to dash up to check on Integrity while it's still light.'

'She and Noble will have everything they need, Shann promised me that if we didn't show at lunchtime, he'd fill their water barrels, muck out the field shelter and fill their hay racks.'

'That's great but I have to give her the draft Adam made to ease her joints through the last of the cold. Save me a place at your table?'

Quinta pulled on her cloak and wrapped her scarf around her neck multiple times. 'Sure, don't be too long though, I want to see you eat a hearty dinner after eating so little of the lunch I brought you.' She lifted a hand as she disappeared through the workshop doorway.

I pulled on my own cloak and gloves, picked up the bottle of Adam's herbal preparation I had left on the windowsill by the door, and made my way up the slippery path to see my horse. Infinity and Oak were grooming one another near their paddock gate, and I was surprised when it wasn't just Oak who paused to stretch his nose out and nuzzle my gloved hand; Infinity did too. Up until then, she had been happier to observe me from a distance, but her gesture left me feeling that I had been recognised for whom I could now be to her, rather than merely one who needed the help she continued to offer to me. I stayed with them until they returned to their grooming.

I continued on to my horse's paddock, breathing in the bitterly cold air and expelling it within dense clouds of moisture. For once, I appreciated the aspects of winter that Quinta had always loved; the silence that accompanied the thick covering of snow on the ground, the lack of scents other than hay and horses, the beauty of a solely white landscape – I even embraced the feeling of the air numbing my teeth and stinging my throat. It was great to be alive!

I found Noble and Integrity munching from almost full hay racks. Their water barrels had been filled to the brim and were free of ice, and it appeared as though their field shelter had recently been mucked out too. I made a mental note to thank Shann for checking on them at the end of the afternoon as well as seeing to them at lunchtime. I ran my hands over Integrity, then over Noble, checking for any heat, cuts or swellings, and stroked both of the noses that sniffed and nuzzled my face.

'I love you both too,' I told them. I drew a syringe full of the draft from its bottle. 'Here you go, Integrity.'

My horse opened her mouth obligingly and swallowed the draft once I had emptied the syringe into it. I felt her satisfaction at the herbs Adam had selected, and also the warmth that spread through her as Adam's peaceful energy added its effect to that of the herbs which carried it.

Her warmth carried me back down to the buildings with a smile on my face. I was just about to enter the dining hall when I remembered that Mason had asked me over breakfast if I would make him a new leather knife, and I had forgotten to add it to my worksheet for the following day. Cursing, I hurried to my workshop. I amended the worksheet and was just slotting it back into its folder when a sense of unease stole over me.

*Integrity?* I sensed her shifting nervously in her field shelter. *Integrity, what is it? What's wrong?*

*Remember,* she told me. *Remember to be everything you know you can be.*

I sensed her trotting out of the field shelter to the centre of her paddock, where she stood with Noble, looking towards the river in the fading light.

*Integrity, what's the matter? Tell me! What's out there?*

She didn't reply. It was only as I walked towards the workshop door that I remembered the only time I had ever felt unease from her before; when the right path to take to get to The Gathering was through woodland where she was at risk of attack from Woeful. But that couldn't be it, we were safe at The Gathering. Woeful stuck to the forests and the closest of those was on the far side of the river. Everyone knew that Woeful avoided immersing themselves in water as if it were fire.

The panic that shot through me all of a sudden wasn't my own. I sensed Integrity cantering through the deep snow in her paddock – she was running from something. No, I corrected myself, a chill going down my spine, she was running from someone. Four someones. I scented her pursuers with her nose. I heard them with her ears. When she spun around in the corner of her paddock to face them, I saw them through her eyes.

It was as though a whole barrel of ice cold water had been upturned on my head. Woeful had left the trees and crossed the river! Integrity's panic became mine. I couldn't move. Until that moment I had thought that being paralysed by fear was a figure of speech, an exaggeration of the effect of extreme terror, but I quickly realised my error. Even Integrity's fresh burst of terror didn't spur me into action. All I found myself able to do was stand on legs I couldn't feel, and witness through Integrity the ungainly yet surprisingly rapid approach of the monsters before her.

It was only when I could make out saliva dripping from the fangs of the beasts, when I could perceive the hungry intent in their eyes, the brown pelts hanging loosely from three of them and the black of the fourth, that I finally found not only my legs but my wits.

*RUN!* I hurled my thought to my horse as I tore out of my workshop. *Integrity, don't let them corner you, get past them and jump out of the field. Come down to the square, there are four Woeful up there and hundreds of Horse-Bonded down here, they won't follow you, you'll be safe.*

The monsters gambolled ever closer to her.

*Integrity, Noble, RUN!!!*

I sensed Integrity burst into as fast a canter as she was able in the snow, Noble at her side. Integrity's longer legs carried her at a greater speed than Noble could manage, a fact which didn't escape the Woeful. Through Integrity's senses, I witnessed all four working together to herd him back to the corner.

I couldn't let them take him from Quinta. From me.

*Integrity, keep going, I'm on my way, I'll open the gate for Noble and find a way to distract the Woeful so he can get past them.*

I sensed my horse continuing on to the fence, which she cleared. She slipped on the ice as she landed, wrenching one of her hind fetlocks and falling onto her knees and chest. She scrambled to her feet and fled towards the buildings – towards me.

I reached the square just as Gas, Spider and Oak tore onto it, blood pouring down both of Oak's forelegs. People were streaming out of the dining room and some of them stopped to calm and inspect the horses while the rest continued running towards the fields. It was Shann who ran alongside me as we passed the first few paddocks. 'Get that shovel,' he said pointing to one leaning against the fence of a paddock just ahead of us. 'I'll get one from the next field down, they're all we have to fight the Woeful off. Watch out!' He shoved me to the side as more horses galloped past us, all lathered in sweat.

I regained my footing, grabbed the shovel and ran after Shann along the fence line so as to avoid being trampled by the horses coming the other way. I sensed Integrity approaching and was relieved that while her instincts ensured her continued flight, her panic was beginning to subside.

*Integrity, thank goodness,* I told her, *just keep going past me to the square, there are people there who'll help you. I'll stop them hurting Noble and be right back.*

*Remember.* Her thought carried a measure of urgency.

*Remember what? To do what's right? I am, I'm going to save Noble, how can that not be the right thing to do?*

*If you need ask then you do not act from a place of truth. Searching For Truth you are ready. You need only choose that which you know you can be.*

Her use of my name had its desired effect. I knew without doubt that Noble had entered into an agreement not only with Quinta but with the Woeful currently hunting him; he had agreed to be prey to their desperate, starving predation. I should allow him to fulfil his agreement without interference.

But then Quinta's scream rang out just ahead of me, carrying her shock, her horror, her agony. There could be no doubt that her Bond-Partner was dead. The panic within me fled before the white hot rage that burned in its place. The Woeful may have killed Noble, but they wouldn't take his body. I would stop them.

*Remember,* Integrity urged me as she slid painfully to a stop in front of me, lame on her right hind, a gash in her chest and cuts all over her front legs. Her hot breath blasted onto my face even as her thought blasted into my mind. *Choose who you can be over who you were. Choose the truth. Choose to help those who need you over the pattern that reaches for you. Choose me.*

'I will,' I snarled out loud, 'just as soon as I've stopped them taking Noble. Don't you see? If I let them take him, they'll come back for more horses.'

*That is not the truth.*

*Integrity, move out of my way, get down to the buildings so the Healers can help you.*

My horse stood where she was, dripping with sweat that froze as it landed on the ice beneath her. She needed help to stay warm as her sweat dried, and to have her injuries healed. And I needed to stop the Woeful taking Noble. My rage burned afresh. I gathered all of myself together, stepped to one side and yelled at Integrity with as much force as I could. 'GO!'

Her eyes widened and she fled. I felt sick as the realisation hit me that it was not from the Woeful she was running now but from me, but I pushed my horror to one side. There was no time for that, Integrity was safe but four Woeful were still running amok and had to be stopped.

Justin overtook me as I started running again. We passed Quinta, who was on her knees, wailing while a Bone-Singer whom I knew to be called Marvel held her close in an attempt to comfort her. I didn't even consider stopping to help him as my fury bore me onward.

When I reached Infinity's paddock, I paid little attention to the black-pelted monster now gambolling after her; Amarilla, Rowena and Shann were already heading in their direction and Justin wasn't far behind them. I would go after the three smaller, brown-pelted Woeful who had heaved Noble onto their shoulders and cleared the far fence. They would not take him from me.

I slipped and slid along the path, my speed nevertheless far greater than theirs now that they were impeded by an awkwardly shaped and dead weight. I rounded the corner of the fence and ran between it and the river, holding my shovel aloft and shouting, 'YOU DROP HIM RIGHT NOW.'

The three Woeful staggered as they turned around to face me, still holding Noble. His head hung lifelessly over one of their shoulders, enraging me further.

'We're more sorry than you can know,' one of them panted, his voice raspy as if he had a cold, 'but we cannot do as you request. Our younglings are starving. We must feed them before we lose them. We ended the life of He Who Is Noble as quickly as we could and now we will honour him by using his body to give life to those he agreed he would.'

Integrity tried one last time. *Searching For Truth. Remember.*

The Woeful was telling the truth. I knew I should let him and his companions leave unhindered, in fact I was pretty sure I should help them. I dropped the shovel. But then Amarilla's scream reached us all. So, the black Woeful had downed Infinity.

We had been happy, all of us. We were primed and ready to bring change, and now my horse was badly injured, Noble and Infinity were dead, and Quinta and Amarilla were no doubt broken. Those who stood, thin, desperate and trembling in front of me had taken everything from me.

I let out a yell and launched myself at the nearest Woeful. I saw the sorrow in his eyes as he put out a taloned hand to stop me knocking him off balance. I heard his intake of breath as four of his talons pierced my chest. I felt pain such as I had never felt before as I crumpled to my knees, but as the Woeful turned to continue on his way, my rage only increased. I grabbed his hairy ankle, causing him to stumble. He reached down and grabbed my wrist, forcing me to let go. His pain-filled eyes leaked tears as he and I regarded the blood spurting between his talons.

'I'm sorry,' he said, and released me.

I tried to crawl after them. I did crawl after them for a short way, blood dripping from my chest and pouring from my wrist as rage spurred me onward.

All of a sudden, I felt better. Stronger. Lighter. Free of pain. I got to my feet and pursued the Woeful again. I reached them just as they were loading Noble's body onto what looked like a raft made from tree trunks.

'NOOOOO!' I could have sworn I yelled out loud, yet I could hear no sound.

All three Woeful turned to me. *You must let go,* one of them said. How was it that I could hear him in my head, just like I could Integrity? And how was it that I could feel his compassion, his sorrow as if it were my own?

I tried to answer him out loud, but found it harder than it should have been. *I'll never let him go, I'll never let you take him,* I thought back.

*We and he are no longer your concern,* another informed me gently, the sympathy that accompanied his thought so intense that I almost believed it. *You must let go of him, of us, of your life here, and move on. Your horse will help you.*

I rallied. *I'm not going anywhere and neither is Noble.* I tried to reach between the Woeful and grab hold of Noble's leg, but my hand swiped through air.

*He Who Is Noble has already released his hold on his body. You must do the same with yours.*

All three Woeful looked past me, and I couldn't help but follow their gaze through the twilight to where my body lay face down in the snow.

# Chapter Eleven

$\mathcal{I}$ was with my body in an instant. How could this be? The Woeful must have knocked me unconscious – this must be a dream. Any minute now, I would come to and look out of my eyes once more instead of seeing myself this way. I supposed I would just have to stay nearby until that happened. But what of Noble?

Footsteps crunched up to me and paused by my side. The black-pelted Woeful looked down at me. *I am sorry,* he told me, *we never meant you any harm.* His devastation swamped me and made me want to console him. Console him? He had killed Infinity!

*I tried,* he admitted, *but I succeeded only in taking the life of He Who Is Spider instead. That is for me to come to terms with just as you must come to terms with your situation. Take your rest from this life and fare you well in your next, Son of The New.* The Woeful staggered onward, as exhausted and broken in mind as in body, to where his friends waited aboard the raft with Noble.

He Who Is Spider? Shann? He had killed Shann but not

Infinity? And Son of The New? How did he know my given name? What gave him the right to use it, to address me as if he were my friend when he and his gang had attacked us all at our home?

I tried everything to wake up as the raft pulled away from the river bank. I tried to pinch both the version of myself that was conscious – my subconscious, I decided – and my body, but my barely visible fingers passed through both without achieving the desired effect. I held my breath... and then realised I felt no discomfort. I cursed myself for an idiot; my subconscious couldn't flaming well breathe! I focused on my body and willed myself to wake. I even lay down inside it and tried to move it. All to no avail.

By the time I had exhausted everything I could think to try, the Woeful had disappeared into the rapidly descending darkness. If rage alone could have picked up my body and made it swim after them, I'd have done it easily, but instead I was incapacitated, exposed and vulnerable.

Voices sounded in the distance. Oh, thank goodness, the Horse-Bonded were coming. I got to my feet and waved both arms in the hope that as the dots of light got closer, they would pick me up – and then cursed myself for a fool again. No one could see the subconscious of another. Except the Woeful had, hadn't they? I couldn't figure out how but when I did, I'd find a way to use the knowledge against them. I'd make them pay for what they'd done to us all.

It seemed an eternity before those brave enough to follow after the Woeful reached me. I recognised Jack first, his almost white hair as bright as ever in the light of his lantern.

'There's someone lying there in the snow,' he said. 'Hurry.'

The lanterns bobbed up and down more rapidly as all ten

searchers ran to my side. At last! Jack was a Healer and there were bound to be others with him, they would sort me out.

'By the wind of autumn, there's so much blood,' someone said as Jack bent down and put his fingers to my throat.

Blood? Well of course there was, I had been injured by the Woeful's talons, but the stab wounds to my chest weren't that deep, and the slash to my wrist... had indeed released a huge amount of blood, I noticed for the first time. No matter, a Tissue-Singer could easily sort that.

Jack rolled my body over so that he could see my face, and clenched his jaws together so hard that the tendons and blood vessels bulged in his face and neck. He stood up and said to the others, 'It's Newson, and I'm afraid he's dead.'

The shock of those present swept through me, adding to my own. No, that wasn't right, I was here. *Someone else check,* I tried to shout to them. *HE'S WRONG, SOMEONE ELSE CHECK!*

No one could hear me. Jack took off his cloak and laid it in the snow by my body. 'We're going to need to roll him onto it so we can carry him back,' he said.

A blond woman handed her lantern to one of the others and bent down by my legs.

'Thanks, Vic,' Jack said. Between them, they rolled me onto his cloak.

Vickery was a Healer too, a Herbalist. Why wasn't she checking my wounds so she would know what she'd need when she got me back to the healing rooms? I jumped around her, shouting, *HELP ME.*

To no avail.

'Right, four of you carry him back,' Jack said, 'while the rest of us carry on and see if we can find where those beasts came from. They're going to rue the day they decided to attack us and our horses here. Keep a low profile as you pass Infinity's paddock,

those tending to her have enough on their plates without having to
see Newson this way.'

I walked behind the four carrying my body until I realised that
I wasn't walking, of course I wasn't. And if I wasn't really
walking, then I could float, couldn't I? This subconscious of
mine? I could float and then I would have a better view of the
carnage the Woeful had left behind. Rage flared in me anew. Just
let them wait until I caught up with them. Until we caught up with
them, I corrected myself. Jack was clearly up for hunting them
down, and Quinta was sure to want revenge for them having taken
Noble from her. I would make sure she got it.

When my carriers reached the paddock in which Infinity lay,
they lowered their lanterns to their knees so that they could see
their way without their load being obvious to those who tended to
the piebald mare. A fire blazed near her and she was surrounded
by lanterns. Those at her side all had their eyes closed as they
hummed their healing to her bones and tissues, supported by the
energy of the horses who also attended her – among whom was a
tall, grey mare.

Integrity. How had she slipped my mind so completely? She
had been lame when she fled from… I couldn't let myself think it,
I didn't want to remember that it hadn't just been the Woeful from
whom she had been desperate to escape. It was of no matter, she
had clearly already been healed and made her way back towards
where she knew I was; she had clearly forgiven me. Relief calmed
me and I became aware of the sense of her I realised I had been
without since I had gone after the Woeful.

*Integrity? Are you alright?* I instantly knew that she was. As I
had surmised, a Tissue-Singer and Herbalist had tended to her. She
was pain free and her surface wounds had been smeared with a
healing unguent. She was aware of me and my situation even as
she made her energy available to support the Healers working

upon Infinity. *Integrity, I'm sorry I frightened you, I just couldn't bear for Noble to be taken.*

*I am aware of the choice you made.* Her thought was as kind and patient as always. *Now you must heed the advice of the Sorrowful and accept its consequence.*

*The Sorrowful? You mean the Woeful? They didn't give me any advice, one of them knocked me unconscious and all of this is just a figment of my subconscious imagination.*

*That is not the truth. You must relinquish your attachment to your body for it can no longer serve you. You must move on and rest. Allow yourself to examine the choices and experiences from this incarnation so that you may learn from them and be better able to choose differently in the next.*

*I'm not going anywhere. I'm staying here in the safety of The Gathering until I'm well enough to go and hunt those monsters.*

*None of that is true. Your body has expired. Our work in this incarnation has come to an end.*

*NO! NO, NO, NO, NO, NO!*

Those clustered around Infinity got to their feet and stretched. Infinity needed rest, but she would be okay. How did I know that?

*Most of your consciousness has returned to All That Is. You can know everything. You merely need allow the remainder to release its hold on your body and you will know everything. You will be able to combine your experience in this lifetime with all others you have lived. Everything will make sense.*

*No, that's not true, I'm not dead, I just need to be healed as Infinity has been.*

*Searching For Truth. Your body has expired. Our work here has come to an end,* Integrity repeated.

I couldn't help but know the truth. Terrified, I pushed it to one side. *Why are you doing this to me? Why are you pushing me away? We're Bond-Partners, we're here to support those who are bringing change, you told me that yourself. Well, they're here, Amarilla and Infinity are here, Infinity's alive, they can still bring change, and you and I can still help them.*

*It is impossible for me to push you away for we are one. I will always be with you and you with me but our time as Bond-Partners in this incarnation has reached its conclusion.*

*YOU'RE WRONG!* I wanted to scream the words at her, but was forced to hurl the thought at her instead.

She didn't flinch. She calmly wandered away from the other horses who stood by Infinity, and followed the group carrying me. There, that was better; she had been forced to face the truth – I wasn't ready to give up on my body as she and those carrying me had been. I'd find a way to make them heal me, and then we'd continue our lives together.

Integrity soon caught up with those trying to keep their feet as they carried my weight, their frozen hands constantly having to renew their grasp on Jack's cloak so that they didn't drop me. One of the two at the back reached her other hand back to stroke Integrity's nose. 'I'm sorry, beautiful girl.'

Integrity followed us onto the square and across it until I was carried into the accommodation block, where she remained outside the door. That wasn't right, the healing rooms were in the adjacent block. Why were they taking me to my room? Torn between staying outside with Integrity and remaining with my body, I resorted to following my body so that I would be immediately reintegrated within it when I woke up. I tried to get through to those who gently lay my body upon my bed, but they couldn't hear me. When one of them fetched a clean, white sheet from the cupboard down the corridor and laid it over the length of my body, I tried even harder.

*WHAT ARE YOU DOING? STOP IT, I NEED HELP, YOU*

*NEED TO FETCH A HEALER WHO CAN HELP ME. FETCH ADAM, HE'S THE BEST THERE IS.*

The four of them lined up along the length of the bed and stood in silence for a few moments, then filed out of my room. I followed them back out onto the square, where each of them stopped to offer a hand for Integrity to sniff, then gently stroked her before leaving her be. As they crossed the square, each was stopped repeatedly by other Horse-Bonded frantic to know what had happened. Their sagging shoulders were mirrored by each of those who stepped in their way on learning the version of my fate that everyone, including my Bond-Partner, seemed so determined to believe.

*Integrity, can't you get their horses to tell them to fetch Adam to me? He'll know what to do.*

Integrity lowered her head slightly and rested the hind leg she had injured earlier. *He Who Is Peace tends to Infinity's wounds. While less serious than those healed by the Singers, they will in time be troublesome without his assistance.*

*You're tired,* I told her. *You shouldn't be out here any more than I should, you need to be in a field shelter with hay and a straw bed.*

*While you choose to remain attached to your body then so will I. While you refuse the rest that you require then so will I.*

*If someone would just heal my flaming body so I can wake up, then I promise I'll rest, but I can't while everyone thinks I'm dead. They've lain a sheet over me, for goodness' sake.* At the thought, I suddenly found myself in my room again. The shock of the mound beneath the sheet sent me reeling back to Integrity. Not wanting any more of her counsel, I immediately returned to my room, only to once again find the shrouded figure unbearable and flit straight back to Integrity. I grew increasingly anxious and afraid as I flew repeatedly back and forth, not just at the inaction regarding my body but at Integrity's inaction regarding her own. She was exhausted and becoming increasingly cold. She needed shelter, water and hay but she wouldn't heed my pleading to look after herself any more than she would heed my begging to get help for me.

Eventually, five figures came hurrying along the corridor and entered my room.

'I don't get it either,' one of them said. 'Newson's body should be left in his room until Integrity sees fit to carry it to wherever he wanted to be laid to rest, not shunted out to a field shelter in the middle of the night, but Rowena's adamant that Integrity asked Oak to tell her that Newson's refusing to move on and she needs to be with his body so that he'll stay with it and accept its condition. Oak said that Integrity needs to get out of the cold and rest, so unless she comes and stands in here, which will only address one of those needs, we need to take Newson to a field shelter. Let's just do it, shall we, then we can try and get some sleep, and escape the horror of this night for a few hours.'

Four of the Horse-Bonded picked up my body, carefully wrapping the sheet further around it as they did so. The fifth hurried ahead of them to open and close both my bedroom and the outer door. I continued to flit between my body and Integrity until the two were together and I no longer knew what to do with myself.

I spun around and around above my body. Integrity had finally asked for help, that was good, wasn't it? And she was following us back to the fields where she could get food and shelter. Relief calmed me slightly and I began to slow my movement. Maybe the best Healers were on their way back from seeing to Infinity now, and they would meet us? Or maybe they were still with Infinity and we would make our way back up there? Yes, that sounded more likely, then Integrity could rest in her normal shelter... but no, that wouldn't work, not without Noble there too. Maybe Oak was waiting for her, maybe he would be her paddock companion now, it was he, after all, who had passed the message for my body to be moved.

Integrity walked past my bearers wearily, tripping twice, so that by the time we left the square, she was leading the way. She walked into the first paddock on the right and headed straight for the field shelter.

'This is for newly bonded,' whispered the only unencumbered of my companions.

'I don't think this is the time to give two hoots about the rules,' one of my bearers said. 'Integrity knows what she's doing, come on, let's get after her.'

Finally, a decision that made sense. Integrity wanted me with her but close to the buildings so that I could easily be tended to. When we reached the field shelter, Integrity was already lying down.

'She's exhausted, bless her.'

'I wonder if she and Spider will leave together with Shann and Newson. I hope they do, it won't be an easy journey at this time of year and at least if they're together, they'll have more chance of fending off Woeful.'

'It's disrespectful to talk of that now.'

'It's not a pleasant topic of conversation at any time.'

'When the four of you have quite finished, you can lay Newson down along that wall and get off to bed. I'll shake that hay up by Integrity so she can eat without getting up, and then we'll leave her in peace.'

I refused to take in their conversation. I focused all of my attention on the stars shining through the doorway of the field shelter, fully expecting them to be blotted out by the Healers' entrance at any moment.

*They will not come. There is nothing they can do for your body,* Integrity informed me from her slumber as the last Horse-Bonded left us.

*They'll come,* I replied. I sat down by her head so that I couldn't see my body, and crossed my subconscious legs.

*There is nothing I can do for your body but there is much I can do for your soul,* I was told gently. *Come and fly the oneness with me. When you allow yourself to experience that which awaits you then that which you will leave behind will lose its hold.*

*Fly the oneness? What do you mean?*

*I will show you.* Integrity was in two places at once. I could still sense her within her body, yet she was also without it. The unattached part of her swirled around me, inviting me to follow her joy, her playfulness. She drifted away from her body and I allowed myself to go with her... no. This was wrong. All of me was coming. All of me was leaving my body while only part of Integrity was leaving hers. I flew back to the tiny part of myself still associated with my body and clung to it.

*You tried to trick me,* I accused Integrity.

*I attempted to show you who you are in truth.*

*You tried to get me to leave my body behind, to believe I'm dead when I'm not. I can't leave it. I can't leave you. I'm Newson, I'm your Bond-Partner and we have work to do here.*

She didn't argue. She merely surrounded me with love, kindness and honesty. Her love and kindness, I welcomed as I waited for the Healers. Her honesty grated on me. I swatted at it continually but couldn't reject it completely without also rejecting the comfort she was affording me.

The light of the following day brought Adam with it. Finally! But he ignored my body and crouched in front of Integrity. He put his palm to her forehead. 'Still trying to help him?' he whispered to her. 'I understand. There's hay right here if you want it, I'm going to fetch water in buckets so you don't have to go outside if you don't want to.'

He left and returned shortly afterward with two buckets of water, which he put down next to the pile of hay by Integrity's head. Then he stood and looked around the shelter. 'Newson, I know you're here and I know you're afraid.'

I was in front of him as soon as I thought about being so. *So then, help me! Why won't anyone help me?*

Adam frowned slightly and appeared to be concentrating. Had he heard me? 'Newson, what can I do to help you? How can I persuade you to move on, to be at peace? Ahh, is that it?'

Immediately, the field shelter was filled with the same sense that everything was alright that I'd always felt in Adam's presence. Now though, it was far more intense. It permeated every stone in all four of the walls, it burst out of the door and surrounded the field shelter, oozing back in through the walls that already were it, that couldn't be anything else.

I started as a large, brown and white horse appeared at Adam's side. *PEACE? How are you here?*

Adam cocked his head a little to one side. 'Peace? Is that you?' He smiled. 'Of course it is. Newson, Peace left his body when it died, but he still exists, if I can feel him here then you must be able to. He's here to help you, to show you that everything's okay, that it's okay to move on.'

*BUT I'M NOT DEAD!*

Adam watched Integrity lower her head back into the straw and close her eyes. He crouched down again and gently stroked the side of her muzzle. 'I'm sorry, my dear, so sorry. We tried.' He turned and left the field shelter with Peace in his wake. No matter, I still had Integrity's energy to sustain me as I waited for the one who would surely come, who would surely realise the mistakes of all the others.

Integrity tried again. She increased the energy with which she was surrounding me until it permeated me too. *Searching For Truth your body is no longer viable. You know this. Accept it and allow me to help you to leave it. I have already shown you that I can lead the way. You will not be alone.*

I did know it. She was forcing me to know it. But I couldn't leave my body any more than I could leave hers. I hurled the truth away from me and focused on that which was more comfortable. I reached out a hand and tried to stroke her cheek, but it passed through her.

*I've already lost so much. I can't lose what we have together here.*

*You are already in the process of losing it. You reject our bond because of the truth it holds. You push me away because you are afraid of who I am. Your focus on your old belief that you need that which is not yourself only gives it a greater purchase on you. The longer you remain here the harder it will be to remember everything you have learnt. Everything you have become. Everything you may take with you that will allow you to progress in your future incarnations.*

Movement by the door startled me. I was surprised that whoever entered the field shelter carried a lantern. How was it dark? Integrity and I had been conversing for only a few moments.

*It merely seems that way,* Integrity told me, *for you yet attempt to hold on to the concept of linear time though it no longer applies to the part of you that is free of your body.*

Heavy footsteps approached Integrity and a large frame knelt down by her head. 'Newson, if you're here, please, my friend, please let go and move on.' Mason glanced at my shrouded body and shuddered, then let out a sob. 'Integrity isn't eatin' or drinkin', it doesn't even look as if she's been on her feet since she got here. She can't go on givin' everythin' of herself to try to give you the energy to leave, please, trust her and go? I don't want you to, none of us want you to – Turi's distraught and so will Quinta be when she finds out – but you have to.' A lone tear ran down his face. 'You have to,' he whispered.

*I'm NOT dead.*

Mason spent some time stroking Integrity, muttering softly to her all the while. She gave no indication that she knew he was there. She was with me, her love and kindness nurturing me even as her honesty probed at me. Soon after he left, it was light outside again and with the light came Rowena.

She looked dreadful. Her pale skin was almost translucent apart from the black half-moons under her bloodshot eyes. She stood and watched Integrity for a few minutes, then scanned the full water buckets, untouched hay and undisturbed straw bed. She marched over to my body and ripped the sheet from it. She stood and glared all around. 'This has gone on long enough,' she said. 'Look at that.' She pointed at my body.

I didn't recognise myself. I lay curled on my side as if I were asleep, but my skin had a grey tinge to it, my mouth hung open and my eyes appeared to have sunk into my skull. I looked like a corpse. A corpse? I shook my subconscious head. No, that couldn't be, I just needed a Healer.

'Your body's dead, Newson, and you need to move on. Look at what you're doing to Integrity, she should have been on her feet, eating and drinking the past few days, preparing to take you to where you want your body left, but instead she's here, wasting away while she tries to help you to stop clinging to it. Spider took Shann this morning, do you know that?' Her voice broke and she heaved a few times. Then she wiped her face on her sleeve and said, 'Do you think Shann wanted to go? Of course he didn't, he'd never have left me given the choice. But he has. He's left his body and that means that when Spider returns, he can get on with his life, whether that's staying here with Gas, or going back to find his family herd. Just look at Integrity wasting away because of your selfishness. After everything she's done for you, you should be ashamed of yourself. Do you hear me, Newson? Do you hear me? Adam and Mason may have minced their words, but I won't. Get yourself gone.' She stormed out of the field shelter leaving me staring after her, stunned.

Integrity was wasting away because of my selfishness.

*It is of no matter. Our work here has come to an end and my body is aged. I would have chosen to leave it after carrying your body to its place of rest. Since I cannot persuade the part of you yet anchored within your body to release its hold while I have a hold on my own then I will leave my body here. With yours. We will leave our bodies behind together. I will ask that they remain together and I will be wholly with you as we leave together. There will be no separation. No loss. Your body will be here with mine and your soul will fly the oneness with mine.*

*But... we belong here. In our bodies.*

*The fact that you no longer perceive time in the same way is testament to the fact that we do not. You believe that you are seeing your surroundings. That you are hearing the voices of your friends. You are merely perceiving them and applying to them the physical concepts with which you are familiar.*

I flitted about the field shelter, changing direction in panic each time a wall failed to ensure that I did. *I don't know. I feel safe here. It's what I know, it's where I've been happy, where we've been happy. You'll really just leave it all behind? Just like that?*

*In truth we are not leaving anything behind. It merely seems that way to you because you are choosing to forget that you are all you need. That you are all there is. The longer you cling to your body the harder it will be to remember.*

I shook my head – or tried to. I couldn't seem to feel whether I had done it. Integrity's honesty grasped hold of my confusion so that I couldn't ignore it, I couldn't discount my lack of physicality. Her kindness and patience reassured me even as her thought struck terror into me. *Searching For Truth you have begun to release your hold. You do well. I am with you. I will always be with you. You know this. You are safe. You are whole. You are all there is.*

*I'm not sure… I need… I mean, how can I leave… I…* I stared at my body, which lost its hideousness as I stopped seeing it and… perceived it. It held no life, no vitality. It was no place for me. *I can't leave it, I don't know how.*

*You merely need to cease fighting the truth. Embrace it. Embrace me.*

It was almost dark again. Mason entered the field shelter with Marvel, the Healer who had comforted Quinta when Noble was killed. He wasn't there to heal me, I knew that now. I perceived the two of them stroking Integrity and then gently shaking her.

'Come on, my lovely, Dili tells me it's time, that you're ready to… to go and take Newson with you,' Mason whispered, and cleared his throat.

Integrity opened her eyes and slowly got to her feet. I cried non-existent tears as Mason and Marvel leant into her, one on either side as she stretched weakly and then wobbled over to my body.

Marvel stroked her neck. 'Are you sure you can do this, beautiful girl? Are you strong enough? Mason, do you think we should walk with her in case she falls? She can barely move herself, let alone carry Newson.'

Mason shook his head emphatically. 'Dili was very clear. Integrity just wants us to lift Newson onto her back and then leave her to it.'

*Where are we going?* I asked Integrity.

*Somewhere that you can be confident our bodies will not be disturbed until the ground is soft enough for us to be buried here. Your friends have conceded to the unusual arrangement so that you will consent to leave with me.*

I was lifted easily and lain across my beloved horse's back. Mason sobbed as he stroked Integrity's neck a final time. 'Goodbye, my lovely. Goodbye, Newson, my friend.'

Marvel gently patted Integrity's rump and said, 'Farewell, you both. Come on, Mason.' He put an arm around my friend and guided him out of the field shelter.

Integrity carried me unfalteringly through the darkness despite the slush and ice underfoot, her lack of energy and my weight. My dead weight, I reminded myself. She turned to walk alongside the workshops and then continued until she reached a small, stone building whose door stood open. She walked inside and barely pausing to stop, lay down atop a large white sheet that had been spread out on the ground. Holes had been created and edged at regular intervals around its perimeter. It was a shroud. A shroud that would presumably be stitched around us once we had gone. Once we had gone? Were we really going to do this?

I perceived our bodies lying together, as they always would. Integrity continued to hold me within her energy, but she now also swirled around me as she had whilst attempting to get me to leave my body before.

*Let us fly.* Where before part of Integrity's energy had remained in her body, this time she left nothing behind. Her joy, her lightness, her sense of freedom overwhelmed me, allowing her love and truth to finally reach me. We flew.

## Chapter Twelve

*E*verywhere was grey. I wasn't sure how I knew that, I just did. It should have felt dreary and monotonous, yet it was anything but. It was dynamic and blissful and full of all of those who had passed on and all of those who were yet to be. We were ourselves and we were all of them.

My sense of Integrity was so intense it was almost painful, as, suddenly, was the truth. I had failed. Despite all of Integrity's reminders, all of my years of practice and my belief that I had become He Who Is Integrity, I had chosen my pattern of clinging to those who made me feel safe and worthy over that which I had known to be true. I had deserted my bond, my Bond-Partner and my purpose in that incarnation when it mattered the most. I was self-centred and vengeful. I was hopeless.

The greyness was replaced by a vivid red. A multitude of figures streamed by, their faces contorted, their fanged mouths emitting silent screams. I tried to scream too as a thousand knives stabbed at me all at once.

*Integrity, where are you? Help me!*

*I am with you as always. You need merely choose me over that which tempts you. As Always.* She was unconcerned but her thought was as faint as the attack on me was intense.

I swiped arms I didn't have at the knives that didn't exist yet continued to fly out of nowhere at me, and at the figures that swooped ever closer. One came straight at me, its maw wide open as if it would swallow me whole.

*Integrityyyyyyyyyyyyy!*

*If you believe that you need me then you have not chosen me.*

The maw closed around me and everything went black. The pain continued, now from an unseen source. Where was I? Was I in hell?

*Only of your own creation.* Integrity was still unmoved by my plight, in fact she felt exactly the same as when we had left our bodies behind; she was a bright light in the darkness, radiating love, peace and joy.

I reached out to her light… and I became it too.

*When you choose the truth over the lies your fear would have you believe then everything becomes simple once more.*

*The truth is straightforward,* I agreed. *I remember. I remember how it felt to choose it, to know I was doing the right thing, but I didn't choose it when it mattered. I let you down. I let myself down. I let Amarilla and Infinity down. And I let the Woeful down. They were suffering enough as it was. Noble knew it and went with them gladly. I fought them and made their ordeal even worse.*

The greyness developed a red tinge again, which quickly grew more pronounced.

*No, nooooooo! Integrity, don't let it take me again, please?*

*There is no it. There is you. Everything here is you. Everything here is me. We are All That Is as much as are all of the other souls who have ever been. If you do not want to create something for yourself then do not create it.*

The red intensified and figures appeared in the distance. *I'm not doing it on purpose!*

*You are not choosing its alternative on purpose. Your earthly pattern yet tempts you with its familiarity even as it torments you with its outcome.* She was as calm as I was panicked.

I reached for her again and the red disappeared.

*Now that we don't vibrate so slowly as to be physical the effects of thought are immediate,* Integrity informed me. *You may create a hell for yourself as easily as you may experience the truth of All That Is. I would that you re-examine the incarnation we have just left. With me. Not with the pattern that yet has a place in your energy.*

*Do we have to?*

*No. But until we do you will continue to conjure your idea of hell for yourself.* The grey became tinged with red once more.

*Come.* Integrity's warmth and light beckoned me and I fled to her.

We perceived my birth, my infancy, my childhood, my parents' loss and its effects on my childhood and adulthood, my bonding with Integrity, my relationship with her, my friendships with the Horse-Bonded and their horses, and all of the choices I had made along the way. Threads that linked me with some in my life had become fainter as our soul agreements with one another were fulfilled. Threads that linked me with others had become more solid as either my actions or theirs took us further away from fulfilling the agreements our souls had made before we incarnated. Those threads would pull us together again until our energies balanced and we could move on to other challenges. The process was neither good nor bad nor happy nor sad, it just was, and we all learnt much along the way.

Integrity began to move through the greyness and I moved easily with her. When we collided with Peace, we moved serenely onward with him for a while before parting ways. When Shann rammed us playfully from the side, we folded ourselves around him, joyfully taking him with us awhile before releasing him into his next incarnation as Victor of Supreme City, where the reminder of the importance of truth he had just absorbed from my perusal of my life would prove useful to him. Then we found Noble and I immediately sensed the agreement with Quinta that he had fulfilled and that would drive her on to be an example to those we had left behind. I should have been there to help her, to help them all.

*Yet we are not. We are here,* we observed as one. The redness that had begun to approach us receded again and all was greyness. *We have observed the truth. We see the threads that yet bind us.*

The strongest of them ran between Integrity and myself; our agreement was the oldest of those I had outstanding, and had the most energy associated with it. The next linked me with both Amarilla and Infinity, as if they were a single soul with two slightly distinguishable halves. I understood. I had agreed to help them bring change and I still could. I still would. Four more threads linked me to the souls of the four Woeful I had hindered. I knew how to make my energy balance with theirs.

Noble peeled away from us, the final part of his agreement to tempt me away from truth complete.

*You are adjusting well to our return to the oneness,* Integrity told me.

*Considering the state I was in when my body died?*

*Regardless of that. You could have chosen to remain in your worst creation with your shame and regret but you have processed it and now see the way forward.*

*It's easy to do that here. Which is why we all choose to try to do it there. It's too easy here. I know what I need to do in my next incarnation but I'm worried I won't be able to do it again.*

*Were there no challenge then there would be no learning as you have already remembered. With each incarnation the energy associated with a pattern gets stronger.*

*So how will I clear it? If I couldn't do it when it was weaker, how will I do it now I've made it stronger?*

*By choosing an incarnation which involves a similar set of circumstances to those in that which you have left but where the stakes are higher. Where there is a greater level of perceived risk and pressure but where you will have a greater level of support.*

At the very thought, new threads burst out from me in search of those who would be prepared to help me. They all found the souls with whom an agreement would be mutually beneficial; that would give them, as well as me, the opportunity to experience in the physical world all that we wanted in order to learn and evolve.

One thread in particular hummed with opportunity. I was fascinated by it and by the fact that the soul to which it was connected had more threads extending to other souls than any other. I was further fascinated by the fact that although incarnate, the soul was aware of my interest. Not aware, I corrected myself, but Aware. The distinction had its own energy, which was familiar; I had agreed to help Awareness enter the human collective consciousness in the incarnation I had just left – it was the change that Amarilla and Infinity were introducing to The New. That was difficult enough. Introducing a version of it to The Old would be that much harder, but this soul could be the difference between me succeeding and failing.

Immediately, I perceived the incarnation that would give me the opportunity – that included all of those who had accepted the threads extending out from me. It would give me both the level of challenge I would need to clear my pattern of clinging to that which I believed external to me in place of acknowledging my inner power and strength, and the support to do it in return for assistance I could provide.

The threads linking me with Amarilla, Infinity, the four Woeful and Tania all glowed brighter as they rejoiced with me in our decision to work together. They were all Aware! All of them were incarnate yet all of them sensed Integrity and me, and knew of the challenge we would undertake together. I felt their excitement, their anticipation as if it were my own – which it was.

Integrity and I whooped and swooped with joy. We would rest a while, fly the oneness until we had fully recovered from the efforts of our recent incarnations.

*One of the greatest challenges of incarnating as a human is the associated belief in separation from All That Is,* I remembered even as Integrity framed the thought. *Once Awareness of the truth has been achieved then both living and dying are much more straightforward.*

I pulled myself slightly apart from her, which felt strange and at odds with whom I was remembering myself to be, but as I wanted so that I could tell her, *Thank you for being Integrity, for showing me how to find the truth in my lifetime as Son of The New. Thank you for helping me to die, to adjust and for being with me now.* With that discharged from my soul, I had no need to be Newson ever again.

We returned to our whooping and swooping, often collecting other souls who added to our joy and exuberance before peeling away to answer an enquiring thread, to incarnate, or to welcome and rehabilitate a returning soul. We were overjoyed when Adam and Peace collected us in their celebration of Adam having released his body following a highly successful incarnation, the four of us continuing the celebrations until the two of them were moved to show themselves in the lives of those we had all left.

Integrity and I observed with interest as the sight of the two of them, and the peace they constantly radiated, gave Aleks the time and energy to act out of love and leave his body for the Woeful younglings so desperate for the deaths of him and his friends. We pulled far away so that as he, Amarilla, their friends and horses all found themselves in the greyness, we would not act as a distraction. We had played our parts in that lifetime and we would leave it be.

When the souls of my parents joined us for a time, our reunion was joyous and held no regrets. They had indeed been trapped by the tide and drowned, exactly as they had planned before incarnating, and both had incarnated since and released the fear of water and guilt at leaving me, with which the experience of drowning had left them. We celebrated their achievements and the pattern that they had awakened in me from a previous incarnation, and when we moved apart they left me with a burst of light and love in celebration of my determination to clear it on my next attempt. Gran's soul was incarnate, and when we came across its anchor in the oneness, I was glad that her success at raising a daughter in extremely difficult conditions was helping her sense of failure, carried with her from her incarnation with me, to fade.

We brushed past multitudes of souls with whom we had incarnated before and each time, the lessons we had learnt from one another were remembered and celebrated. When I was finally full of my time in the oneness, I felt myself drawing away slightly from the soul who had incarnated as Integrity even as she pulled slightly away from me.

*It is time,* we agreed.

She streamed away from me and immediately infused into the body of a filly still forming in her mother's womb, making it easier for me to plunge into the still developing body of a baby boy.

## Chapter Thirteen

*I* gasp as the blinding white light fades, and try to focus on Tania, who adds her other hand to the one that already grips mine. 'It's okay, Nathan, I'm still here. Just breathe.'

The quad bike rider looks between us both in confusion, which is nothing compared with mine.

'How did I…' I begin to whisper.

'There's no time for that,' Tania interrupts in a low voice. 'You remember now.'

Integrity. Infinity. Amarilla. Tania. I am here to do what I couldn't do before. What I wouldn't do before, I correct myself. I nod. 'I do. But Honour…'

'Is still honouring her side of your agreement,' Tania says. Warmth blasts from her hands into mine and spreads throughout my body.

I feel calmer and more accepting, a little more like I did while in the oneness. Everything was so simple there though. Here, our horses are being taken from us. When last I faced this challenge, it was my friend's horse being taken away. This time it is Honour. This time it is the horse I now know to be my Integrity.

I take an involuntary step towards the quad bike rider, who has begun to sink back down onto his seat. He is back standing on his pedals in an instant, ready to spring on me. If he does, I'll die. I'll make the same mistake in this incarnation as I did in my last. Tania's warmth intensifies and I search my mind for my memories of Integrity – and find that which she instilled into me. If I'm to help bring change, I have to live. I have to allow not just Honour, but my honour, to be taken. Again. I step back. It is the most painful step I have ever taken.

*You've done what's right instead of what's easy.* Tania smiles up at me. *Your Gran was a wise woman.*

*How am I...*

*Hearing me? Because you haven't remembered that you can't.*

A thought occurs to me and I reach for my horse. *Integrity? I mean, Honour?*

*Searching For Truth.* She is trotting out of the newly erected city gates.

*Integrity. I know you now.*

*And you know yourself,* she observes. *All will be well.*

I take another step back from the quad bike and turn away from its rider, who revs his bike, trying to provoke me. I turn my back on him and walk away. *How did I remember all that in, what, seconds?*

*The same way you have reincarnated into a lifetime that appears to be taking place before your previous one,* Tania replies, keeping hold of my hand in just one of hers now as she walks beside me. *All time is now.*

*Like in the oneness.* I feel a sudden homesickness for it; for the ease of being there, the togetherness, the knowledge I had while I was there that already seems a little fuzzy.

*Exactly. Your memory of being there is already beginning to fade, but you'll remember who I am to you, who Integrity is to you, and most importantly, who you are to you. You're Newson and all of your incarnations, but most importantly, you're Nathan. You've learnt from your other incarnations, and now you're here not just because you need to be, but because you're needed. The horses have attracted here, to this centre, some of those who are capable of helping you to resist the energy of The Old, and they need a leader – someone who can encourage the sensitivity they already possess, and who can stoke it within those we have yet to find.*

My mind spins with everything she is telling me. I try to relate it to that which I can remember of my previous life and the choices I made whilst in the oneness, frantically grabbing hold of details of both in an attempt to prevent them from slipping away from me as I sense myself becoming rooted in my current lifetime once more. My parents flicker into my mind and I remember that they died trying to help others. I am their son. I may live in The Old but I am a son of The New.

*I need to form a resistance,* I affirm to myself as well as Tania, *and I need to get everyone who's been coming here to visit the horses to help me. But how will we do it? None of us would have made it this far without the horses, and now they've been taken from us.* Grief catches at my throat and my eyes fill with tears, but I blink them away as anger begins to churn in my belly.

*The horses will stay just beyond the wall, out of sight but close enough for you to get to once I have the means in place,* Tania tells me. *You'll all be able to visit them for the support you need, but first things first. This centre and its land have been requisitioned.* She takes the piece of paper that was given to her by the police from where she folded and secreted it in her breast pocket, and flaps it. *I have a list here of everything they expect us to do before we vacate the property, and we'll need help. You need to convince everyone to come every day as they're used to doing, and help us clear up and out, so that we can keep them calm and plan. Here comes Helen now, I'll have her and everyone else assemble in the house while you go and change your trousers. When I release your hand, you won't feel as calm as you do now but you'll retain the Awareness I've wakened in you. You'll be able to communicate with me, Integrity, and anyone else who is Aware of you. Remember that, Nathan. Whatever happens, remember who you are and what you're here to do. Remember who I am and that I'm here to help you.*

Helen hobbles up to us as fast as her spindly and slightly bowed legs will carry her, bending over the sticks she is now forced to use and wheezing so hard, I'm worried she'll keel over. 'I couldn't… get… here… in time,' she gasps, 'I was… up… at… the… far… end.'

Tania releases my hand and rushes to Helen's side, telling her, 'Not to worry, it wouldn't have made any difference, in fact it would have made things worse.' She grasps the old lady's elbow to support her and almost immediately, Helen appears more stable and a little less likely to collapse. And I am suddenly very aware of my sodden trouser leg and the smell emanating from it. Tania comes to my rescue as heat floods my face and neck, saying to Helen, 'The police have taken the horses and there's nothing we can do about it for now. We'll gather the others and go to the house, and Nathan will be along in a few minutes.' She winks at me – or tries to. One eye closes more tightly than the other, but they both definitely close, giving her a comical appearance. I almost smile.

Tania helps a now sobbing Helen towards the two-storey, red brick house that has been her home for the past thirty years,

waving to those now flooding into the yard from where they were
tending the horses in the fields, to follow them.

I am left standing alone. My acceptance of the situation flees
as Tania warned me it would, and is replaced by all of my old fear
– and a whole lot more besides. A darkness lashes at me,
wounding me with every strike as it encircles me, taunting me
with its ability to hold me prisoner inside my body. Not content
with that, it penetrates my skin and spreads within me like poison,
trying to make me its own.

Terror grips my stomach and spreads, clutching hold of my
diaphragm so that I feel as if I can't breathe, then my jaw, which
clamps shut so that I can't scream even if I could find the breath.

Where I have always been affected by the madness and
violence with which I am surrounded, they have always lurked at
the periphery of my senses, threatening to take me if I let them in
but kept at bay by my refusal to acknowledge them, and by the
peace I have always managed to feel when around the horses.
Now that I am fully Aware of the energy of The Old, I have no
defences against it.

*Remember.* The thought is so faint that I wonder if I've
imagined it; if I've finally gone insane. I grasp hold of it just in
case.

*Integrity?*

The second I choose her over the insanity of The Old, it is not
only she who infuses me, pushing the malevolence out, but all of
the other horses too. They're with her! It's just like Tania said, our
horses are all together, just outside the city gates – well, the far
side of the hill that is a short distance beyond the city gates,
anyway. They're grazing in the valley. They have water from a
nearby stream and they even have shelter in the form of a huge,
three-sided barn left empty when the farmers who owned it were
forced to surrender their livestock and abandon their farm.

*They have everything they need,* agrees Tania, *as do we. We just have to get organised.* Her words have what I can sense is their desired effect, and I finally manage to get myself moving towards the barn.

*I'm here to help,* I remind myself. *However hard it is, I have to help.* I remember that which Integrity has just helped me to stave off, and shudder. Being Aware makes things harder as well as easier.

*It does make everything seem more acute,* Tania tells me while also settling Helen into a chair, answering those hysterically firing questions at her, and having a mental conversation with... Will. He's her father, and... Amarilla's nephew. All of a sudden, I'm Aware of Amarilla and Infinity observing me with amusement. Who else is Aware of me? Who else witnessed me peeing my pants?

*As it happens, I missed that bit,* Amarilla tells me. Only it isn't just Amarilla, it's both she and Infinity, but with more of a sense of Amarilla than her Bond-Partner. *Only we, Will and Tania are directly Aware of you, Nathan, no one else can sense what they perceive to be the past and future. They can pick up varying amounts of what we're Aware of in your time, but only if we leave them unhidden.*

Relief allows me to ponder my Awareness of her. *You're different from when I was with you both last. Infinity is... oh, I'm sorry.*

*Infinity is now discarnate while I'm incarnate,* Amarilla agrees. *Don't be sorry, Fin chose to be as she is so she'd be in a better position to help, just like you did. We're here for you, Nathan. You've chosen a difficult path but we're all here for you, Fin and I, Integrity, Will and Tania. You've got this, just as soon as you change your trousers.* Her teasing lifts rather than embarrasses or annoys me, which is strange as I'm a twenty-five-year-old man and she's just a sixteen-year-old girl... except she isn't. She's nearly as old as Helen, which makes sense if Tania is her great-niece. Some other things begin to make sense too.

*You achieved Awareness without me, you achieved the change you and Infinity were trying to bring about, without needing my help,* I observe as I climb the wooden stairs of the barn to the hayloft, where I keep clothes and often sleep at weekends if there's a lot of work to be done at the centre.

*You helped us at the beginning of our journey together, when it mattered the most,* Amarilla tells me. *You played the part you were meant to play, just as you're doing now. If you ever get changed, of course.*

I frown, trying to remember when and how I helped them, and failing as my previous incarnation becomes ever fainter in my mind.

*That is as it should be.* It is Infinity who counsels me now. *Your attention is needed in your present. Anything else may act as a distraction. That includes your Awareness. It will serve you to commit yourself to focusing on that which is immediately before you.*

I sigh. *My trousers. Got it.*

I peel my current pair off along with my underwear, wrinkling my nose as I drop them into a pile as far from my sleeping bag as possible. Selecting replacements from a bag hanging from a cross beam, I quickly descend to the ground floor of the barn, where there is a tap at the far end. I quickly wash and re-dress, noticing as I do that I feel cleaner than the change of clothes alone should account for.

*You have more protection now against that which has plagued you since you were born,* Integrity informs me and I am Aware again of my connection with her helping me to keep the malevolence of The Old at bay. *So long as you continue to choose*

*your bond with me over that which would convince you of its
power then you will feel as you do now.*

*Thank you for helping me before I knew who you are to me.*

*You knew.*

I think back to the first time I met her. It's true, I recognised
her love and kindness without having any clue as to how that
could be possible. I feel lighter still. Integrity has stuck with me
through everything, even different lifetimes. While I find that I
can now remember little about our previous one together, I know
it happened and that we both died and were reborn at a time that
has enabled us to be here together now. I smile as I walk across
the yard to the house.

'Well, that's better,' Tania calls out from where she's holding
open the back door. 'Come on in, everyone's waiting for you.'

*What shall I say to them?* I ask as I take the door from her and
follow her inside.

*The truth. Happily, this place hasn't been judged a necessary
candidate for any surveillance, so you can speak freely.*

*And you know this because…*

*My Awareness exceeds yours.*

*So then why do I need to be the leader of the resistance? It
seems to me that you should be, and I'll just help you.*

Tania grins at me over her shoulder as we enter Helen's
enormous kitchen. *I'm more of an instigator than a leader. I'll be
here as long as you need me and then I'll be off to cause trouble
somewhere else. Be yourself, Nathan, you're everything they and
this city need.*

Everyone is staring at me.

*What have you told them?* I ask Tania.

*Just that nothing is as bad as it seems, and that you know of a
way forward for them all. The floor is yours.* Tania jumps up onto
the end of a kitchen counter that runs along one wall, joining those

already sitting on it and the long counters lining two of the other walls. Helen and eleven others sit at chairs around the table, leaving me the only one still standing.

I look around at them all and count twenty-five plus Tania and me. 'Well, I guess at least having our horses chased away on a Sunday morning means that we're all here to talk about what happens next,' I say.

'How can you possibly see that as a positive thing?' Shauna replies, her voice weak and trembling. Like most here apart from Helen, she's younger than I, and like everyone apart from Tania, her pale face is blotchy and tear-stained. She scrapes her fingers through her black, cropped hair, and rubs her eyes.

I check for Integrity and find her where she's always been. I take a deep breath and say, 'Because it is.' I raise my hands as a multitude of voices object. 'No, wait, let me talk.' When they continue to gabble with an increasing level of hysteria, I find the strength afforded me by the truth of what I am about to say, and raise my voice. 'Let. Me. Speak.'

They quieten down. I am Aware that some of them feel chastened, others are mortified and a few are a little scared.

I soften my tone. 'Helen's horses – our horses – have never been safer than they are now. I can't be the only one who's been too scared to think about what would happen to them when the hay and feed run out now that we can't get any in from the countryside and there's no green space available to grow any, or what would happen when the governors decide to take this place as they now are. Well, now the worst has happened and our horses are absolutely fine. They're just over the hill beyond the gates, they have grazing, water and shelter, and they're no longer at risk of being shot. What they are, is as ready to help us cope with living here as they've always been.'

'How can you possibly know all of that?' Shauna says. I sense her desperation to believe me vying with her feeling of utter hopelessness now that Tango, the horse who has been her lifeline for the past four years, has been taken from her.

My interest in that of which I am Aware about Shauna extends to everyone else in the room. Aside from Tania and Helen, I sense little vigour or verve in any of them, not even the smallest hint of desire to fight the regime that has taken our choices, and now our horses, from us.

*We will need to look elsewhere for those like Helen,* Tania agrees. *You're looking a little vacant, Nathan. Remember what Infinity told you and don't allow your Awareness to be a distraction. Carry on talking but as you do, notice what these people have rather than what they lack.*

I blink a couple of times. Everyone is staring at me. 'Um, sorry, what was that, Shauna? How do I know the horses are okay and waiting for us?' I glance at Tania, who gives the faintest of nods. 'Because I'm Aware of them. I know that Int... I mean, Honour, is grooming with Shandy.' I gaze at eighteen-year-old Alanna, who is devoted to my horse's preferred grooming partner, and hold eye contact with her until she brightens a little. 'I know that Rocket and George are currently drinking from a stream.' I look between Saul and Primrose, who have become close to one another as a result of Rocket and George's pair bond. They both lean towards me a little as they stare back. I work my way around each and every person there, telling them what the horses they have taken on as their own are currently doing.

No one challenges me or tells me I'm being fanciful or ridiculous. No one speaks at all and as I continue relating their horses' activities, I am Aware of why. They believe me. Not because they are desperate to, though they are, but because they sense I'm telling them the truth. It's as if a small part of them reaches out to the words I'm speaking and wraps around them, drawing them inside where they almost seem able to taste them, to know whether they are true or false. By the time I've spoken to all but Helen, the atmosphere in the room has changed from barely contained hysteria to anticipation for what I will say next.

Helen, however, is a mass of grieving, simmering anger. Her eyes, which have become almost colourless in recent years, now appear to have regained some of their old green as they fix on me, daring me to say that her thirty-seven-year-old mare, Silver, is fit and well and enjoying her new utopic life.

Helen has been like a second mother to all of us, never asking for anything in return for allowing us the company of the horses who have kept us alive. I don't want to hurt her with the truth. Integrity pushes at me from within and I know that I have to. Helen isn't reaching out to me, ready to capture and examine my words as did the others; she isn't that sensitive, but she's sensitive enough and she knows me well. If I lie to her, she'll know, and that will cause her almost as much pain as that which I can sense she already knows. My stomach wrenches around on itself as I tell myself, *Do what's right, not what's easy.*

I hold Helen's challenging gaze. 'Silver's passed on,' I say as gently as I can. 'She made it as far as the gates, but collapsed just outside them. They have a machine out there now, digging a hole to bury her in. I'm so sorry.'

Immediately, the two sitting closest to Helen leave their seats and rush to her side. Still grasping her sticks, she puts a hand out to either side, holding them away. Her face is wet with tears as she gets to her feet, her eyes retaining the hint of colour that appeared with Silver's passing. 'I couldn't have shared thirty-six years of my girl's life with her and not known when she left it,' she announces to us all, almost in a whisper. 'I didn't need you to tell me she's gone, Nathan, but I'm glad you did.' She clears her throat and her voice is a little stronger as she continues, 'Now, you said that the rest of the horses are ready to carry on helping everyone here to cope with living in this hellhole. Since they can't get in here to us, I imagine that means we'll be needing to find a way to get out there to them, and for some reason, I'm finding myself in no doubt whatsoever that this new you standing before us all knows exactly how we're going to do it.'

My heart swells with love and admiration for the woman whose strength, courage and determination to continue helping us all is greater than ever, despite the grief I can feel battering her from within.

'Silver's with you, Helen,' I manage to say. 'She's left her body, but she hasn't left you.' My voice breaks as I realise that the same goes for me; I am Aware of my parents' love, their pride in me as they observe the person I'm trying to become.

Helen nods at me and manages to smile. Then she raises her eyebrows as she always does when expecting an answer.

'Yes, er, sorry, you wanted to know how we're going to get out of the gates to see our horses,' I say and tell Tania, *You need to take over.*

*It's important that they get used to looking to you for the answers they need, and that you get used to looking for those answers where they can always be found,* Tania replies. She holds my attention until I've picked up all of the information I need from her.

'Okay,' I say, 'so Tania and her dad are going to create tunnels under the wall in lots of different places, so we can vary where we leave. We'll also need to vary when, so we don't create any kind of routine that'll draw attention. The first tunnel will come out on the far side of the hill beyond the city gates, exactly where the horses are at the moment. All of the other tunnels will also end in spots where we won't be observed leaving them, but we'll have to figure out how to get to the entrances on this side of the wall without being caught – oh, hang on, I know how to do that.' I stop and turn to Tania with a frown. *There are others already doing this? In other cities? Are they Aware of me like I'm Aware of them?*

She smiles sweetly. *Don't get distracted by your Awareness. Concentrate on what's in front of you.*

*Well it's flipping well hard when there's so much else...*

*No one said it was easy, just that it's necessary.*

'How?' Saul asks me.

'Huh?'

'How will we get to the wall, to the tunnel entrances, without being shot?' Though he's racked with terror at the very thought, he doesn't doubt anything I've said. Part of him wants to know how it might be possible to get to his horse, the rest of him is adamant he won't be going anywhere near the wall.

'The same way you've all known I've been telling you the truth, despite how ridiculous it's sounded,' I say, looking around at them all. 'By using your sensitivity. Thanks to Helen, all of us here have come to trust that when we're with the horses, we're safe. How did we know that? None of them could tell us that if we opened ourselves to them, to what we felt for them and from them, we'd be immune to the vileness that bombards us everywhere else; we reached out to them instinctively. We sensed that they were our only refuge and we've hung on to that sense. You sensed I was telling you the truth when I told you your horses are alive and waiting for you, and you sense it now. We've all been using our sensitivity instinctively. The time has come to use it intentionally – to practise sensing when we're being observed and when there are those nearby whose energy doesn't resonate with ours.'

'I can do that already,' Alanna says. She flushes red when

everyone turns to look at her, but I sense her relief when many of them nod in agreement.

'That's great. When do you do it?' I ask her.

'When I'm on my way here. I'm always scared someone will follow me, and I don't want to draw attention to myself by keep turning around, so I make sure I always know if someone's watching me. It's horrible at home, I can feel them watching me and my family through the wallscreen.' She shudders.

Helen waves one of her sticks. 'This is all very well. I've had lots of kids and young adults come to my yard over the years and I've always been able to recognise which of you would stick around; the horses have always told me by their responses to you all. Those of you here now are different from everyone else, me included, and now that Nathan's put words to it, I get what it is the horses have always sensed in you. I accept what you can do and actually, I think it's more than possible that we've only just touched the surface of it. But am I the only one who thinks it strange that Tania and her dad – who I believe wasn't able to reach our "City Of Glory" before the wall was finished and the gates locked last week – are planning on digging tunnels under the wall? Without being seen? And not short ones either, if their exits are going to be out of sight? Even if you had the machinery and engineering knowledge to do that, Tania, which I can't believe you do, it doesn't seem possible.'

Tania grins. 'It wasn't so much that Dad couldn't reach the city in time, as that he was otherwise occupied.' She leans towards the centre of the kitchen and tries to wink conspiratorially. 'He keeps disappearing with his horse for days on end and it's driving Mum mad.' She sits up straight again. 'He'll meet me outside the wall when we're ready to begin excavating, but I'm afraid that won't be until tomorrow. Nathan and I have a few things to organise first.'

Helen shakes her head. 'In the five weeks you've been here, Tania, I've come to appreciate that you're a far more capable young woman than your years should suggest. But trying to get out over the wall on your own to meet your father? That's foolhardy, not to mention impossible, as those who've already been shot for trying would assure you were they able.'

Tania says, 'Well, this is the first time I've done this in front of so many people at once, but I have faith in you all that you won't panic; the sensitivity your horses have encouraged in you should see you through. Hold tight, and please, no one scream. We might not have cameras and bugs here but we soon will if anyone walking past hears anything suspicious. Back in a tick.'

She disappears. Just ceases to be sitting on the counter beside Saul, as if she never was. Mouths open but before anyone can say or do anything, she reappears. Saul jumps so violently, he slides off the counter and lands in a crouch at Tania's feet. She jumps down beside him and offers him her hand, telling him, 'That wasn't the most sensible re-appearance I've ever made. Sorry.'

I sense the burst of light she sends through their contact, and Saul's instant reaction to it. A smile replaces the shock on his face and he says, 'Is this a dream? It feels real, but I'm beginning to think it can't be.'

Tania chuckles. 'You want to be glad my dad isn't here, he delights in tying people up in knots with his answers to that question. Suffice to say that you're awake and rapidly becoming more so. Dad and I can increase the vibration of our physical energy until it matches the part of us that is physically insubstantial. Then we can slow it down again somewhere else – or in this case, right where I was when I sped it up. When I'm ready to, I'll take myself outside the wall to meet Dad, who'll get there in the same way. We'll excavate the tunnels by resonating our energy with the earth and moving it with the strength of our joint intention. We'll create and move metal supports into the tunnels in a similar way so that they'll be safe for you all to use. We'll work from the far end, so no one on this side of the wall, or on top of it come to that, will have a clue we're doing it. Any questions?'

'Yes,' Helen says. 'Who are you, exactly? You're a good person, the horses have already let me know that, but where are you from and why are you here?'

Tania doesn't flinch as she says, 'I'm from the future in order to continue helping those of you who'll ensure it exists.'

No one speaks. No one moves. Everyone except Helen can feel that Tania is telling the truth and they have absolutely no idea what to do with it. For my part, I remain quiet as I fit Tania's display, explanation and admission with the memories they draw up from deep within me.

She's using her Awareness in ways I can barely grasp, even with her explanation. But her description of moving earth and creating supports from metal, I understand. Tania and her dad are Metal-Singers, like I was. But they're Earth-Singers too?

Tania grins at me. *We have Adam and Amarilla to thank for that. We can all do all of the Skills now, and we don't need to sing out loud, which is fortunate when excavating secret tunnels.*

Helen bustles around the table towards Tania, unsteady on her legs even with her sticks, her determination making up for her lack of co-ordination. When she reaches Tania, she stares at her, attempting to see the truth that the rest of us can sense.

When she eventually takes a step back, she says, 'You said you're continuing to help. Who else have you helped?'

'Those in other cities who were chosen by their horses in the same way your horses have chosen you,' Tania replies. 'The horses know what they're doing.' She looks past Helen at all of those still seated. 'They have chosen all of you for your sensitivity.' She looks back at Helen. 'Silver chose you for the same reason many other horses who have just been evicted from their livery yards chose their people; for the kindness, strength and determination you and your Kindred Spirits combine with sensitivity to overcome the fear that overwhelms everyone else. Sensitives and Kindred Spirits are both needed if you're all to resist the regime that will otherwise crush you.'

While Tania is speaking, I am Aware of the first city dwellers she helped coming to the forefront of her mind. Pamela is to them as Tania would have me be to those in this room and those we have yet to find. There are sixty-four people and horses at the core of Pamela's resistance. Eight groups of eight. I'm almost blown off my feet by the power that surges through me as I become Aware of what that means. They have the energy of infinity. No, they ARE the energy of infinity. They work individually at their tasks but they are connected to one another within and between their groups, and the energy that flows between and from them is self-perpetuating.

*We need to be sixty-four if we're to be as unstoppable as they are,* I observe, *half of us Sensitives and half Kindred Spirits, as you call them.*

*That's not necessary,* Tania replies. *Pamela's was the first group Dad and I worked with. Its energy fuels the pattern which calls to you and everyone else here – the Sensitives in this room would never have been as open to their sensitivity as they are if it weren't already doing so. So long as the sixty-four continue to exist as they are, it's unnecessary for the infinity energy to be created anywhere else; infinity is infinity, there can be no more of it due to multiplication.*

*The pattern?* I shudder involuntarily as I remember the one I have been trying to leave behind me for so long. *Which pattern are they fuelling?*

*The pattern for living according to The Way Of The Horse,*
Tania tells me. *You'll like this one.* She finishes speaking out loud
to the others and there is silence as everyone digests her words.

Then Helen says, 'I'm in. What do you need me to do?'

Tania looks at me. 'Nathan?'

I combine that of which I am Aware with that which Tania told
me I needed to do, and think on my feet.

'For now, Helen, it's important that you please organise
everyone here to help you clear and pack everything up according
to the requirements on that list.' I point to the paper Tania has left
on the kitchen table, then look around at everyone. 'Let what
we've told you sink in and don't behave in any way that will lead
anyone to think you're doing anything other than helping Helen
follow those instructions. Over the coming days, go to work as
normal and come here as normal.

'We have twenty-four Sensitives here and only one Kindred
Spirit.' I nod at Helen, who raises her eyebrows at me. 'Okay, um,
maybe two, including me, although I'm kind of... anyway, Tania
and I will need to go and find enough Kindred Spirits to give you
guys the support you'll need in order to be able to do as your
horses want you to. When we have everyone, we'll be back. Any
questions?'

'Yes,' Helen says, sticking her chin out. 'What are the two of
you still doing here?'

Tania chuckles and backs out of the door, her hands lifted in
surrender. I rush to hug Helen, who hugs me back firmly before
pushing me away and nodding towards the door. I hurry out onto
the yard.

'So,' I say to a waiting Tania, 'we need to go to the remaining
livery yards, where presumably there'll be people as devastated as
everyone here was, and identify which of them were selected by
their horses to be Kindred Spirits. Catchy name for them, by the

way. I guess they'll be obvious to your Awareness even if they aren't to mine?'

'They'll be obvious to both, not least because their horses are waiting for them outside the city gates with those from here, while the rest have taken off and are heading for pastures as far away from humans as possible.'

'Huh?' I reach for Integrity and am instantly Aware of all the horses in her recently expanded herd, rather than just those who left the city with her, as I was before. 'Huh. Awareness is confusing.'

'You're managing it pretty well considering you came to it in the middle of a situation,' Tania says as we walk towards the yard gates which still hang open.

'A situation? I nearly died. Again. The details are fading as you said they would, but I remember that much.'

'Aren't you glad you chose to live?' Tania says, beginning to skip. 'Come on, this'll be fun.'

# Chapter Fourteen

*I* still find it strange, even after so many years, to leave the peace of the yard by walking straight onto a busy street. When I first came to the centre, this was a tree-lined road with fields on both sides. Now, the trees are no more and the fields are home to high rise apartment blocks. Back around the corner, where Integrity saved me from the police on the day my parents were murdered, is the only stretch of road for miles that isn't shaded by the monstrous grey buildings in which we have gradually all been forced to live. My heart sinks as I realise that soon, it will be as grey and miserable as everywhere else.

'It's a fair walk to the closest yard, we could take a PV,' Tania says cheerfully, pointing to a waiting passenger vehicle.

'Errr, you're not from here.' Though I don't doubt it, I can't bring myself to actually say out loud that she's from the future. 'The PV won't move until all of its occupants have had their identities checked by eye and hair scanners, and you aren't in the city's database. Go anywhere near the scanners and there'll be riot police here before either of us can blink.'

'The scanners won't want to check me if they don't know I'm inside the PV, will they?'

I shake my head and chuckle. 'You can make yourself weightless and invisible. Fair enough, we'll take PVs later on then, but are you okay to walk to the first yard? I could do with some time to clear my head, and besides, I don't think it'll be very long before we don't have the choice of walking.'

'Fair enough.' We begin to wend our way between everyone else hurrying along the pavement. *You're right, by the way. They'll take away the option to go anywhere other than by PV so they can constantly monitor and log your movements. It'll make your mission far more difficult, but you'll find ways around it.*

*Our mission being to help victims of the regime, and recruit more people like us where we can,* I reply. *Like the sixty-four are already doing.*

As I think of them, I am Aware of their high level of organisation, their infiltration of government departments that allows them to offer clandestine help and support, whether it be – in the case of the Kindred Spirits, or the Kindred as they are now known – gathering and distributing food, medicine and clothing to the elderly, whose rations are otherwise drastically reduced in the hope they will perish more rapidly; sabotaging government surveillance systems and research into methods of gaining ever more control over the city's inhabitants; or even helping those most at risk to escape the city and take their chances alone.

The Sensitives support the efforts of the Kindred dotted across the city by passing telepathic messages between them via their horses, helping them to evade the guards patrolling the city walls so that they can visit their horses, and offering friendship and their horses' counsel to anyone open to and in need of it. While I admire the willingness, the determination, even, of the sixty-four to put themselves at risk in order to help others and undermine the city governors' control, I have a strong sense of that which is at the root of everything they do.

'The Way Of The Horse,' I say out loud, then flinch and surreptitiously look around myself to check that no passers by are showing any reaction to my words. *Their horses have helped them to feel connected to one another, to trust their intuition, to be kind, forgiving and resilient. You're right, I like it. It's daunting, though, knowing what they've achieved and thinking about doing the same.*

*They didn't get there in a day,* Tania tells me, *they were riding their horses together for years before they were ready to accept what the Sensitives of this city took in today. They've speeded up the process for all of you who are following in their wake, and those in other cities who've already begun to follow the pattern they established have speeded it up even more – as will you and your friends here. Don't worry about the future, focus on the present and the reason we're going to give anyone who is watching and listening to the people on the yards we'll be visiting, for why we're there.*

*Hmmm, good point. We could always say that our horses have been taken and we have to clear the yard in a hurry, and are wondering whether anyone wants to take any of our equipment? The police didn't tell us that all of the horses have been run out of the city, just that they were taking ours, so there are no lies in there.*

'Yep, that'll work,' Tania murmurs. 'Time to test the theory,' she adds as two policewomen appear in front of us, one of them swinging a baton menacingly at a man scurrying away from her. Judging by his level of dishevelment, he's just been searched.

'What are you two doing wandering the streets on a Sunday morning?' the baton swinger demands, her tone suggesting that she has already decided. I am Aware that, having been humiliated by her superior in front of her colleagues at the beginning of her shift, she is desperate to feel less small by humiliating everyone who crosses her path today.

'Our horses have just been run out of the city and we have to clear the yard, so we're just visiting other livery yards to see if any of them have a use for our stuff,' I say.

'PVs not good enough for you?' the other policewoman says. 'Turn around, hands against the wall and spread your legs.'

I grit my teeth. I've been the subject of numerous body searches before, all under the pretext of searching for illegal weapons and substances that could compromise the safety of my fellow citizens, but usually because the police in question just happen to feel like it. I've been groped and assaulted in the process, in attempts to get me to resist and give them a reason to arrest or abuse me further, but so far I've survived them all. Tania hasn't grown up here, she isn't used to this. I can't let them assault her, but I don't know what to do to stop them.

'Problem, is there?' the woman asks. Her partner lifts an eyebrow.

My mind racing, I am about to turn around when Tania takes hold of my hand and moves across in front of me so that I turn with her, giving her strange version of a wink once she is facing away from the policewomen. The warmth from her hand spreads through me, lightening the darkness that had begun to cloud my mind. Everything is okay.

We put our hands against the wall, and Tania finally moves hers away from mine. Immediately, the warmth is gone... except it isn't. It may not be coming from her anymore, but it's still there. Integrity.

*The Way Of The Horse,* I remember. *I have to follow The Way Of The Horse. So, what do I do?*

*Feel your connection with those who would harm you,*

Integrity instructs me. *Feel how you are similar instead of focusing upon how you are different. Help in any way you can. She Who Is will show you.*

The baton swinger holsters her weapon and grabs hold of my hair with one hand while feeling roughly around my neck with the other. I want to turn around and punch her in the face, but I stay with Integrity and remember her advice. I sense what Tania is doing, and smile. Of course, this is how she stopped the policemen assaulting her at the yard earlier. As soon as the other policewoman touched her, Tania began sending her the same warmth – the same light, I realise – that she was sending me when she held my hand. I sense something stir inside the policewoman; it is buried very deeply within her, but it's there and she feels it. She releases her grip on Tania's ear and gently pats down her neck and back.

*How do I do that?* I ask Tania.

*You're Aware of her. You understand the motive for her actions. Empathise with her and send her everything you feel for Integrity. Wherever she touches you, send your love for your horse through the connection. It's as simple as that.*

It may be simple, but it isn't easy. The woman's breath smells as she almost pants onto the side of my face while pinching the skin that covers my ribs. I think of the sixty-four who already follow The Way Of The Horse. I feel their determination, I feel the strength of the pattern they have established... and I am back with Integrity. Light blasts out of me in all directions.

*Just through your connection with her,* Tania tells me, her thought ringing with amusement. *It's visible otherwise and has the potential to create as many problems as it will solve.*

Both policewomen step back from us. 'What the hell was that?' Tania's searcher says.

'I don't know,' mine replies. 'It looked like lightning, but I don't hear any thunder, do you? There aren't even any clouds in the sky.'

'Well, anyway, I'm done, this one's clean.'

There is a tap on my shoulder. 'You're clean too. You can both step away from the wall.'

I can't believe it. My body search is far from over and I doubt Tania's progressed much further than mine. She smiles brightly at the two women and her voice is warm as she says, 'Thank you.'

I sense their confusion. No one looks at them with such an obvious lack of fear – they don't even look at one another that way – and it affects them. I can feel the parts stirring within them again that my and Tania's light awoke. Their faces soften and their shoulders relax so that they feel awkward and unfamiliar, and neither seems to know what to do with their hands. Both women simultaneously link their thumbs through their belts. 'On your way,' Tania's searcher says with the barest hint of a smile.

'Thank you,' I say to them as they move to the side to let us pass. Once we are well clear of them, I begin to let out a deep breath, then hold it as a passer by gives me an odd look.

Tania laughs. 'You're allowed to breathe, you know.'

I let out the remainder of my breath. *That was amazing, I can't believe it just happened. Hopefully they'll go easier on everyone else they stop. Will we show the others how to send light to people here? Not like I just did, obviously, but how you do it? So it's invisible? Wait, the sixty-four don't do it. Why don't they do it? Why didn't you show them how to do it?*

*For the same reason I didn't take them to Awareness or try to teach them – or you – how to drop their physical boundaries and disappear and reappear at will. They aren't ready. You're here fresh from The New, if in an unconventional way, and thanks to Integrity, your soul retained everything you learnt in your incarnation there; you brought that energy with you. You were ready for Awareness, and to find and use the light within you, but, open as they are to the pattern that's calling to them, they're entrenched in The Old. It will take a little help from us and a lot of help from their horses to get them to where they'll be able to do as they need to.*

*Do I tell the other Sensitives that I'm Aware of what they're thinking and feeling? Of what's uppermost in their minds?*

*I find it best to let people figure it out for themselves. A bit of mystery gets them thinking and then feeling their way. It's easier to accept a realisation when you've arrived at it by yourself.*

*And then what? They won't trust me when they know what I can do, I'm invading their privacy.*

*By the time they realise, they'll also have realised that you only ever use what you know to help them. Don't ever pass what you sense on to anyone else, or make light of it, don't even retain it, just pick it up and either discard it or use it and then discard it, just like the Sensitives do when they're using their intuition.*

*Okay, well it was definitely useful back there. It was weird seeing someone in a black uniform as a victim though.*

*Few things are as they seem where humans of The Old are concerned,* Tania observes. *It's good that they bought your explanation of where we're going and why.*

*You were right that we should have taken a PV though, we'll definitely do that once we've been to the first yard.*

*If we ever get there. Like I said, it's a fair walk, I might just meet you there.* Tania punches my arm lightly when I look sideways at her in horror at the thought of her suddenly disappearing from the busy street. *I'm kidding. It's actually a great time for you to practise balancing your Awareness with your sense of everything that's going on around you, so you get used to using both at the same time and not allowing one to distract you from the other. I want you to peruse your Awareness of everyone and everything around you, while also playing I spy.* 'Okay, I spy with my little eye, something beginning with "p".'

My horror changes to bemusement at my companion. Tania is beautiful. As we pass countless others hurrying the other way, I am Aware that there's not one who doesn't remark upon it to themselves. But what I sense from her as she instructs me – what I sensed from her even before I was Aware, I realise all of a sudden – diverts my attention from her physical appearance. Where my eyes form an image of a striking young woman of similar age to me, I sense someone who is... ageless. Someone who carries herself with the bearing of someone very much older yet like no elderly person I've ever known. Someone who speaks with authority, as if she's my superior, whilst teasing and joking. Someone who behaves as if she's invulnerable, powerful, yet incorporates that behaviour into that which is expected of someone of our age so that hindsight is necessary in order to identify it.

As if to prove my point, she whispers, 'Okay, so you know I literally just said that you need to practise balancing your Awareness with your sense of what's going on around you? Well, you're not doing it. Carry on dissecting me in your Awareness if you like, but at the same time, you're looking for something beginning with "p".'

I roll my eyes. 'People.'

She tilts her head sideways towards me and lifts her eyebrows. 'Seriously?'

'Okay then, pillar.'

'Nope.'

*Why can't I pick up the answer in my Awareness?*

*I'm hiding it from you. There are two people who have the tiniest chance of finding anything I hide, and you aren't one of them so don't waste time trying.* 'Guess again, Nathan.'

'Pedestrians.' *Amarilla and your dad can find things you hide!*
'No.' *Yes, sometimes.*
'Post.' *It annoys you that they can do it.*
'No, try again.' *It annoys me that I can't do it back. They never examine anything they find that I've hidden, they just let me know they've found it – but when I know they're hiding something, I can't find it. It's a game between the three of us and I always lose, like you are now.* She squints both eyes shut.

*So, you can't wink and you can't find bits of knowledge that two people in the whole universe hide from you. There are only two things you can't do, and that annoys you?* 'Pigeon.'

*I can wink. There's just one thing I can't do and yes, it bugs me.* 'No, not pigeon.'

A loud bang makes everyone around us jump and crouch down, shielding their heads. I instinctively grab Tania and pull her behind me as laughter erupts. A policeman holsters the gun with which he has just shot the pigeon now lying bleeding at his feet. He points at me. 'You. Clear that up.' He swaggers away, confident that I'll do as he ordered.

Tania reaches the fallen pigeon first. The bird flaps her wings forlornly as Tania picks her up, gently folds her wings to her sides, and tucks her down the front of her coat. I sense the light she sends her – and something else. Where the bird was fading, now she is strong again.

*This way,* Tania tells me and heads for a side street. When we are out of the stream of people scurrying away from the shooting as fast as they can without running, Tania unzips her coat and allows the pigeon to sit in her cupped hands. 'Go up and away, little one,' she breathes, 'and take your family with you, this is no place for you all anymore.'

I sense the energy of her suggestion, if not the words, settling within the healthy bird, who immediately flaps her wings and flies upward until she is but a speck in the sky. A multitude of specks joins her, forming a black cloud which arrows towards the city boundary.

'You healed her without singing, like you said you all can now,' I whisper. 'You removed the bullet and dissolved it, you healed her and you showed her where to take her family. You didn't have to sing because you resonated yourself with her – no, you were her, as well as being you.'

'And you still haven't found something beginning with "p". There's no excuse for being distracted, Nathan, not here where you need your wits about you. Come on.' She grabs the sleeve of my pullover and pulls me back into the throng.

By the time the livery yard gates come into view, I have exhausted my vocabulary of words beginning with "p" and still haven't found what Tania's "little eye" can see. 'I give up.'

'Pupil.'

I frown. 'I suppose you mean me.'

'And the eyes of every single person we passed. You had two meanings to choose from, doubling your chances of getting it. I'm beginning to consider choosing another leader.' Her eyes are bright with mischief and I can't help laughing. 'We should be serious now,' she says, returning to her role as my teacher, 'we'll shortly be on camera and the yard is bugged. Remember that we've just lost our horses and we're as devastated as you were before you knew what you know now. Here.' She hands me some slips of paper. 'These have Helen's address on them. You'll know who to give them to.'

I stuff the slips into the back pocket of my trousers and straighten my face. I picture Integrity and her herd disappearing from sight, and remember how I felt. By the time I sense that we are being watched with intention rather than just noticed by those hurrying past us, I'm suitably sombre. I unlatch the yard gate and hold it open until we are on its other side, wondering who closed it and why, now that there are no horses in danger of escaping onto the road. Force of habit, probably; anyone who has been around horses for any length of time will close an open gate without being aware they're doing it.

We walk up to stables arranged around three sides of a concrete yard, from within many of which emanates the sound of sobbing. Women appear in the doorways of two of the stables, both slamming forkfuls of dung and straw into barrows with far more force than is necessary, before disappearing into the stables again. Tania and I head straight for the two of them and I realise that it isn't only their behaviour that is drawing me to them, but the invisible threads that I am Aware stretch between them and horses in Integrity's expanded herd. No threads any longer connect those sobbing out of sight with the horses taken from them; the agreements that existed between them, whatever they were and for whatever purpose, have been fulfilled.

A forkful of dung comes flying through the nearest of the doorways and lands in its intended barrow, followed by the sound of thumping from within the stable. When we peer inside, a middle-aged woman is beating the remainder of her horse's bed with her pitchfork. Tania nods for me to go on to the next stable, and says, 'Hi, I'm Tania,' to the woman, who flinches and turns around. I sense her terror fading as she sees Tania standing there in place of the police she feared were witness to her temper, which rapidly rises again.

A woman of around thirty slams another forkful of soiled straw into her barrow while glaring at me as if daring me to tell her to take it back out. I sense her channelling her grief, her devastation at having watched helplessly while her horse was taken from her, into fury and a desire for revenge. Her anger swells as she pictures what she would like to do to those who laughed as they hooted the horns of their quadbikes and threw stones at the rapidly retreating backsides of the fifteen horses taken from the yard less than an hour previously, but is replaced by hopelessness as she remembers what will happen to her if she does… which fuels her anger all over again.

'I'm Nathan,' I tell her.

'Good for you.' She disappears into the stable and I follow her in, relieved to sense that I am no longer in view of those watching. They can probably still hear me though.

'I'm from Helen Baxter's yard. We had all of our horses taken this morning and Helen's yard has been requisitioned. We have to clear everything out within the next week, so my friend and I are here to ask if you'd like to come and see if we have anything you need?'

The woman gestures wildly around with her arms. 'Does it look like it? Do you see any horses here? They took ours too, so no, Nathan, you don't have a single thing I need.'

There was a time when I would have been angry at being spoken to like that, but my sense of her devastation leaves me with an overwhelming desire to take her pain away. My love for Integrity blasts out of me and surrounds the woman as a bright white mist. I put my forefinger to my lips as she flinches and then visibly begins to relax.

'I'm sorry,' I say to her. 'I know how hard that would have been for you. So you have to clear out of here too?' I move close to her and whisper, 'Your horse is just outside the city walls along with mine. He's okay, in fact he's better than okay, he's safe and happy. We know how to get out to see the horses. If you want to come with us, here's Helen's address.' I hand her one of Tania's slips of paper. 'Answer my question now, they're listening.'

She glances frantically around at the mist still surrounding her, confused both by its existence and by the effect it's having on her.

'Um, well, yes, obviously,' she manages to say. 'They've requisitioned this place too.'

'You just had the one horse?' I ask, then smile and whisper, 'You still do.'

'Yes, er, just Barney.' At the thought of him, she stands straighter. I sense her gathering her wits.

'Okay, so you won't have too much to clear. If you have time and wouldn't mind helping out some fellow horsey people, Helen's yard is bursting at the seams, she's been there such a long time and has had so many horses and people come and go, you see. If you could spare any time to help us clear everything out, we'd really appreciate it.' I continue in a whisper, 'Your horse has opened you up to be able to feel more than everyone else in this city feels. You can trust me, but don't take my word for it. Hold Barney in your thoughts and then think of me and what's happened here between us. Then if you want to, come to Helen's after work tomorrow. We're not just going to get out to see our horses, we're going to be coming back in again. We're going to defy the regime.'

She lifts her chin and puts her shoulders back as she would if she were sitting astride her horse. 'I'll see what I can do. I'm Maggie.'

I nod. 'I hope to see you again soon, Maggie.' I join Tania back on the yard. 'Well, they don't need any of our stuff here, we'd best hope the next yard still has horses on it,' I say to her.

'They couldn't have taken all of the horses in the city, not all at once, surely?' she says for the benefit of our listeners.

'I guess we'll find out.'

We leave the yard and head for a PV that has pulled off the main rail track to a side track and, having discharged its previous passengers, is ready and waiting for more – although it would be more accurate to say that it's waiting to gather more information on the city's inhabitants, from their pick up and set down points, and the conversations they have whilst inside.

*You're sure about this?* I ask Tania. *It'll know you've entered it and it'll register your absence when you suddenly disappear before having your eyes and hair scanned. That'll be registered as suspicious behaviour and we'll have police raining down us.*

She grins. *I'm sure.*

I press a button by the door on the side of the PV and it opens outward and upward. Tania bends towards its interior and lifts her foot to step inside... and disappears before landing in the vehicle. To anyone on the outside, it will have appeared as if she stepped inside, but there is no beeping from scanners demanding that she place her eye in front of one and her hair against another; the PV is oblivious to her presence.

I hastily step inside and press the button for the door to shut, willing it to close quickly enough that those approaching can't register the absence of the young woman who should be there. I'm relieved when it closes rapidly so that by the time anyone draws level with us, all I can see of them through the doorway is their legs. The door shuts, its tinted glass making the inside of the PV invisible to those outside. I let out the breath I hadn't realised I was holding, and present myself to the scanners whose beeps change from constant, high-pitched and irritating, to just three which are more pleasant and approving.

*Okay, phase one complete. Watch yourself now, we're about to move,* I warn Tania, and immediately sense her amusement.

*I don't need to stay in the PV, you nutter. I'll see you there.*

I key in my destination, feeling a little silly. As I sit down and watch this crazy world of ours flit past the windows, I frown, trying to make sense of how my life can possibly have changed beyond recognition in the space of, what, four hours? I've existed in two lifetimes and a kind of one in between, I've had my whole world view changed, I have abilities I would never have dreamt were possible, and now I'm suddenly the leader of a resistance? And I feel absolutely fine about it? I mean, how on earth?

*You released almost all of your old pattern in the instant you chose to do that which felt true to everything you have learnt instead of that which your fear wanted you to do,* Integrity tells me. *Though your present situation and course feel unfamiliar and difficult you have confidence in them because they follow the pattern you have chosen in its place.*

*The Way Of The Horse. Your way.*

I sense Integrity returning her attention to selecting an area to graze. We're just doing as we agreed, I know that, but still I feel humbled by her consistency, her dedication to her side of our agreement.

*We both continue to honour it,* Integrity observes.

*We're both still hanging in there, but we both know that's down to you.*

*We are one and the same. We choose to appear differently while we are here but you know that is not the truth. You are all you need.*

The PV comes to a stop outside the yard whose name and rough area I selected.

*Tania, how are we doing this?*

*The same as before. Just act as if I'm there in person and I will be.*

I open the door and Tania steps out of the vehicle in front of me without having set foot inside it. She flicks her long, almost white, blond hair back over her shoulders and walks purposefully towards the yard gate. *There are three here. I'll have a chat with the one currently throwing brushes against the wall in the tack room, shall I, while you talk to the two who are sabotaging the toilet?*

I sense the intentions of the two towards whom I begin to head. Any police unfortunate enough to have the need to relieve themselves when they return to inspect that the yard has been cleared, will have a nasty shock. It isn't worth it; the police will easily trace the pranksters, and the two who have the exact temperaments we need and whose horses are waiting to help them see how better to use it, will be imprisoned and tortured. I pick up my pace.

# Chapter Fifteen

y the end of the day, Tania and I have visited all of the yards that until this morning had managed to hang on to their land and horses, and we return to Helen's with the knowledge that all twenty-three riders whose horses graze with ours will be on their way within the next twenty-four hours.

When Tania and I appear on the yard, Helen invites us to join her and the others for the huge buffet she has managed to prepare in between hobbling to the various areas of the therapy centre to check on the five groups of Sensitives she directed to begin the task of organising and clearing. As she tells us of their progress, it becomes clear that she has made very sure they have kept their minds on their jobs and on looking forward to when they will see their horses again, rather than backward at everything that has happened. 'I'll have them all going home this evening excited and uplifted about the turn our lives all took today, if it's the last thing I do,' she tells us breathlessly.

All I can do is hug her. She's put her life into helping us and the horses – none of which could be ridden for one reason or another when she took them in, and would have been shot if it weren't for the sanctuary she offered – and she's still doing it even though, unlike the rest of us except Tania, the horse of her heart isn't waiting for her on the other side of the wall. I sense her determination to be optimistic and look forward, but also the self-protection she has buried beneath it; the busier she is, the less space she has to miss Silver. The pattern stirs up memories within me – memories that were fresh this morning but are now almost out of reach.

'Helen, you need to let yourself grieve,' I murmur as I continue to hug her. 'If you don't, if you put protection up around yourself to keep the pain away, you'll only shut yourself away from all of us. Believe me, I know.'

Helen pushes me away. 'I don't have the time to grieve.'

'You don't have time not to,' I reply, recognising Integrity's advice as it passes my lips.

Helen stares at me for a long time. Finally, she says, 'All this time I've kept going, helping more horses, more people, it's been because of Silver. I always felt there was nothing I couldn't do when she was here, looking at me with so much trust in her eyes, so much belief in me that whatever happened, I could measure up. I can't think of her not being here. If I do, I won't have the strength to go on.'

I gently take hold of her arms. 'You are all you need, Helen. Silver was, and still is, a part of you; all she did was show you the part of yourself that already existed. If you shut out all she was to you, you shut that part of yourself away. Grieve for her physical loss and you'll be able to feel that she's still where she always was – that you're still everything you've always been.'

I frown slightly as the truth I've just told her cements itself inside me, as if its ingredients were always there but have just come together in the right amounts for the first time and reacted to become something solid, substantial. Real.

'Thank you, Helen, for being you. Please, don't stop now?' I beg her.

Helen's eyes fill with tears. 'I found her in a ditch when she was just a yearling, you know. I didn't have any money, I didn't have anywhere to keep her, but I couldn't leave her there.'

I guide her to a seat at the food-laden table. 'So, what did you do?'

She hastily wipes away her tears as voices sound through the doorway. 'I can't do this now, I can't let them see me this way.'

'Yes, you can,' I say. 'Don't hold them away from you, let them in, let them and me help you as you've helped all of us.'

Tania hurries to the door, calling out, 'Hurry up, you lot, Helen is going to tell us about Silver's life while we eat this amazing food she's prepared for us all.'

By the time Helen reaches the end of Silver's story, the dishes have been cleared of food and there isn't a dry eye in the room, including, I'm glad to see, Helen's. We all, at different times during her account of her time with Silver, felt moved to go to her side and hug her as she talked and cried, and she hung on to the arms around her, appreciating their support and releasing them when they were replaced with new ones. For our parts, it felt good to be able to offer our love to the woman who means so much to us, even if in such heart-rending circumstances.

I sense the exhaustion that settles over her now, partly from the stress and efforts of the day but mostly as a result of the emotion she has been brave enough to release in front of us all.

Tania is Aware of it too and gets to her feet. 'It's been a

privilege for all of us in this room to have been included, by way of the memories you've shared, Helen, in your life with your very special mare, and to have been able to comfort you in your grief at her passing.' She raises her glass of water and we all do the same. 'Without Helen and Silver, none of us would be here, none of us would be planning to do what we're going to do, and all of those you'll be able to help as a result would have been left to flounder. Silver is as much with us as she ever was, giving Helen the strength to carry on being the force of nature she's always been. To a very much loved Helen and Silver.'

'To Helen and Silver,' we all echo.

'And now I'm going to help Helen to her bed,' Tania says, 'while you lovely lot clear away all of these dishes and organise them so they're ready for you to pack up tomorrow. I know you all have work to go to in the morning, but come here as normal afterward and you can get to know the newcomers while you're showing them how they can help.' She passes Helen her sticks. 'Come on, wonderful lady, there's only so much anyone can take on in one day.' I sense the light she sends to Helen as she puts a hand under the elderly woman's elbow and helps her to her feet.

Everyone else stands and takes it in turns to hug Helen a final time before Tania guides her out of the kitchen, leaving us all to do as she instructed. In no time at all, the mountain of plates, dishes and cutlery has been washed, dried and organised into piles ready to go into boxes in the morning once Helen has selected what she wants to take with her to her new apartment.

'I think it would be better if we leave in ones and twos, rather than altogether,' I say as the first of the Sensitives select their coats from the hooks by the door. 'When you come back tomorrow, come at your normal time and exactly as you normally would, so that no one is given cause to think we're any sort of group other than just people who used to come and spend time with the horses, and are helping to clear the place as instructed.'

'It'll be horrible, arriving without any horses being here to welcome us,' Primrose says.

'And wonderful when we get to see them outside the walls,' I say.

Many heads nod, but all of the faces turned towards me are riddled with worry. 'I want to do that, I'm desperate to see Shandy,' Alanna says, 'but I'm scared. I need her in order to feel like I have any kind of strength to keep going here, and without her, I'm not sure I'll be brave enough to get to the wall. I can feel it all coming in on me even now, and once I'm home, it'll be worse. What if I can't find enough courage to even come here tomorrow now that I know Shandy won't be here to make my panic go away when I get here?'

Most of the others nod in agreement. I sense the fear that pinches their brows, as well as their relief that someone else has voiced that fear. And I sense their shame.

*We will assist,* Integrity tells me. She doesn't mean tomorrow. She means now. My heart lifts as I pick up her intention and relate it to how I know the horses at the other cities have helped their humans.

'None of you have any reason to feel ashamed,' I tell the Sensitives. 'Everyone who lives in this city is scared of what they can see and hear going on around them every day. You have the added burden of being constantly frightened by what you can sense, which is a hundred times worse. You can't hold it away from yourself by going into your apartment and closing the door, because it follows you in.'

Heads nod again and a few wipe away unbidden tears.

'Up until today, being sensitive has been a curse for all of us,' I continue, 'a curse we've only been able to live with because what we could sense from the horses was more powerful. Well, it's even more powerful than we knew, and we don't need to be with them to sense it. Stand still for a moment. Think of your horses and everything they are to you.'

'Okaaaaaay,' Saul says after a few minutes. 'I'm still scared.'

'Just wait a bit longer,' I say. It's taken the horses a little while to form a herd and negotiate the hill that has been hiding them from the city, but now they are between the hills and the city wall. Now they have begun cantering around the city.

All of those in the kitchen, including me, look towards the open door, sensing something stirring, something that carries the promise of something far more powerful. No one is scared of it. They all sense that whatever this is, it is gentle, loving, even. No one speaks and I sense them instinctively reaching for more of what they can feel. The pattern that has been reaching for them in return grasps hold of them all and pulls them further out of themselves to where the horses are cantering as one giant moving, breathing being that whips up the energy their humans need, gradually enfolding the city within its blanket. It fuels their sensitivity so that they know exactly how their horses are, where their horses are, and why they are behaving as they are. Smiles replace frowns and laughter breaks out.

'They're still with us even though they aren't with us,' Shauna says. 'I can feel where Tango is. I should be with him. I want to go to him.' She looks at me, her eyes bright and shining. 'How soon will the first tunnel be ready?'

'I'm not sure, but at least now you know you can survive until then.' I glance around at everyone. 'When you're feeling wobbly, and you will again once the horses have gone back to the hills, reach out to your horse and get a sense of them like you are now; it'll help you keep out everything you don't want to sense. I'll see you all back here tomorrow?'

There is a murmur of excited voices as they all confirm that I will.

'Okay, the closest two to the door, get on your way now.'

When only Primrose and Shauna are left, Primrose says, 'There are other horses with ours, I can feel there are. They belong to the people coming tomorrow?'

'They do,' I say.

'Can they feel what we can feel? The horses are nearly halfway around the city,' she adds breathlessly.

'They're sensitive enough to feel something that will lift them and help them get through this evening after everything that's happened, but you guys will need to explain to them exactly what's happened, once they're here tomorrow.'

'We can do that,' Shauna says. 'Come on, Prim, let's get home while the horses are still carrying us. See you tomorrow, Nathan.'

I wave at them both. 'See you tomorrow.' I shut the door behind them and call out, 'You can come back in now.'

Tania appears in the kitchen, grinning. 'That went well, honestly, this is so much easier now the pattern has so much more strength.'

'I take it you mean that you had to do a lot more in the cities you've helped before this one, rather than hovering outside the door while someone else does it?'

Her grin broadens. 'Exactly. And once you're all riding, things will speed up even more. This is so much fun. Isn't this fun?'

'Riding?' I frown. 'I'm sure the horses from the livery yards are all rideable, but ours aren't, that's why they were here at the centre; Helen took them in rather than let them be shot. And anyway, none of us who visited them can ride.'

'I healed all of the horses as soon as I got here, and they're very keen to be ridden so they can show everyone what they need to know,' Tania says, filling the kettle. 'All of their people will be

able to ride if you help them. Want some hot chocolate? It won't
be long before you won't be able to get it, so I'd make the most of
it while you can.'

'You got here weeks ago. You healed them weeks ago? Why
didn't you say?'

'It wasn't the right time. Now it is. We should let the
Sensitives know over the next few days, it'll be an extra thing for
them to hold on to when they're panicking about getting to the
wall.'

My mind is racing so fast, my thoughts almost block out my
Awareness… almost; the horses' energy takes me back to it. I feel
the power of their circle as they continue to race around the city. If
it's affecting us all from here, then if they move in a circle – when
they move in a circle, I correct myself – while we're riding them,
it won't just affect us temporarily, it will change us. It will embed
The Way Of The Horse within us all, as has already happened in
the other cities Tania has visited.

'How can I help the others to ride when I can't ride myself?' I
ask Tania, the horses' energy powering me to the answer so that I
know it as soon as I've spoken. 'I can ride. As soon as I'm on
Integrity's back again, I'll remember.'

'You'll remember how you used to ride, and once I've
tweaked that a bit, you'll be good to start helping the others,'
Tania confirms.

'Can't you just teach us all?'

'I can while I'm here, but after that, they'll need you.'

'How long are you going to be here?' It hits me how much I'll
miss her once she isn't.

'Long enough.' She pours boiling water into two mugs. 'I'm
taking your lack of response regarding the hot chocolate as a yes.'
She stirs the contents of the mugs and passes me one. 'Here
you go.'

We sit in silence, sipping our hot chocolate while revelling in the forcefield that now surrounds and infuses the city as a result of the horses' efforts.

'They're almost done,' Tania says eventually. 'They're tired and the therapy horses will be sore, they're not used to so much exercise. I'll finish this and get out there to the hills for when they get back.'

'I wish I could come with you, I could try to do some healing now I'm Aware.'

'You won't need to try. Just be Aware of what I'm doing, and you'll be able to do it.'

'But that won't work for being able to disappear like you can?'

Tania smiles sympathetically. 'No, your Awareness won't stretch that far, I'm afraid, and even if it did, there's that to consider.' She nods at my wrist, where the cuff of my shirt has shifted back to reveal my wrist safe. 'You'd leave it behind and then you wouldn't be able to re-implant it when you got back here.'

'How are we going to overcome the wrist safes showing our locations when the tunnel is ready and we're wanting to leave the city?'

Tania grins wickedly. 'I know of a nasty little virus that will sort your wrist safes out. In the first few cities, the Kindred released a virus that scrambled the wrist safe's location data, but then they had to keep updating it as it was fixed. Every time they interfered, they were in danger of being discovered. In the third city, one of our people came up with a virus that's enabled and disabled by a passcode. When the code is spoken into the wrist safes of those who know it, the virus locks their location until the word is spoken again. The Governors can't set people to fixing a virus if they don't know it's there.'

I find myself grinning with her. 'Nice.'

'Isn't it? We just need to sort out who is in a position, or can quickly get into a position, to release the virus into the system here. When I say we, I mean you. When I go out to the horses in a bit, I'll stay there and begin work on the first tunnel with Dad. You won't see me again until you bring everyone out. I'll be available to chat any time you want, but it'll be down to you to look out for Helen and work with her in organising the others. You're Aware how the initial sixty-four are organised and why. Delve a little deeper and get a good idea of where in their government they have people placed, and how that came about, and set your lot here on the same path.'

I nod enthusiastically, the horses' energy giving me the strength to believe that I can do everything that is necessary.

'The horses have given you all a reprieve and a promise of what they can do for you,' Tania says. 'When their energy disperses, and you begin to think you can't climb the mountain ahead of you, remember what you did when you had an actual mountain to climb.'

I stare at her, her words having stimulated a plethora of images and feelings in my mind from the lifetime I have all but forgotten. 'I stick to the path that feels right. The one that's straight and forward,' I murmur. 'I stick with Integrity.'

'And remember that I'll be available to chat any time you want. See you, Nathan.' She puts her mug on the table and disappears.

'I'll wash up, then,' I say with a chuckle.

When I arrive back at the apartment I still share with Gran, having had to make myself walk at the same hurried, anxious pace as everyone else when I wanted to jog and leap, and keep the smile

off my face that also would have marked me as behaving
unusually, it's late.

'Oh, Nathan, you're back, that's good,' Gran calls out as I
close the front door behind me. She hurries into the hall so that
she can only be heard by the wallscreen and not seen, and says,
'Here, let me take your coat. You really should start wearing a
thicker one now that the evenings are drawing in.' She hands me a
note as she continues to chatter, giving me time to read it. 'Thanks
for calling earlier, I was just about to put the dinner on, so it saved
me cooking needlessly for you…'

---

My poor love, I heard about the horses, I'm so sorry, and
even more sorry that we can't talk about it here. I'll have a
hug ready for you whenever you need it, I hope you'll feel
how much I love you in every one xxxx

---

'…I was thinking of watching a film tonight after the news has
finished, what do you think?'

I smile at her. 'Sure, is it your turn to choose or mine?' I hold
out my arms and she practically hurls herself into them. 'Thanks,
Gran, I'm okay,' I whisper directly into her ear.

'It's mine, but you've had a hard day, so we'll make it yours,'
she says, and whispers, 'You won't do anything silly, will you?'

'Okay, thanks,' I reply, and whisper, 'Absolutely, but it's not
what you think. I'll write it down for you. You'll love it.'

Gran pulls back from me in horror, then cocks her head to
one side at the smile that I can't take off my face. I mouth,
'Honestly, you'll love it,' then say, 'Come on then, I'm thinking
one of those old comedies in black and white? I could do with
cheering up.'

I lead the way into the living room. 'I'll just get the kettle on. Want some tea?'

'Yes please,' Gran says, 'by all accounts we'd better enjoy it, what we've got is the last we'll be able to get of the real stuff. The food factories are capable of producing substitutes for pretty much everything now.'

While the kettle is boiling, I use the notepad and paper we keep in the kitchen for exactly the purpose to which I'm putting it. I write down for Gran my initial plans for the resistance, and let her know that we already have a way out of the city to see the horses, about which I'll tell her once we're out of the apartment. I have no idea what to write about Tania and her abilities, but this should satisfy Gran's curiosity and concern for me over losing the horses, for now.

I sit down beside her on the sofa and hand her a mug. 'Dammit, I forgot the biscuits,' I say.

She hands me the remote control. 'I'll get them. Here, I've got the menu up for the old movies, choose which one you want.' She hurries to the kitchen, eager to read the note she knows will be waiting for her.

I sense Gran's initial shock and fear for me give way to a thirst for rebellion... and then to pride. I hoped she would react this way. She was an enthusiastic supporter of her daughter and son-in-law's attempts to do exactly as I am planning, but since they were caught and murdered in front of me, she has dedicated herself to keeping me as safe and sane as possible. There is a large part of her that still wants to put that above all else, but her steely determination to live according to the values with which she was raised, and by which my mother also tried to live, won't allow her to ignore the feeling she has that whatever the risk, she has to support me. Once she has acknowledged that to herself, I sense her determination to go further. She wants to be involved.

Knowing I am being observed via the wallscreen through whose menu I begin to scroll, I fight to keep any kind of expression off my face as Gran returns to the living room with fire in her eyes. She nods to me while still out of sight of the wallscreen, her jaw clenched just as my mother used to whenever she was about to do something illegal. She puts a hand over her heart and blows me a kiss, and I sense again the pride she feels, not just in me but in the daughter and son-in-law who died trying to do by themselves what I am planning to do on a far larger scale.

I blink as a memory flashes into my mind from the lifetime I relived and released only this morning. Then, Gran died feeling despondent, as if she had failed me. As I look into her eyes again now, I sense that feeling, brought with her into this lifetime, fall away from her completely even as the guilt I felt at her death falls away from me. She knows not what it is that she feels, exactly, but I do because I feel it too; we are free. Free to be everything we could have been to one another the last time we incarnated together. I will do what I know is right, and when that gets tough, I will have Gran as well as Integrity to make sure I remember myself. This time, I will listen to them both.

'There are only two chocolate chip cookies left.' I admire the elderly lady for the calm with which she manages to infuse her voice when she is a mass of questions and excitement. 'After the day you've had, I think you should have them and I'll take the plain ones.'

I smile at her. 'There are times when you just have to do what's right instead of what's easy, aren't there?'

Her face breaks out into a broad smile in return. She sits down beside me on the sofa and hands me the plate.

I wake the following morning to a sizzling sound and the smell of what can only be a fried breakfast. I smile to myself, Aware that Gran has been up for several hours and was down at the shops for when they opened to get the ingredients for the plate of food she is now cooking for me. Much of the fear that has assailed her for so long is being held at bay by the new sense of purpose with which she woke, and the remainder doesn't affect her nearly as much as it did.

I turn my attention to Integrity and am filled with her sense of contentment as she dozes in the dewy, early autumn grass, her nose resting on one of her forelegs, her ear twitching as a leaf tickles it on its way to rest on the ground by her knee. Through her ears, I hear the snort of a nearby horse, the munching of many more, and the trickling of water from the nearby stream. I leave her to rest.

The day passes quickly, my usual distress at having to work alongside the particularly nasty individuals in the scientific research department, in which I am a research assistant, assuaged by a new interest in its workings and employees. As Gran's note reminded me this morning, the amassing of knowledge has to be my first step – both that which I can achieve myself, and that which those I will be leading can undertake and feed back to me. I need to build a picture of which departments do what in the medical, security, scientific, social, education and planning sectors; who among our number already works within them and who can apply for roles in departments not currently infiltrated; which people are candidates for joining our resistance in time and which gaps they already, or may in time, fill; and eventually, who needs our help.

When I get to the yard after work, I turn my attention away from my initial distress at Integrity and the other horses not being there, to moving between the five groups of Sensitives whose numbers are quickly swelling with Kindred Spirits. As their members sort through and either clear out or pack up the equipment, rugs, tack and detritus accumulated during a lifetime of running the equine assisted therapy centre, I learn as much as I can about each and every one. I write nothing down of the lives of those who attended the centre as clients alongside me, or of those whose anger and determination have doubled our number; I won't compromise anyone's safety by leaving a written account of who they are and what they can contribute to our cause.

As I walk home that evening having had dinner with Helen on the pretext of getting her up to date with my findings, but actually so that I could make sure she sat down, ate and talked about Silver some more, I sort through the information I have gathered. I file it away in my head in such a way that I will be able to retrieve it when I need it. I begin to see which of the Kindred I need to ask to apply for certain jobs, and know they'll do it without hesitation. I'll need to go much more slowly with the Sensitives as, overloaded as they already are with everything they can sense and everything that will be happening over the coming weeks, they won't be able to cope with any other changes just yet.

I am happy that, at my request, the Sensitives and Kindred Spirits have paired up so that the Sensitives will have a ready source of strength and encouragement when they need it, and their Kindred partners will have help to get out to see their horses undetected. I was pleased to be able to sense threads of different thicknesses flaring to life between the members of each and every partnership as they agreed to work together; some have big issues to clear together, others have lesser ones, but each and every partnership will serve its members as well as all of the people they will help.

When I get home, Gran puts on another movie so that I am free to carry on thinking without looking suspicious, and when I go to bed, I can't sleep for all of the information I continue to peruse and sort in my mind. When I finally do, it's because Integrity infiltrates my thoughts and gently pushes them to one side so that my exhaustion can take over.

By the end of the week, Helen's things have either been moved to her apartment, surreptitiously dispersed among the resistance and stored ready for those we will identify as needing them in the future, or heaped in a single rubbish pile on the yard as our instructions dictated. The fields, stables and barns have been cleared of dung, which is heaped in another large pile. The Kindred Spirits have set up a network between themselves along which to pass information, and the Sensitives have been practising reaching for their horses so that they know exactly where they are, and honing their abilities of knowing when they are being observed and when there are others in close proximity to them.

Our fledgling resistance has formed. Helen is ready to leave for her new home and start the menial job for which she insisted on applying despite her age, in the social sector, so that she can be a fully operational Kindred Spirit. The rest of us either know what we need to do in the jobs we will retain, or which jobs we need to apply for, and we know our horses will help us. We also know, because Tania told me just before I left work this evening, that the first tunnel is ready and our horses are waiting for us. The code for the virus – which will allow members of our resistance to move around while appearing to be in our bedrooms at home – that I took down from Tania several days ago and passed to the Kindred Spirit who was confident she could upload it, has been installed. We have the guard rotas so we know when they will be changing over and not atop the city wall. Everything is in place.

We are too many to fit into Helen's kitchen, so the forty-nine of us stand in a circle, hand in hand, in what was her indoor arena.

Helen stands firm without the sticks that she has thrown

behind her, and her voice is strong as she says, 'Thank you all for everything you've done here this week. Thank you for your hard work, your willingness to channel your grief at the horses being taken, into forming something so important. And lastly, thank you for supporting me. I won't be coming with you all to see my horses – your horses, now – because I've realised that's not my place anymore. I'll be the head of the Kindred communication network as we agreed, and I'll be happy doing it while knowing that the horses will be helping you all to do so much more.

'This is the last time we'll ever all meet in one place inside the city walls, and while that makes me feel sad, it also fills me with pride because it's for the same reason that Silver and the other horses brought us all together in the first place – we'll be resisting everything that's wrong with this city. Go now, all of you, get home, get some food in you and then get out to see your horses, taking all of my love with you.'

It is some time before only Helen and I are left in the arena; desperate as everyone is to see their horses, they feel for Helen being the only one not coming with us, the only one who will never see her horse again, and wait their turns to give her a hug before leaving singly or in pairs.

'Come on then, you,' I say to her, picking up her sticks and handing them to her. 'Let's get you home.'

She shakes her head emphatically. 'I can get myself there. There's bound to be a PV waiting nearby or at least somewhere along the way. You need to get home to your gran. She's barely seen you all week and she'll want to spend some time with you before you leave to go outside the wall. It'll be hard for her, being here while you're out there.'

'Yes, it will. She's meeting us at your apartment block with dinner for us all because she thought you'd appreciate the company after being booted out of here – would you mind asking her to stay on with you for the evening? I'll go home before setting my location on my wrist safe, then if I'm caught where I shouldn't be, neither you nor Gran will be complicit.'

Helen begins to hobble towards the arena doors. 'That sounds like a fine plan. Come on then, we'd best not keep her waiting.'

There is indeed a PV waiting near the yard gates, which Helen closes behind us both with a sigh. I open the PV door and get inside, and once the scanners have beeped their recognition of me, sit down to wait while Helen regards the place that has been her home for so long. Her mouth is set in a straight line when she enters the vehicle, and I sense her continued determination to only look forward, keeping Silver with her in her heart. She allows herself to be scanned, then keys in our destination. We travel in silence, each contemplating that which has happened and is yet to happen today.

Gran is waiting for us outside Helen's apartment block, two bags at her feet. She smiles warmly at us both and links her arm through Helen's, leaving me to pick up the heatproof bags containing our evening meal and follow them both into the building. Gran comments on the day's weather, the convenient location of the apartment block, how much she enjoyed preparing dinner, how much smoother the lift is than those in our block, and then, once we've entered Helen's apartment, how lovely and airy it is. Then she offers her help with unpacking and any decorating Helen wants done.

Despite her determination, Helen wipes tears from her eyes every now and then before bracing herself again and answering Gran. When she sees the meal Gran has cooked, she relaxes and the smile she gives my grandmother is full of her usual warmth. The two of them chat about anything and everything as we divide the food and eat, leaving me free to run over and over the plan I have agreed with the others for getting out to our horses.

When I refuse the coffee that Helen offers to make, she says, 'You're wanting to get off home after a hard day's work, I can see. Gwen, why don't you stay on here for a while with me? We've known of each other for so long but we've never taken the time to sit down and chat properly, and with Nathan out of the way, we can talk about all the things that'll make his ears burn.'

Gran laughs and glances over to where I am now standing in the doorway, out of sight of the wallscreen. I nod once, keeping my head tipped down for longer than normal so she knows it's important that she does as Helen has suggested. I mouth, 'Horses.'

Gran says to Helen, 'That sounds lovely. I'll see Nathan out and be right back.'

I lift a hand in farewell to Helen, who returns my wave as if she hasn't a care in the world. Gran follows me into the hallway, her hand resting on my back.

'You'll take a PV?' she asks, rubbing my back as I bend over to put on my shoes and whispering, 'You're sure everything is in place?'

'Yep, it's getting chilly. You'll get one too later? I know you like to walk in the dark, and I know the streets are safe now the police are always patrolling, but you look a little tired.' I stand up and whisper into her ear, 'I'm sure. Don't worry, I'll be fine, we all will be.'

I return the hug she gives me as she says, 'I will. I won't be too late, but I'll be quiet so I don't wake you. Get an early night, Nathan.'

I kiss her cheek. 'I will. See you in the morning, Gran.'

## Chapter Sixteen

*a*s soon as I get home, I change into dark clothes and dig out my black woollen cap, glad that the temperature has dropped enough to warrant me wearing it as I pull it down low over my brow. I check my watch. Ten minutes past eight. I'm on time.

I slowly twist the handle on my bedroom door and then release it every bit as slowly once the door is enclosed within its frame. I move to the furthest corner of the room so as to minimise even further the risk of being overheard by the wallscreen in the living room, lift my wrist safe to my mouth and say in a low voice the word we all agreed was unlikely to be uttered by anyone outside our group. 'Serendipity.'

As Tania assured me would happen, my wrist safe flashes white, once, to confirm that my location has been set. My heart leaps. I'm actually going to do this, I'm going outside the wall to see Integrity! I take a breath. I have to concentrate. I have to go and pick up the most sensitive of the Sensitives, who at this moment I know will be freaking out, and get us both to the spot on the wall that is closest to where I know Integrity is waiting for me, for that will be where Tania and her dad have created the tunnel entrance.

Even had I not been Aware of the dense thread linking Avril and me – even had I not been Aware at all – I would have known that she was the Sensitive with whom I, as a combination of Kindred and Sensitive, should partner. She's the closest to being able to communicate with her mare, Dolly, but the least able to hold the energy of The Old away from herself and the one most likely to fall apart at any moment. It's very possible that the terror with which she wrestles all day, every day, will escalate to the point of blocking her completely from being able to sense her horse on our way to the wall, so I'll need to be her guide as well as hopefully being a source of strength for her.

I attach a note to my bedroom door asking Gran to wedge the apartment door ajar once she's home, so that I won't need to submit to an eye scan on my return in order for it to open. I check my Awareness for anyone in the corridor outside and, finding it empty, hurry to the lifts. I'll need to exit the building as someone else is leaving or entering, so that I can again avoid the eye scan that is normally necessary to open the main doors.

I get out of the lift on the first floor and take the stairs to the ground floor to slow my descent, so that my arrival in the foyer coincides with two people who have just exited the other lift. I slip through the doors to the street behind them, hoping that the others have all managed to do the same while knowing how much more difficult it will be for the Sensitives without the level of Awareness I have, and even more so for the Kindred.

I reach for Avril in my Awareness and find her huddled in the corner of one of the lifts in her block, paralysed with fear. I curse under my breath. We don't have much time to spare if we're going to get across the bare ground between the city and its wall while the guards are changing shifts, and I can't miss seeing Integrity. A small part of me wants to leave Avril and get to the wall on my own, but the larger part prevents me from diverting away from the path I know to be right.

I pick up my pace as much as I dare, glad that Avril's block is just around the corner from mine. I sense whom of those in the vicinity are intending to enter her block, and time my arrival so that I slip in behind one of them. I hurry past him and towards the lifts, reaching Avril's just as its doors open. I quickly step inside and press the button to close the door so that no one can enter behind me. I select the first floor on the control panel and kneel in front of Avril, who is looking down at the floor with vacant eyes, ghostly white and shaking.

'Avril, it's me, Nathan.'

She doesn't answer. She doesn't even register my presence. I'm Aware that in reaching for her sense of Dolly in order to try to give herself the strength to get to her, she reached beyond the thin barrier she had been working so hard to hold up against the malicious energy of The Old, with too much of herself. It grasped hold of her and when she tried to retreat back into herself, it held fast, creeping along her energy until it gained hold of her from the inside out. If I don't do something quickly, she will be lost to us.

I think of Integrity and send everything she is and everything I feel for her to Avril. White light bursts out of me and surrounds and infuses my friend, who begins to gain a little colour in her cheeks. She blinks, but her eyes are still vacant as she fights the horror inside her. We'll reach the first floor in a moment and then we'll need to go straight back down to the ground floor – I'm not going to be able to give her enough energy by the time we get there, I can feel it, I'm not strong enough.

*On it.* Tania adds her strength to mine and I'm almost blinded as the lift fills to bursting with light.

The lift pings to announce our arrival at the first floor, and I slam my hand behind me to the button which will keep the doors closed, then turn and select the button for the ground floor.

'What's… happening?' Avril murmurs. *Dolly? Is that you?*

I shouldn't have been surprised. If Tania could give me enough light to relive nearly forty years of another lifetime in a few seconds and bring me to Awareness on my way back to this one, she can blast The Old out of Avril and tip the balance so that she can communicate with her horse.

*You are never a victim of the energy that assails you,* Dolly tells her. *Only of your beliefs about its capabilities. Come to me and we will work to dispel those beliefs.*

The lift bangs to a stop and the doors open. I hold my hand out to Avril and she takes it. We hurry to the door, which I catch from someone hurrying in. Once we're on the pavement, I put an arm around Avril's shoulders and hurry her to where we both sense our horses are waiting. She continues her conversation with her horse, and I sense her wonderment and delight keeping her terror at bay.

I glance at my watch. The guards changed five minutes ago. We now have ten minutes to reach the tunnel. I am Aware of two sets of police patrols in our path. One should be out of the way by the time we reach their current location, but the other pair seem content to loiter.

'This way,' I whisper to Avril and steer her away from the direct route to our horses.

'What? No, they're that way.'

'As are some bored police. We need to take a detour.'

'What about the others?'

'As far as I can tell, they're all ahead of us so they should be fine.'

'Nathan, I don't know about this…'

'Dolly does and she told you to go to her. Come on.' I try to send her some light through the physical connection between us, but my worry about missing my chance to get to Integrity has turned to frustration and irritation, and I can't seem to generate any.

'Maybe we should try another day.' Avril's feet begin to slow as she looks up at me, her face orange under the street light.

'Avril…' My scowl causes her eyes to fill with tears. The thread between us thrums as our current situation resonates with the one in which we interacted before. I let her down then. I won't do it again. This time, I'll do the right thing. 'I'm sorry.'

I begin to reach for Integrity and find that I don't need to for she is part of me. Light flows easily through the physical connection between me and Avril, who blinks away her tears and responds to Dolly's reminder. *Come.*

By the time we pass the last apartment block, we only have two minutes to cross no man's land and reach the wall before the guards will be back atop it. This part of the wall was built months ago, so most of the rubble piles that would have hidden us have been cleared, and the grass is long and slows us down – but we're both determined. We reach the wall just as we both sense a guard appearing directly above us. I push Avril in front of me to where we both hope the tunnel entrance is, and when she pulls some brambles to one side and disappears, I follow her down the steps that I can just about pick out in the moonlight.

When we reach the bottom of the stairway, arms enclose me in a tight hug. 'We did it! We made it! Thanks, Nathan, I'd never have been able to do it without you.'

'Nor I without you.' Avril isn't Aware of my exact meaning, but I sense that her soul is; I can feel the thread between us thinning slightly even as it continues to link us. I'm not done making my reparations just yet. I sense a storm brewing, and my need to see Integrity, to be with her physically as well as in mind and essence, suddenly intensifies.

*Storms are necessary for the transfer of negative charges back to the earth,* Integrity informs me pointedly.

*They're unpleasant though,* I reply. *Anyway, it isn't an actual thunderstorm I'm sensing.*

*It is not an actual thunderstorm to which I am referring.*

'Nathan? Are you coming?' Avril's voice reaches me from further along the tunnel. 'I can't sense you behind me.'

'I'm coming.' I put my hands out to either side so that I can feel my way along the tunnel in the dark, and hurry after Avril, trying to convince myself that the thumping in my chest is due to exertion alone.

When Avril emits a grunt and then giggles just in front of me, I stop so as not to bump into her. Her voice comes from below me as she says, 'I've just found the steps that'll take us back up.'

I chuckle. 'I'd give you a hand up if I could see either of our hands.'

'No worries,' she replies, now from just above me, 'just take small footsteps until you find the bottom step.' There is the sound of spitting. 'There's no need for both of us to eat dirt.'

When we reach the top of the steps, we are able to see one another again in the moonlight that permeates along the short, horizontal section of tunnel.

Tania's voice reaches us. 'Well, about time too, everyone else is already riding.'

We step out of the tunnel onto the side of a hill and look across a flat, wide valley covered with tackless horses carrying riders in the grey-blue light. They, Avril and Tania are all forgotten as I sense Integrity approaching. I run to her and put my forehead against hers as I stroke her neck.

*We have much to do,* she tells me. *Allow yourself to be assisted onto my back.*

'Will you allow me?' a man asks from behind me.

I turn to him and he holds out his hand. 'I'm Will, it's good to meet you, Nathan.' When he smiles, his teeth and white-blond hair seem to be all of him, favoured as they are by the moonlight. I shake his hand and know that he can be no other than Tania's father; just like when I am with her, my Awareness serves only to let me know how little I can ever know about him rather than how much. I should be daunted by him, yet it doesn't feel necessary or even possible; his relaxed openness doesn't allow it.

'It's good to meet you too. Um, that's some tunnel you and Tania have excavated, I don't know how to thank you.'

'No thanks are needed,' Will says, still smiling. 'I'm always pleased when the opportunity presents itself for me to feel vaguely necessary in my daughter's life, and if I'm going for full disclosure, it got me out of doing the washing up. Anyway, will you allow me to give you a leg up onto Integrity? Once you're up there, your riding experience will all come flooding back but I think vaulting on from the side of a hill in the dark before that has come to pass is a little ambitious.' He talks to me as if he knows me – as if he's always known me, and I get the sense that he has, though, try as I might, I can't think how that could be. I just stand next to Integrity and stare at him.

'Don't ask him what you're about to,' Tania warns.

'Do I know you as well as you seem to know me?' I ask Will.

'Yes of course,' Will says, 'although we're all only seeming to know one another here, aren't we? That's part of the fun. The tricky part is seeming to know oneself.'

Tania sighs and says to him, 'You used to warn people not to ask Amarilla and Infinity stuff like that, and now you're worse than they ever were. Nathan, I did warn you.'

Their humour makes light of the answer I sense they both want me to have. An answer that confirms the sense I already have that the storm – my storm – is coming.

'Yet unlike Integrity, the storm isn't here,' Will says. 'I'll ask a third and final time before slinking away to wallow in rejection. Would you like a leg up?'

'Er, yes please.' I'm glad he can't see my frown even as I realise that he doesn't need to; he'll be fully Aware of my disconcertion at him answering my thought as if I had said it out loud.

'Bend your knee and jump on the count of three,' Will says. 'Once you're over Integrity's withers, swing your right leg over her back and sit up. You and she will be able to take it from there.'

I do as he says and the moment I'm astride the horse I've known as Honour for so long, any thought of that name disappears for good. It's as if the almost white neck in front of me and the dappled neck I can just about remember merge into one – and as if the person I am now and the person who rode the dappled horse finally merge into one.

'Okay, ride as you know how to,' Tania says, 'but I want you to focus on helping Integrity to carry you in such a way that won't cause her any harm, as all of the sixty-four do with their horses. I know you're Aware, through them, of how that feels, and I'll give you any help you need while I'm helping some of the Sensitives to ride over there.' She nods to where she and Will have all of the Sensitives except Avril riding their horses in two circles. 'When you and she are feeling connected, I want you and the other Kindred to canter a large circle around the Sensitives. You know how I love a circle.'

'I know what happens when the horses circle,' I say. 'Okay, I've got it.'

I waste no time directing Integrity to where the Kindred Spirits are riding their horses a little further away on the valley floor. Many of them are talking to their horses as they ride, some are crying and some are just leaning forward along their necks, hugging them.

*Focus on your posture, Nathan,* Tania instructs. *You need to sit straighter than you used to so your weight is off her forehand. Then you need to slow her pace a little while asking her to keep her hind legs pushing on through, so that it's they that take more weight and not her front legs. Good, that's a little better already. Concentrate now on your Awareness of the sixty-four. Feel how they ride and let that Awareness spread through your body so that they almost ride through you.*

I spare a fraction of a second to marvel at the ease with which she's able to guide me whilst also calling instructions to the brand new riders circling her, before doing as she told me. A sense of wonder steals over me as not only an Awareness of how to ride settles within my body from the sixty-four, but Awareness of their energy. I invite it in. I know exactly how to use it.

I don't recognise how I ride Integrity, but I know that the increased connection I feel both within her body, and between our two bodies, is the result of it. As we trot on, my body and hers work together to maintain our connection and balance. When we move up to a canter, we have the presence we need. We canter slowly, powerfully around the outside of the Kindred, drawing the infinity energy from the sixty-four around them until they are enclosed within it.

Their horses all spin to watch us in the moonlight, their ears pricked, their breath puffing in small clouds from each nostril. They know what we are about. Their riders don't... but they feel it. The pattern created by the sixty-four, and strengthened by those following it in other cities, calls to those Integrity and I circle now. It teases them with a sense of possibility, a sense that they are where and with whom they need to be for something wonderful to happen.

'Follow me,' I tell them.

None of them hesitate. I am Aware of each and every partnership as they fall in behind me. None of the riders are as connected with their horses as they need to be – as they will be – but thanks to the sensitivity the pattern has already encouraged within them, they're all able to help their horses to balance well enough to canter in the same slow, steady rhythm that Integrity is achieving.

I circle towards the last horse and rider so that the Kindred Spirits canter a large circle of our own, whipping up the power of both the circle and the horses to join the energy of infinity. When it is a maelstrom, I peel away and head for the two circles of horses carrying the Sensitives. Those horses are all walking while their riders listen to Will and Tania and adjust their positions whilst becoming accustomed to the sensation of a four-legged animal moving beneath them. The horses are desperate to join us in our dance with energy, to experiment with their newly healed bodies in connection with their riders, but they know they must wait just a little longer.

If the Kindred reacted well to Integrity and me circling them, it is nothing to the reaction of the Sensitives as we canter around them. They are as open to the energy with which we surround, infuse and lift them, as they are to that which drags them down whilst in the city. It carries them with us so that their bodies shift to match ours, their knowledge and experience of riding expands to match ours, and the terror that blocked their horses from their minds is left with nowhere to reside. They hear their horses' encouragement to ride as we do, to join us in abandoning ourselves to that which is showing us all we need to know. One by

one, they accede until Will and Tania are left standing alone at the
centre of our single, enormous circle.

The horses who were previously considered to be broken
down wrecks move with as much soundness, purpose and grace as
the rest. The Sensitives, who find negotiating everything else in
The Old such a challenge, ride as if they've been doing so for
years. The Kindred, who are only here rather than in a prison cell
or dead because their love for their horses kept them from open
rebellion, ride with lightness and sensitivity. For my part, I ride as
if I've never struggled with anything, as if I've always known that
all of the answers I need are within me.

I can help the others. I can coach them when they ride, until
their bodies have sufficient muscle memory and strength that they
can achieve by themselves that which the circle is helping them to
achieve now; until their connection with their horses isn't
dependent on all of us being here together; until they can come
and ride alone whenever they feel a need to be reminded of the
strength, sensitivity, connection, honesty and consistency that is
The Way Of The Horse.

*Well, I guess we'll just scoot off and get on with digging more
tunnels then,* Will tells me. *Good on you, Nathan.* I swear I hear a
dog bark as he disappears.

*I'll let you know when the next tunnel's ready,* Tania tells me.
She turns slowly and waves at each of the riders, then disappears
too.

*Thank you, both of you.*

*Thank you, Newson.* It is neither Tania nor Will who
answer me.

*Amarilla? Or Infinity? I think Amarilla?*

Amusement accompanies her thought. *At least there are two of
us, just about. You answer to two names even though there's only
one of you. Nathan, Newson, thank you for helping us when we*

*were newly bonded, and thank you for helping us now, what
you're doing is speeding things up here no end; this has been the
easiest city so far.*

*It's down to Integrity.*

*Remember that.* Amarilla and Infinity's thought is faint but no
less powerful for it. It stays with me as I call out to everyone to
slow their tiring horses to a stop and dismount, and during the
hours we all choose to spend with them afterward.

We decide unanimously to miss the next guard change in
favour of spending five extra hours with our horses, and split our
attention between them and one another. We firm up our Kindred-
Sensitive partnerships; confirm communication networks when
the Sensitives realise that they can all now pass messages to one
another via their horses; give moral support to those due to
interview for new, carefully selected jobs; and agree to not come
out to see our horses again until the next tunnel is ready – we want
to ride together again and won't risk any kind of pattern forming
regarding our movements out of the city.

When not only the next guard change, but dawn, is
approaching, we know we have to tear ourselves away from our
horses, each other and the incredible experience of which we have
all been a part.

Yet Amarilla's comment has continued to poke at me from
inside. *What did she mean?* I ask Integrity before leaving her. *I
mean, I know what she meant, but there's something else – she
added something to the thought.*

*She merely spoke with intention in order to assist you.*

*Something's going to happen, I can feel it.*

*Something is always going to happen.* Her calmness assures
me that all is well.

I smile to myself as a flash of memory shows me a time when
I sought reassurance over assurance; when I wanted relief from

my fear rather than confirmation of the strength my horse has helped me to find. I rub her forehead and turn towards the tunnel. 'Okay, everyone, groups of around ten need to be going back every three minutes from... now. Hurry up, or we'll be trying to cross no man's land in daylight with a full complement of guards watching from the wall.'

I time everyone in ahead of Avril and me, sensing her relief at every extra minute she has with her horse while she waits. When I can't delay any longer, I call out to her, 'Hold her in your mind with you as we leave and it won't seem so bad. Stay with her in that place for as long as you can and then keep finding your way back to it, and you'll be okay – in fact you'll be better than okay.'

Avril leaves Dolly reluctantly and enters the tunnel in front of me. 'You sound like you know that from experience. Like you've been doing it forever.'

'I have,' I murmur, 'it's down to Integrity.'

I'll remember.

# Chapter Seventeen

*I* get home just as the workers on the early shift are leaving for work, giving me perfect cover to re-enter my apartment block. I creep into my apartment and am relieved to hear gentle snores emanating from Gran's room; she isn't awake worrying about me. I discard my clothes, crawl into bed and say, 'Serendipity,' to my wrist.

The next thing I know, Gran is whispering urgently, her mouth right next to my ear. 'Nathan, PLEASE.'

'Huh?' My eyes feel as though they're glued shut. I rub them but it makes no difference, I can't seem to lift my eyelids.

'You have to wake up and get up. What if the others are like this? What if none of you make it to work? I can't think of a quicker way for you all to be linked as a potential group of subversives than if all of you who lost their horses within the last week are late for work on the same day. If you're linked, you'll all be watched more closely and then you'll never get out to see your horses again.'

My eyes open wide and I sit up. 'What time is it?'

She smiles wearily and whispers, 'It's alright, you're not late yet, I just couldn't wake you and I was starting to panic. I take it everything went well?'

The events of the night flood back and I feel a sense of wonder all over again. 'Better than well,' I whisper, 'it was amazing. I rode Integrity as if I've always been able to do it, as did all the other Sensitives with their horses. All of us, Sensitives and Kindred, rode together in a circle with this incredible energy that made us feel as if we can do anything.'

Gran squeezes my hand and smiles as she gets stiffly to her feet. 'Then get yourself ready so you can go out there and do it. I'll get a decent breakfast on to cook, and the last of the real coffee.'

I bounce out of the apartment an hour later and run down the stairs, high on caffeine and the lingering exhilaration of what we achieved last night. The caffeine ceases to have an effect by mid-morning, but my continued delight combines with a heightened Awareness of Integrity to carry me through the day with so much energy that I keep having to check myself and make sure I appear to everyone else as the same reserved, meek, obedient Nathan they think they know.

I put my ability – hammered into me by Tania – to continue interacting normally with my physical surroundings while perusing my Awareness, to good use when checking in with those Kindred being interviewed today. I find that all three are more energised and clearer of thought than normal, all three impress their interviewers and all three are granted their new jobs, one a secretarial position in the education sector, one an admin post in the food production sector, and the last a managerial position in the security sector.

I have to fight to keep a grin from my face as I fit those pieces of information into the flow chart I have in my head that details who can feed what type of information to the rest of us, and where they can insinuate our misinformation. The irony isn't lost on me that for someone so intent on acting from a place of integrity, duplicity appears to come very naturally to me.

*Integrity is being consistent with that which you know to be true,* my horse is quick to inform me. *Do not confuse it with being true to those who act according to falsehoods.* I sense an unusual steeliness accompanying her thought; a determination where up until now there has been only patience. I have a sense of time running out.

*Not running out for that is impossible. Merely converging. All is well.*

I can feel that it is. I make it to the end of the day without giving myself away and on my way home rejoice, through our horses, with the Sensitives, all of whom are relieved to have been able to do the same. It feels strange to have to wait for Integrity to shift her focus away from her individuality as my Bond-Partner and towards her connection with her herd, in order for me to be able to converse with the others, rather than merely thinking thoughts directly to them as I do with Tania and Will, but nice at the same time as it gives us all a strong sense of unity both with our horses and with one another.

*That was so much easier than I thought it would be,* Avril tells the rest of us as we hurry along different streets, each heaving with people trying to make it home before the current drizzle gets heavier.

*Me too, I'm so tired after last night, but today was the easiest day at work I've ever had,* another Sensitive replies. *Does anyone know how the Kindred got on?*

*I do,* I say, sensing that they all immediately know who I am and turn their attention towards me as if it's normal for us to converse this way – which it is, I realise. Normal for Sensitives attuned to The Way Of The Horse, anyway; those who have gone before us have created a normality into which we have all easily slipped.

*Um, so, how did they get on, Nathan?* Primrose asks.

*Sorry, I got distracted. All three did brilliantly and got the jobs they went for. The resistance took another step forward today.* There is jubilation all around, which I feel dutybound to interrupt. *Pull back to yourselves now, wait until you're out of sight and earshot to celebrate, we can't afford to appear happy in public. It'll only take one informant to file a report before we have someone in place to intercept it, and one of us to be arrested and tortured, for everything to come crashing down. Be happy, but with a straight, preferably miserable, face.*

I sense their minds quietening as they focus on their surroundings and ensure they are blending in.

*Nathan?* Avril's thought is faint.

*Still here.*

*Do you also know how Will and Tania are getting on with the next tunnel? I know it's been less than twenty-four hours since we saw them, but now they'll have started on it, I just wondered whether it might be in an easier location than under and up into a hill – whether it might be finished quicker than the last one?*

*We'll have it finished in five days' time,* Tania tells her.

*Tania? Oh, thank goodness.* Avril's relief turns to confusion. *How am I hearing you though? I can hear the others through our connections with our horses.*

I wait for Tania to answer, then realise I already know. Avril knows Tania's thoughts via her link with her horse because Tania is the horses. All of them, as well as being herself. I can't conceive of how that's possible.

*I'll let Nathan fill you in on that,* Tania replies to Avril. *Lots to do, five days to do it in!*

*Nathan?* I sense all of the other Sensitives focusing on me.

*I'll let you know when I've figured it out. Sleep well tonight, everyone, and when you see your Kindred partners, let them know we'll be going out again in five nights' time. Not you, Avril, I already know.*

Her mirth almost makes me smile, but I hold my face straight as I hold my eye to the scanner at the entrance to my apartment block.

The five days that follow are filled with joy, anticipation, excitement and misery in equal measure. I revel in being able to communicate with my friends whenever I want to, and as another two Kindred get the jobs for which they are interviewed, we all feel a sense of momentum building.

But when all of the city's dogs, then the cats, then all other pets are rounded up and dumped outside the city gates as unceremoniously as were our horses, we all feel for those grieving their losses, to the extent that the other Sensitives increasingly struggle to keep their sense of their horses uppermost in their minds so that they aren't swept away by the grief pervading the city.

Their Kindred partners check on them as often as they dare, reassuring them, reminding them that the grief they feel isn't theirs and that their horses can give them sanctuary from feeling it, but by the end of the third day, the horses feel a need to intervene by once again circling the city. Their energy dilutes the grief emanating from one in three households, lifting it, changing it to a softer energy; an energy that is easier to bear and that allows us to be clear enough in our minds to easily identify those whose grief has turned to simmering rage and thoughts of rebellion – the future members of the Kindred are in our sights.

On the fourth day, it is the animals from the city zoo who are taken outside the city gates and abandoned. The guards coming off their shifts of wall duty are full of bloodthirsty tales of watching predators hunting and feeding on the prey animals released with them, and while I would love to assure the other Sensitives that the stories are exaggerated, they would only sense the lie. It takes everything I have, all of my practice and experience from this lifetime and the last, to stay with Integrity when fear for her and rage at the guards and city governors would otherwise have incapacitated me.

Fear for their horses spreads quickly among the others though; they are terrified of what will happen when the wolves, bears, lions and tigers have slept off their current satiation. Will they disperse? Will they go off and hunt the prey animals who have fled the city surroundings, or will they stay nearby and hunt our horses?

I am quick to intercede before they can slide towards being unable to feel their horses again. *Calm down, and you'll be able to sense that the horses have all moved around the city to the furthest point from the gates, where the zoo animals were released. There's a whole city's worth of smells between them and the predators, and by a happy coincidence, the horses aren't far from the new tunnel exit. We'll see them tomorrow night. Hang on to that thought, and to your sense of your horses. We don't want them feeling the need to help us out by circling the city, until the zoo animals have gone. If we're to keep the horses safe, we need to stay calm and let them help us from where they are.*

When the night passes and our horses are not only safe but completely unperturbed, we all find it easier to remain calm. When another day passes and there is still no hint of a threat to them, excitement begins to take the place of fear as we all anticipate getting out to see our horses and one another again – to ride and allow the energy we hope to create once more to chase away the stress of the week.

I am Aware that most of the surviving zoo animals are as far away from the city and its inhabitants as their legs have been able to carry them since they were freed. Only a few have taken the time to explore their new surroundings more fully as they've travelled, but their focus is ahead and not back to the city they have left.

When it is time to collect Avril, I find her waiting for me outside her block. Her face lights up when she sees me and she links her arm through mine. 'It's going to be weird, hearing the other Sensitives' voices when we've got used to hearing their thoughts, isn't it?'

I sense her fighting hard to keep her connection with her horse at the forefront of her mind so that her anxiety over whether we will reach the wall is held at bay, and her need for conversation with me to help her in her efforts.

'It is,' I agree, 'and weird how quickly we've all become used to communicating that way. It kind of makes you think anything is possible.'

I sense Avril instinctively reaching for Dolly afresh as she agrees with my observation. She relaxes a little and her grip on my arm loosens.

'I'm glad Tania and Will made the next tunnel on the opposite side of the city from where the zoo animals were released,' she says. 'It's almost like they knew it was going to happen. I trust Dolly when she tells me she isn't in any danger but even so, I feel better knowing we're as far away from where it all happened as possible.' She shudders and almost loses her grip on her horse.

'All of the horses are relaxed,' I observe. 'It's great timing.

The zoo animals have dispersed, it's a clear night again so we'll be able to see what we're doing when we ride, and our horses are rested and waiting for us. Here we are at the edge of the city, right on time. Walk purposefully, as if we have every right to be here, help me keep a sense of whether we're being watched and whether there are others close by, and in about twenty minutes, we'll be with our horses.'

The only others we sense are a group of four Kindred Spirits and Sensitives who converge on us as we're crossing no man's land. The six of us arrive at the second tunnel without issue until there is a thump and a surprised 'Oooof!' as one of the Kindred suddenly stops in front of us, causing us all to knock into one another. 'Sorry,' she says, 'it looks like Tania and Will have branched out into making doors. Let me just find the handle… ah, here it is. The door opens into the tunnel, so, last one in, be sure to push it shut after you've pulled the brambles back into place in front of it. I'd hate to deprive those coming along behind us of a bruised forehead.'

We all chuckle and follow her into the dark hole that appears in the otherwise grey wall, and down the steps that fall away from our feet. As we walk in the dark, we all wonder where we'll exit when we finally do, and marvel at how Tania and Will have managed to not only excavate another tunnel, but shore it up so that it is safe, in less than a week.

*It's no big deal, we have a system now,* Tania tells me.

*What she means is, she tells me what to do and I do it,* Will adds. *We're off home now, we'll be back tomorrow to start on the third tunnel. Use that one next time since you'll all still be coming out to ride together. It'll mean waiting a week as it'll need to be a bit longer than the one you're in now, but until you're coming out in smaller numbers, it's sensible to carry on mixing it up.*

*Thank you, both of you, honestly, knowing we're coming out to see the horses is what's keeping everyone going.*

*Honestly, we know,* Tania replies, her amusement making me smile.

*What's it like, being a literal know-all?* I ask her.

*Ask your horse, I'm tired. See you, Nathan, oh and tell Fowler there's a door at the other end of the tunnel too. They're to stop animals getting back into the city and alerting the guards to the breaches in the wall, although the cats will still manage to slip through... oops, too late. Sorry.*

*No you're not.*

There is laughter up above me as I begin to climb up some steps and Fowler lets out a string of curses.

*No, I'm not,* she admits. *At least there's one among you who'll remember to feel her way with her hands as well as her feet – or to bring a torch.*

*We can't risk being stopped with torches in our pockets.*

*So develop new ones that look like something else, a pencil or something – don't you work in a research lab?*

*Don't you have a home to go to?*

*We do,* Will interrupts. *Come on, Tan. Have a great evening with your horses, Nathan.* I definitely sense a dog with him this time just before he disappears from my Awareness.

*He likes to have Maverick's help,* Tania explains.

My mind fills with Awareness of who Maverick is. Was. *He had a dog.*

*He still has dogs, both incarnate and discarnate. The incarnate ones are trying to lick him to death right now. Have a good night's teaching, Nathan.*

She is gone from my Awareness but her words stay with me. They remind me that this evening isn't just about me being with and riding my horse or even about channelling the energy of infinity to us all as we ride, but about me teaching the others to increase the level of connection both within their horses' bodies as they ride them, and with their horses, so that they adhere more strongly to the pattern established by the sixty-four and channel the energy of infinity for themselves.

I exit the tunnel to find the others standing, looking around themselves. Where before we found ourselves on the side of a hill and looking across a valley, this time we have emerged in what appears to be a substantial woodland glade. The grass is grey-blue in the moonlight, while the surrounding trees appear black and foreboding. None of us are afraid; our horses are grazing or snoozing peacefully, and their calm infuses us all so that we feel confident and safe in our surroundings.

'Looks like we're the first ones here,' Avril almost whispers. 'This is amazing. Will and Tania are amazing. They made the tunnel come out where there's no chance of us being seen from the city, it's just perfect.'

We all stand for a few minutes longer, then when voices sound in the tunnel behind us, we move away to make room for those at the foot of the steps.

I can't see Integrity but I can feel her. I make my way through the herd, stroking and patting the horses I pass until I see her shining brightly in the light reflected by the moon. My heart feels as if it is swelling in my chest at the sight of her, and I see double as my mind flickers between the Integrity I once knew and the one in front of me now.

I sense her enthusiasm for what we are about to do, and after a quick mental check of her body and stroke of her neck, I am on her back. My body settles into the same position and balance I achieved the last time I rode, but this time, rather than purely allowing my Awareness of how the sixty-four ride to guide my actions without any thought, I focus intently on what my body is doing to assist Integrity's to connect more and balance both her and my weight. It's hard not to get carried away by the infinity energy that once more swirls around and through me as Integrity and I follow the pattern of the sixty-four, but I manage it. And when I sense that all of the others are astride their horses, I call them to me.

Part of me is surprised by how easily they accept my instructions – particularly the Kindred, many of whom are older than I and all of whom have vastly more riding experience – but the rest of me takes it as a given; it isn't to me they are responding, but that which they can't help but sense emanating from me.

The Sensitives, despite having only ridden once before, easily follow my instructions – carried not just to their ears by my words but to their souls by the energy that I am channelling – and are soon channelling the infinity energy themselves, from the pattern to the circle in which we all now ride. The Kindred aren't far behind them once the pattern strengthens in our midst and combines with their previous knowledge and experience of riding.

We are connected with our horses, with one another, with the sixty-four and with all of the others in the other cities who are determined to stay sane and help others to do the same by adhering to The Way Of The Horse.

When we peel away from the circle to ride by ourselves, we take its energy with us. There isn't a sound in the glade apart from the light thumping of hundreds of hooves, the outward breaths of ninety-six sets of lungs exerting themselves, and the beating in harmony of ninety-six hearts – for we can all hear them, the horses due to natural ability and we humans through our horses. Forty-eight human minds are given the opportunity – the gift – by the horses of not only feeling connected to one another in mind and spirit, but through the organs that pump life through us all.

As one, we sense our horses' approaching need to rest, and slow them gradually, gently, to a halt. We drop to the ground in a single thud. There is silence.

We continue to ride together once a week for another ten weeks, using a newly completed tunnel to exit the city each time. Each time we ride, we become more connected with our horses and one another. Each time we ride, we get stronger. And each time we ride, we become more attuned to The Way Of The Horse until the pattern of sensitivity, strength, tolerance, loyalty, and confidence feels like a more obvious point of reference, a comfort to which we all return and cling when we have need.

All of our number are now in positions where we can either influence, disrupt or provide information to the others, and several have made subtle overtures towards some of those we identified as being potential members of our resistance following the seizure of their animal family members. Though the mountain we all have to climb in order for our efforts to flourish is no less tall, it no longer feels overwhelmingly so; between us, and with our horses' help, we know we will navigate it.

When all of the twelve tunnels Tania and Will promised us are complete, we agree that our time of riding as one large group must come to an end. There is nothing more I can teach the others with regard to riding their horses, it is now merely a case of visiting our horses so that they can continue to remind us of The Way Of The Horse until it is so embedded within our makeup that it will survive in our descendants long after we have perished.

Our last ride together is an emotional one. While those of us who are sensitive enough will remain in constant contact, we know it is likely – and indeed sensible – that most of the

Sensitives will never see most of the Kindred again. The Kindred will need to be in regular contact with their Sensitive partners and a few others either side of them in the Kindred communication chain, but other than that, for their safety and all of ours, they will need to keep their distance. I sense their sadness and trepidation constantly rising and dissipating in the face of the infinity energy that swirls around and through us as we ride.

When we, as always, bring our horses to a halt in the same heartbeat, I call out, 'We're connected, all of us. You can all feel it in your minds and your hearts as well as I can. Like the sixty-four whose example we follow, we're attuned to The Way Of The Horse. We're fuelled by the energy of infinity, and that means we won't fail. Come out here to see your horses whenever you need to, and if you need me, know that I'll be out here too. Between us, we'll make sure that everything the horses have done, and continue to do, for us, will be put to good use.'

There is cheering all around. We all dismount and hug our horses and one another.

'Can anyone join in?' Tania's voice reaches us from behind some bushes, around which she subsequently steps with Will just behind her.

There are shouts of delight as everyone rushes to hug them both and thank them for everything they've done for us all. It is only when the majority of the others have left for the city that I finally reach the pale-haired father and daughter.

'You're done here,' I say to them both, Aware of their satisfaction at another city now having a fledgling, but well-equipped and determined, resistance in place.

'We've done what we needed to,' Tania says, 'but we'll be Aware of you all and what you're up to, and if you need us, we'll know.'

I frown at them both. 'You've said that to those you've left behind in every single city you've set up like this one, and yet I have no trouble believing that you mean it – that you actually are Aware of all of us at once.'

'Tania was born like it,' Will says, his teeth showing white in the moonlight. 'I had to work a little harder, but neither of us would have the abilities we have were it not for the leader of the sixty-four. You're every bit as able and determined as she is, Nathan.' He stretches out his hand and draws me into a hug. 'Remember that when you need to, and remember what Tania just told you.' He releases me, and Tania hugs me before I can answer her father, or question the sense his words stir afresh in me, that my storm is almost overhead.

'Fare you well, Nathan.' Tania releases me and this time I actually see the ghost of a black and white dog with upright ears and a frantically wagging tail, before Will and Tania disappear.

'Come on, Nathan, or we'll miss the guard change,' Avril calls out from by the tunnel entrance.

I glance at where Integrity is grazing peacefully alongside Dolly. Whatever is coming, I can handle it.

## Chapter Eighteen

*a*s I sit in front of my wallscreen, watching the news with Gran, I am horrified at the announcement that paper will no longer be available to us. I am also relieved that only two days have passed since we were all with our horses; we have reserves of calm and strength to help us cope with the shock and to trust that we will find new ways of communicating silently with our friends and families, and of passing messages to and between the Kindred. When terror erupts across the city as its inhabitants all realise what the announcement means, however, I sense Avril's reserves quickly running dry.

I am Aware of her request for Dolly and Integrity to help her reach me, moments before she blasts into my mind. *Nathan, what will we do? If they're stopping us having access to paper, they must know we've been using written notes to tell each other things, and this is their answer. I bet they can now not only monitor emails and phone calls on tablets and wrist safes, but anything we write down on our tablets for each other to see...*

*We'll find ways around it, is what we'll do,* I tell her. *We just need to hang tight and not panic, because they'll be watching for anyone who does. Hold on, others are joining us.* I sense more horses linking their humans into our conversation and by the time all of the Sensitives are with us, I have a plan. *Okay, everyone, this isn't good news, but it's just the first blip of many we can expect, all of which our horses have prepared us to be able to overcome.* When I sense their panic receding, I continue, *We're going to have to use the paper we have left sparingly and with the sole purpose of setting ourselves up to be able to operate without it. Shane, you're due to meet up with Maggie in a few days' time, aren't you.*

*Er, yes, yes I am. I know lots of you are nervous about meeting your Kindred partners regularly, but Maggie and I, well, we're, um...*

*Dating, we know,* I finish for him and sense his embarrassment and the others' amusement at his having forgotten that, linked as we are by our horses so that we can communicate, we can all know everything about one another. *So, when you see her, you're going to need to pass her a note asking her to step up her overtures to the woman she was talking about who works in tech support; the one she thinks will join the Kindred.* I explain to the other Sensitives, *The woman's constantly been denied the job she was demoted from when her husband was thrown in prison, and now they've taken her dogs and her cat away from her. Maggie's befriended her and is sure she's angry and driven enough to work with us, but stable enough to not give herself away. She's an expert programmer and Maggie has access to the servers, so between them, they can hopefully get some code written and uploaded that will allow us to send communications and write messages on our tablets that aren't viewable by the authorities.*

We all discuss the plan, and several of the other Sensitives suggest people they or their Kindred partners can approach in order for our resistance to grow and strengthen in concert with the increased measures for control.

As we're winding down our discussion, I say, *Regardless of when you're next due to meet your Kindred partners or leave them a written message, you're going to need to arrange to bump into them over the next few days, so you can let them know what we've discussed. I'll get my gran to visit Helen. Can you all do that?*

All except four of them gather strength from the horses who continue to link them into our conversation, and tell me with varying degrees of confidence that they can. When the others leave our conversation, the four, including Avril, remain. I sense Avril's relief that she doesn't have to fight her own fear as well as that which she can constantly feel trying to find its way through the protection that Dolly affords her, in order to devise a plan to "accidentally" bump into me. Her relief wars, however, with her terror that the new control measure is the first of many that will gradually overtake our ability to overcome them, and the time will come when we're prevented from leaving the city. The other three Sensitives have no such relief to temper their fear, and indeed are only just about hanging onto their senses of their horses. Their thoughts are faint as they all beg the same favour of me.

*Nathan, you have to help me get out to the horses, I need to be with George,* Primrose pleads. *I'm losing my sense of him and if I lose that, I'll lose the plot completely, I'll never be able to pull off finding Charlie and telling her what she needs to know.*

*Me neither,* agrees Alanna. *I'm losing my strength. By tomorrow I won't be able to leave my apartment, let alone go to work as normal and contrive a way to speak to Dean, I need to get to Shandy.*

*And me.* Saul's thought is barely discernible to the others but I'm Aware of it, and the effort it costs him to add, *Help me, Nathan.*

*We'll both help you, won't we, Nathan?* Avril's thought is firm but has a tremor attached to its tail. She knows as well as I that the two of us meeting and walking to three other blocks to collect three terrified Sensitives so soon after the announcement is dangerous by itself, let alone getting them to the wall without being questioned as to why they look so terrified, and the risk of them breaking down on the way. I sense the courage that she managed to muster beginning to desert her. I have to act now.

*Okay, I'll collect Avril in ten minutes then Saul fifteen minutes after that, Primrose ten minutes after him, and Alanna in an hour,* I tell them all. *The horses are shifting to the gate nearest to Alanna's block, you can all feel that, right?* I sense their assent. *They're waiting for us. Hold on to that thought, hold on to them until I get to you. You too, Avril. Okay?*

Saul's thought is a little stronger. *Okay, yes, I can do that. Okay.*

*Yes, thank you. I'll be ready.* Primrose is telling herself rather than me.

Alanna panics. *Will we make it? What if one of us has a meltdown and we're all arrested? Oh, I'm not sure I can do this.*

I sense her terror reaching and filling the others – and me. No. I hold firm to Integrity and tell them firmly, *We can all do this, our horses chose us because we can. All five of us are sensitive enough to know where our horses are and to know when we're being watched. I also have the ability to be Aware of how to reach the wall without bumping into anyone we don't want to bump into. Remember how your horses behave; they stick together, they look out for each other, they lend each other strength and they never forget who they are or why they're here. They chose us as their humans because we're capable of being the same, so BE THOSE PEOPLE.* The strength I send to them along with my thought surprises me as much as it does them. All four regain their hold on their horses and assure me that they'll be ready and waiting.

I turn to Gran and say, 'It's been a long day and I'm feeling sleepy, I think I'll turn in.'

She takes the mug I have just drained of tea. 'You do look tired. Sleep well.'

Once at the living room door and out of sight of the wallscreen, I mouth to her, 'I'll leave you a note.'

Her eyes flick to me just long enough for her to register my message, then immediately back to the wallscreen. 'Goodnight, love,' she calls as if I have already left the room.

I tiptoe to my room, grab my coat, scarf and hat, then quickly write Gran a note and leave it on my bed. I say, 'Serendipity,' to my wrist, and silently leave the apartment.

I actually enjoy myself as I evade my building's scanners, collect Avril – who grips my arm far more firmly than she has for some time – and evade each and every police officer out looking for anyone behaving as if they have been spooked by the news announcement, as we collect the other three Sensitives. By the time we reach the wall and are safely in the first tunnel Tania and Will excavated for us, I am jubilant. The Governors may think they have us all trapped like fish in a bucket, they may think they are all powerful, but they are no match for the versions of ourselves that the horses are helping us to be.

'Well done, all of you,' I say to the others, all four of whom have come to a stop at the bottom of the tunnel steps, exhausted from the effort of holding themselves together while hammered by terror from both without and within. 'Nearly there, just a few minutes more and then you'll have the relief you need from everything in the city.'

I am Aware of them gathering themselves together for the easiest part of our journey to see the horses… and in focusing on them as a group for the first time, become Aware of something else. How did I miss it before? How did I not see it? Why didn't I look for the connection between the four of them, especially knowing how and why Avril and I are connected? I turn my attention to the thread that runs between the two of us and find that while it isn't quite as thick as it was, it's the same thickness as those that connect me to the other three. All four threads are humming, vibrating, as if they themselves are Aware and know something I don't.

When the four Sensitives begin to move along the tunnel, I remain where I am. The storm is directly overhead. What have I brought them to?

I'm Aware of Integrity, Shandy, George, Dolly, and Saul's horse, Rocket, waiting patiently for us near the far end of the tunnel while the rest of the herd graze in the valley below. Integrity. It feels right to follow the others, so I do. When we emerge onto the side of the hill, I glance upward, almost expecting to see and hear evidence of a physical storm, but the sky is clear, the air crisp and there is silence apart from the sound of horses grazing nearby.

The weight that has been bearing down upon us all drops away as we run to our horses. The sound of Integrity munching on a mouthful of grass soothes me almost as much as does the warmth emanating from her both physically and emotionally.

*When the challenges you will face increase in difficulty you can be assured it is because you are ready for them. Your energy attracts that which it needs to rebalance in any given moment.* Her counsel is familiar. While I can't recall her giving it before, I know she has. And I know that she is reminding me of my strength.

I lean against her shoulder as she continues to graze. When she's ready, I vault onto her back and immediately feel the remainder of the effects of The Old fall away from me. We are all there is; everything else is just a distraction from whom we are.

As we move off, the others fall in behind us, sharing my desire to move further away from the distraction of The Old, to discover new territory, to lose myself completely in my connection with my horse. Integrity walks down the hill and when she reaches the valley, canters across it and up the shallower incline on the other side. When we reach its brow, we all canter a circle for several minutes, revelling in the burst of energy that doing so always affords us, then canter down the long, even shallower incline to the valley beyond. Once there, we laugh as we weave slowly between old, wide-girthed trees, the horses' hooves rustling through the thick layer of fallen leaves.

My eyes water due to the crispness of the air, a sharpness that is blunted in the city by the warmth of its closely-packed buildings and the smell of fear. Out here, it is clean, fresh and unspoilt, and makes me want to stay, to breathe it all day every day alongside Integrity. But that isn't her reason for being here, or mine. We have work to do now that my old pattern has been replaced... at the thought, a slight sense of unease jabs at me. *That is not the truth.* I have no idea whether the thought is mine or Integrity's. It doesn't matter. I am now as Aware as she of the tiny part of me which yet refuses to believe that I am all I need.

My acknowledgement of the fact sparks the storm, which I thought would originate outside of myself, to explode from within, attracting the lioness and her cubs who, having struggled to hunt in competition with the larger groups of the other cat species released from the zoo, have slowly made their way back towards the city.

They hone in on me, the beacon who has drawn their attention, then by extension, on the four riders and five horses in my company. I am Aware of the lioness's keen intelligence as she stands, sniffing the air. She is now, thanks to me, fully Aware of our location, and that of the rest of the herd of which our energy is a part. She would cut us off from them. Only having been captured and imprisoned in the zoo relatively recently, her hunting instincts and skills are yet sharp, and she would pass them on to her cubs.

Integrity changes direction at the exact moment the lioness and her cubs commit to the hunt; she gallops in a straight line towards the herd as the hunters move to intercept us.

*No, Integrity, turn around,* I urge her, grabbing two handfuls of mane to help me keep my balance. *The other horses are already starting to flee, the lions will never catch them. We need to go in the opposite direction, we need to get away, you're doing exactly what the lioness wants.*

*She will prevent you all from returning to the city this night. You are needed there. You know this.*

'Woohoo, I've never been this fast before,' Saul yells from behind us.

'Me neither, I had no idea Dolly could go this fast,' Avril shouts breathlessly.

*But then what?* I ask Integrity. *If you and the other horses get us to the tunnel, what will happen to you? Integrity, please don't do this, I can't be here without you.* There it is. My old pattern stabs me in the stomach. It catches in my throat. It almost blinds me with tears.

*That is not the truth.* Integrity falters and almost goes down on her knees, just about managing to right herself in time to keep going. I'm not keeping her connected and balanced. In not helping her, I'm hindering my Integrity.

My realisation causes me to remember. *It's all down to Integrity.*

I know what I have to do. I have to put my fear of having her taken from me to one side so that I can put all of myself behind her, or it will be me who kills us both as surely as will the lioness and her cubs… and it will be down to me that the other four won't make it back to their homes on this dangerous night, if at all. It will be down to me that their and my disappearances and associations will be investigated, and down to me that our resistance will crumble before it's had a chance to make a difference to the people of The City Of Glory. I have to do what's right instead of what's easy.

*Go, Integrity, go!* Strength at knowing I have chosen the right path surges out of me to my horse. She powers onward without faltering despite the slope we are now negotiating.

'What the…? George, what's wrong?' Primrose says behind me. 'Nathan, what's happening? George is scared.'

I turn and call over my shoulder, 'So, you can't be. It's okay, we'll be okay, the four of you just need to give back to your horses all of the strength they've just given you so that they can keep up with Integrity, I mean Honour, oh, it doesn't matter. We need to get back to the city urgently, and we will, you just need to trust me and your horses.'

The threads linking me to the four of them vibrate to the point of feeling they will explode as our energy, unbalanced by me in our previous lifetime together, prepares to rebalance. Integrity's neck flickers in front of me between white as she is now and dappled as she was before, as I live both the scene unfolding in front of me, and the one in which Avril, Saul, Alanna and Primrose were four Woeful whose bid to survive I hindered.

It was Avril who had to live with the guilt of killing me when all she and the others were trying to do was keep themselves and their families alive. Their actions were crucial to the development of the people of The New – if they hadn't attacked The Gathering, Amarilla wouldn't have felt compelled to find and help the Woeful communities, Awareness wouldn't have come to be widespread among the people of The New, Will and Tania wouldn't be the forces of nature they are, and all of us in The Old would be lost. Just as all in our city will still be lost if I can't help the four behind me as I should have the last time we met.

I sense their confusion, their fear, and turn my head so they can catch my words as their horses gallop close on Integrity's heels. 'Remember how to help your horses stay connected within their bodies so they can carry you without injuring themselves,' I call out. 'Absorb the energy, the power you feel from your horse beneath you and channel that back into your efforts to help them stay balanced. That's it, Avril, that's brilliant. And you, Primrose. Can you feel that your horses feel stronger when you do that? Great, Saul, keep going. Alanna, sit up a bit, your weight's a little too far forward. That's it, that's better.'

The more instructions I yell out, the more the four behind me fall back into the familiar, comfortable place of focusing on my voice and on their horses' reactions beneath them. As their balance and connection with their horses improve, their horses move more surely. We rapidly approach the intersection with the line the lions are taking, and Integrity senses that she needs to increase her speed even further if we are to get there first. All four horses behind us are able to come with her as I keep their riders focused on helping their balance and connection, and on giving them strength. I have to trust Integrity to keep going, to use the strength that I'm able to keep channelling to her as a result of knowing I'm doing the right thing.

We crest the last hill before the tunnel and are galloping down it when we all sense that not only are we being observed, but that those observing us are behind us – and closing. Having narrowly missed us at the top of the hill, the lions are now streaming down it on our tails.

I can't let the others lose focus, I can't let any of them scream; not only will it cause the other three to lose themselves in terror, but a piercing noise like that could carry to the guards on the wall through the still, crisp night.

'All four of you, stay with your horses, keep them balanced and connected, don't let them down,' I call back. I have to keep talking, I have to give the four of them energy even as I'm doing my best to give as much of myself as I can to Integrity. 'You can feel their energy, you can feel their strength. Absorb what you can feel, then turn it around and give it back to them. You've brought them this far, you can keep going, come on, keep going.'

The horses, breathing hard now, begin to carry us up the final incline. When the tunnel looms in front of me, Integrity interrupts my constant discourse with the four still behind us. *You must dismount by the tunnel. I will lead the hunters away.*

I sense her intention. The instincts of her species warn her that the lions will act together to separate one of the horses, or one of us, from the group. She will sacrifice herself so that the rest of us will survive. I see her logic; we five humans need to survive, and I'm the only one who has a chance of doing it without my horse. It doesn't mean that I will.

*The final shard of your old belief yet fights for survival,* Integrity informs me as she judders to a halt near the tunnel. *That is all it is.* She's tired but she doesn't waver from who she is – and who she knows me to be in truth. We are all we need. We are Integrity.

Tears pour down my face as I slide from her back. I can't even watch her go, I have to help my friends, I have to make sure they get to the tunnel in case the lions decide they are an easier target than Integrity – I have to make sure they survive so that our resistance will strengthen instead of flounder.

'Get off your horses, they know what they're doing,' I tell

them all. 'Quickly, you have to get off and let them go, they'll be able to run much faster without your weight.'

I grab the hands of an exhausted Avril and Alanna, and shove them into the hands of Saul and Primrose, of whose hands I take hold so that I can pull them all behind me towards the tunnel.

'Dolly…' Avril moans.

'Will be fine. Integrity will lead the lions away,' I manage to tell her in between gasping for breath.

'LIONS?' Saul roars. 'Those were lions behind us? Why didn't you say?'

I pull them into the tunnel, wait for them to stagger past me and then reach for the door, slamming it shut moments before something rams it from the other side.

Avril screams.

'Our horses are being chased by… lions?' Alanna says weakly as Avril's scream echoes off the tunnel walls.

'No, my horse is being chased by them,' I reply. 'Integrity knew they'd try to pick one of them off, so she…' I swallow hard. 'She went in the opposite direction from your horses so they'd follow her.'

'Why do you keep calling Honour, Integrity?' Primrose says with a tremble in her voice.

'Because it's who she really is,' I reply. 'She'll always do the right thing, just like she's doing now.'

'I can feel Shandy slowing down,' Alanna says. 'He's shattered, but he's okay, he and the others are moving towards where the rest of the herd are, and they're not being followed.'

'Yes, okay, I can feel that Rocket's alright too,' Saul says, 'and…'

I zone out of their conversation. They're safe. I gather together everything I feel for my horse and send it to her, willing her to keep going as her exhausted legs gallop on. I try not to cry out as I sense the lioness right behind her and the cubs flanking her on either side. I have to focus, I have to help her and hope that the lions, desperate as I am Aware they are for food, run out of stamina before she does.

I jump at the sound of gun shots. My hands fly to my ears before I realise that it isn't my ears that are hearing them, but Integrity's. She's led the lions over the hill, straight into the sights of the guns on the top of the wall!

I sense the glee of two guards as they shout to one another which targets they will take so that the sport is shared evenly; one will take down Integrity and the lioness now tiring rapidly on her heels, the other will aim for the equally spent cubs. There is nothing I can do except continue willing all of my strength into my horse, and hope that she can evade both her predators and the guards' bullets.

I keep my integrity, my strength, to the very end. It is only when I feel the bullets pierce my horse's flesh that I scream and allow my heart to break.

# Chapter Nineteen

*a*rms embrace me from in front, behind and both sides as the Sensitives intuit what has happened. I am Aware of them flinching internally as my agony invades their senses, but they don't balk from me. They surround and enfold me in the only way they can, letting me know that I am not as alone as I feel. My Awareness of them, of everything, fades as grief takes its place, sitting heavily in my stomach, pounding within my head and tearing at my heart.

The arms around me tighten, holding me in place as I try to move towards the tunnel door, to tear out of it and run to where my soul mate has fallen. My sobs turn to shouts of rage when I am thwarted, then return to those of agony at the emptiness in my mind; the quiet where there was always potential for conversation, the confidence that always assured me of myself, the kindness that always soothed me, the honesty and consistency on which I could always rely. I have no idea how long we all stand huddled together.

When exhaustion finally quietens my cries and halts my tears,

I begin to realise that I feel… different. While my mind still feels empty, I am not. I feel a quiet strength sitting within me, a knowing of what I need to do and a quiet determination to do it. While Integrity's absence from my mind hurts like hell, I no longer need her constant presence in my mind for me to grasp whenever I need to remind myself of who I'm trying to be, because thanks to her, I am that person. I am all I need.

And I'm who the four with me need if they're to get home when the guards change. 'I'm… I'm okay,' I say, my voice hoarse. 'Let go of me, I'm okay.'

'Nathan, I'm so sorry,' Primrose whispers, and the others add their condolences.

I glance at the luminous hands of my watch as the four of them release me. 'We need to pull ourselves together. The guards will be changing in a little under twenty minutes, so we need to be at the far end of the tunnel by then, ready to cross no man's land.

'But, Nathan, you're d… devastated,' Alanna says, 'as all of us would be if it had been our horses who… who… anyway, you can't try to get home as you are. We should wait here until the next guard change so you have more time.'

I take a deep breath. 'And then we'll be wandering around in the early hours of the morning at a time when the police will be even more watchful than usual for abnormal behaviour. No, we need to go now, I need to get all of you home safely. I know what's just happened was a shock, but you can't let that take away from you everything your horses gave you this evening. Focus on how we all felt before we turned to come back to the tunnel, and on how you all gathered your strength and gave it to your horses so that they could escape the lions. You're stronger than you knew you were, I hope you can all feel that within yourselves, because I can feel it in me. Come on, let's get back.'

I put my arms out and gently push my friends away from me so that I can feel the tunnel walls, and begin to walk.

*He Who Is Integrity you have done well.*

I stop in my tracks. *INTEGRITY?* I sink to my knees and put my hands to my face as I am not only Aware of my horse in my mind once more, but of the fact that she's still incarnate – she's still here, in her body, with me.

'Oooof, Nathan, are you alright?' Saul says as he walks into me. 'Hold on, Prim, Nathan's collapsed.' Hands find me in the dark and I am quickly enfolded in hugs again.

I am Aware that my horse is completely exhausted, but otherwise well. 'Integrity's alive,' I whisper.

'WHAT?'

'How?'

*I healed her,* Tania announces. *You might be He Who Is Integrity, Nathan, but you have a little to learn about not jumping to conclusions.*

*But I couldn't feel her in my mind.* 'Tania's here,' I tell the others. 'She healed Integrity. Ask your horses to help you hear her.'

*Grief does tend to block out everything else,* Tania tells me. *I told you I'd know if you needed help.*

*We needed it a lot sooner, as it happens.* A sudden heaviness in my stomach contradicts my words. I add, *That's not the truth. What happened was necessary for the five of us. Thanks, Tania, for coming when you did. Thank you.*

She brushes off my gratitude the same way Integrity always does, replying, *You might like to know, I healed the lions too.*

*WHAT? Then Integrity's still in danger?*

*No, Dad and Maverick drove the four of them away. To coin one of your phrases, they've got form for doing it. The lions are currently heading for an area where they'll have much easier hunting than around here. They won't dare return, your horses are safe.*

*Who's Maverick?* Primrose asks.

While Tania explains, I pick up from her Awareness how a single man, his dog's ghost and a whole lot more besides, drove away four lions. I don't understand it, but decide I don't have to. Integrity is alive!

*Didn't the guards try to shoot you and your dad too?* Saul asks Tania.

*They didn't notice us, they were too busy congratulating themselves and talking into their wrist safes, inviting the other guards to come and see what they'd done,* Tania explains. *They felt pretty stupid when their friends arrived and there was no sign of either a dead horse or four dead lions.*

I leave them to their conversation. I gather all of my relief, my admiration, my love for my horse and send it to her as she walks slowly, tiredly to where the other horses are waiting for her. *Integrity, I'm so glad you're still with me.*

*I can be nowhere else. We Are Integrity.*

Hearing her thought in my head makes my heart sing. *We Are Integrity,* I repeat. Speaking of which… 'Come on, you lot, you can chat with Tania while we walk, we need to get to the other end of the tunnel. This should be an easier exit than any of the others as the guards are still distracted by the lack of physical evidence for what happened, but even so, we need to get back. We have work to do.'

As I hurry the four of them along, I am Aware that the threads linking me to them are now the same thickness as those linking me to everyone else in the resistance. I have returned to them that which I took when the five of us were together last time around, leaving us all free to focus on moving forward – and move forward we will. I'll make sure of it.

# Epilogue

$\mathcal{I}$ get home from work to find Tania sitting cross-legged on the sofa, talking to Gran. I'm unsurprised; her visits have become regular, if not frequent, occurrences.

'You disabled the wallscreen again?' I say to her while lifting a hand to Gran. 'That's the second time this month, they'll be coming to arrest me at any moment.'

Gran chuckles and gets to her feet. 'They'll have to arrest the whole block then, and the one across the street, Tania's had something of a field day. I'll get some dinner on for us all, just pretend I'm not here.'

I can't help but laugh. 'Thanks, Gran. So, you can stay longer than normal this time then, Tan?'

She squints. 'I would say so.'

'Still not got the hang of just the one eye, huh?' I hold up my hands. 'Just teasing, I love you the way you are.'

She rolls her eyes. 'It's not enough that Dad still can't let that go, now it's both of my favourite men?' She kisses me as I sink onto the sofa beside her.

'You've had a busy few weeks,' I tell her. 'They're a strong bunch in Supreme City, aren't they? It wasn't just me who felt the pattern strengthening this time, all of the Sensitives did too. Saul and I were out riding Rocket and Integrity when you had them riding in a circle for the first time, and I swear that by the time we'd finished, Saul was feeling strong enough to join the Kindred.'

Tania smiles. 'That's not just because of what my current bunch are doing, Nate, it's because of what you're doing here.' She moves behind me and massages my shoulders, Aware as always of exactly where I'm holding tension and how best she can ease it. 'You're a good leader and your resistance is flourishing because of it. It's only been two years, but you have people in all of the positions necessary to counter each new control measure with another to limit its effect, and your Kindred are keeping the elderly alive who would otherwise have starved or frozen to death, and getting medical help and supplies to those deemed unworthy of them. You're there for every member of your team even though they have their horses helping them too – I know being Aware helps, but it also makes more work for you when you use it to check in with each of them every day and get help to any of them who're struggling.'

'It would be easier if I could monitor everyone and everything at the same time like you can, but I've had to accept the limitations to my Awareness; I'll never be like you.'

'I wouldn't want you to be like me. Can you imagine?'

I chuckle. 'I see your point. Two know-alls who can't wink? No, there's only room for one of those.'

Tania moves her hands down to my ribs and tickles me until I manage to turn and grab hold of her. I tickle her back until she begs me to stop. I wrap my arms around her and hold her close.

'I wish I could stay for longer than I can,' she murmurs.

'Do your parents mind that you snatch time with me when you can, rather than going home to someone in The New?'

Tania pulls back from me a little so she can look up into my eyes. 'Dad's happy that I'm happy, and he likes you. Mum would love it if I settled down and had a family in Rockwood, but she knows I was never going to do that. No, they're both okay with me choosing you, it's Delta you should be glad you'll never have to meet.'

'Your cousin.'

'My cousin, closest friend and self-appointed guardian and biographer. She's just bludgeoned her way to being a Master Collator for the Histories. If she actually met you, she wouldn't know whether to examine you as an antiquity or throw you into the nearest tree. She was thrilled to be able to document that you and Integrity have helped not one catalyst for change and not even two, but three in your two lifetimes together, but she's far from thrilled that you're here and not there where she can "keep an eye on you".'

'It's weird to think that everyone in The New knows about me being here after I blew it there,' I say.

Tania reaches up and pokes me on the end of my nose. 'There's no such thing as blowing it, and you know it. You were Newson in your previous life, and I was a horse. And here we are.'

She can't lie any more than I can, but I'm incredulous nevertheless. 'You were a horse?' I stare at her and she stares back unblinkingly. I'm Aware that she's never told anyone else that; only her dad and Amarilla know. I'm also Aware that she's purposefully making a whole lot more about herself available to my relatively limited Awareness. 'You and your dad are descended from the leader of the sixty-four,' I murmur. 'The Way Of The Horse was embedded in your body before you were even born, which meant that your body had no resistance at all to the experiences your soul brought with it from your lives – lives? – as horses. Your DNA, your upbringing and your soul have combined to make you the best, the most powerful, that a human can be. So why are you with me?'

Her eyes sparkle. 'Because you make me laugh.' She becomes more serious. 'And because you don't need me. You love me but you leave me free to do what I need to do. There's only one other person I know who is as much her horse as you are yours.'

'And you find me more attractive than Amarilla,' I say with a grin.

Tania rolls her eyes again. 'I'm trying to say that I was born into The Way Of The Horse, Nate. You chose it. You chose Integrity over everything else, and that makes you the best a human can be.'

# Books by Lynn Mann

### The Horses Know Trilogy
*The Horses Know*
*The Horses Rejoice*
*The Horses Return*

### Sequels to The Horses Know Trilogy
*Horses Forever*
*The Forgotten Horses*
*The Way Of The Horse*

### Origins of The Horses Know Trilogy
*The Horses Unite*

### Prequels to The Horses Know Trilogy
*In Search Of Peace* (Adam's story)
*The Strength Of Oak* (Rowena's story)
*A Reason To Be Noble* (Quinta's story)

### Companion Stories to The Horses Know Trilogy
*From A Spark Comes A Flame* (Novella)
*Tales Of The Horse-Bonded* (Short Story Collection)

*Tales Of The Horse-Bonded* will take you on a journey into the lives of some of your favourite characters from *The Horses Know Trilogy*. The book is available for purchase in paperback and hardback, and is available to download for free. To find out more, visit www.lynnmann.co.uk.

A regularly updated book list can be found at
www.lynnmann.co.uk/booklist
(The QR code below enables quick access.)

## The Horses Unite (Origins of The Horses Know Trilogy)

When FE88 qualifies as an enforcer of The City Of Power's rules, her life becomes marginally more secure, not least because she has the love and support of a member of the city's underground resistance to help her stay sane.

But then she discovers that the only light in her otherwise dark existence will be assigned to her as her next kill. She resolves to resist the regime that gives her no choice but to obey, and save the life that is hers to take – but is shocked to learn that it is her own life that must be preserved at all costs. Without her, the future of both enforcers and humans is uncertain. Even with her, it isn't guaranteed, for her hatred of human nature runs deep.

When the city falls, it is a horse who proves to be the two races' best chance of co-existing. If he can succeed, the pathway laid down by the horses of the past will remain open. But some tasks are too great for one horse alone…

## In Search Of Peace (A Prequel to The Horses Know Trilogy)

Adam is on the verge of grief-induced insanity when a horse chooses him as a Bond-Partner and refuses to leave his side. He tries to rid himself of his unwanted companion as he has everyone else, but finds it more difficult than he could have imagined.

Just when it seems as though the horse has managed to find a way through Adam's grief and bring him back to himself, Adam rejects him in the worst possible way, resulting in catastrophe. In order to save the Bond-Partner who has tried so hard to save him, Adam must remember what his would-be saviour tried to teach him. And he must do it soon, before it is too late for both of them…

## The Strength Of Oak
## (A Prequel to The Horses Know Trilogy)

Unloved and unwanted by her parents, Rowena is desperate for a way out of the life she hates. When a horse chooses her as his Bond-Partner, she thinks she has found one – but she soon discovers that while she can leave her family behind, there is no escaping herself.

With patient guidance from her horse, Rowena begins to accept the truth of her past, and to believe she can change. But then her past catches up with her at the worst possible moment, leaving her with a choice. She can be the person she was, or she can find the strength to be the person her horse has shown her she can be. One choice will give them both a future. The other will be the death of them…

## A Reason To Be Noble
## (A Prequel to The Horses Know Trilogy)

Quinta is crippled with anxiety and can barely leave the house, so she is terrified when she senses the touch of a horse's mind on her own and realises that he has selected her as his Bond-Partner. She manages to find the courage to leave her home and her village, and meet the horse whose mind calls to hers. A bond settles into place between the two of them, and Quinta's outlook on life begins to change.

With her horse's guidance, Quinta's confidence slowly increases, but she has a long way to go if she is to leave all of her fears behind, and her horse is a relentless teacher. When it seems as though he has pushed her too far, Quinta must find a way to trust that everything he has taught her still holds true. Their lives and that of a young boy will depend on it…

# From A Spark Comes A Flame

When Fitt leaves Rockwood with her horse to take Awareness to the villages of The New, she knows it will be a challenge, not least because those she wants to help are terrified of her kind.

Upon arrival at the village of Bigwood, the worst of Fitt's fears about her mission are realised. She takes the only way forward that she can see, but her actions go against the advice of her horse and the cost to herself is high. It is only when the cost to the people of Bigwood is higher that Fitt is forced to acknowledge her mistake. If she can rectify it, she will discover the extent of her power. If she can't, the consequences will be deadly…

Did you enjoy The Way Of The Horse?
I'd be extremely grateful if you could spare a few minutes
to leave a review where you purchased your copy.
Reviews really do help my books to reach a wider audience,
which means that I can keep on writing!
Thank you very much.

I love to hear from you!
Get in touch and receive news of future releases at the following:

www.lynnmann.co.uk

www.facebook.com/lynnmann.author

# Acknowledgments

*The Way Of The Horse* practically wrote itself, the first time that has happened to me since my first book, *The Horses Know*, erupted out of me! I've so enjoyed moving my fingers across the keyboard in accordance with the words that wanted to flow out of them, and am hugely grateful to my editorial team – Fern Sherry, Leonard Palmer, Caroline Macintosh and Cindy Nye – for giving me the help and feedback necessary for me to be able to release a novel that was so much fun to write.

Thanks as always to Amanda Horan for her fabulous cover design. She didn't have an easy brief this time but I've learnt to trust her talent, and she delivered as always.

At the time of writing this, four years and three months have passed since my beautiful blue-eyed mare, Pie (Coxstone Infinity), moved on from this world. At the time, I really thought that the book I wrote in the aftermath of her passing, *The Horses Return*, would be my last, so I can barely believe that another seven have now followed it – yet at the same time, I'm not surprised. Pie was a mare on a mission and always pulled me out of my head to the part of myself that was much calmer and stronger, so that I could accompany her. She's with me still.

Printed in Great Britain
by Amazon

35003926R00165